KT-102-973

11

The Complete Encyclopedia of Cooking
Supercook

Marshall Cavendish · London Sydney New York

Symbols in Supercook

'Low-Calorie' Recipes

The description 'low-calorie' has been given to recipes in *'Supercook'* which contain fewer calories than other comparable recipes in the book. For instance, the pudding recipes marked 'Low-cal' have the fewest calories when compared to other pudding recipes in *'Supercook'*. Some – but not all – of the recipes labelled 'Low-cal' would be suitable for people who are following strict slimming or low-calorie diets. Each recipe should be examined carefully to ascertain whether the ingredients are permitted for a particular special diet.

The labelling 'Low-cal' will be more helpful for those aiming to lose weight slowly by reducing their calorie intake slightly or those who frequently experiment with new recipes but wish to avoid a very high consumption of calories. These recipes can also guide the person entertaining for weight-conscious friends. However,

thought should also be given to what is to be served *with* the 'low-calorie' recipe. An over-enthusiastic combination of these recipes will not guarantee a low-calorie meal!

In deciding which recipes to consider in the 'low-calorie' category, each ingredient needs to be considered for its calorific contribution. Low-calorie ingredients such as vegetables, fruits, white fish and eggs may be combined with a moderate amount of fat or fat-containing foods and still be relatively 'low-calorie'. A generous combination of fats and fat-containing foods will produce a high-calorie recipe. Similarly, recipes which rely heavily on sugar, alcohol, flour or a combination of these foods with or without fat will be excluded from the 'low-calorie' rating.

In some recipes it may be possible to make further reductions in the amount of fats and sugars used, such as substituting low-fat yogurt for cream, or to grill [broil] food and drain off fat rather than frying, although the end results will differ slightly.

The calorie chart under the alphabetical heading CALORIES (p. 302) may be used to work out the approximate calorific value of individual recipes.

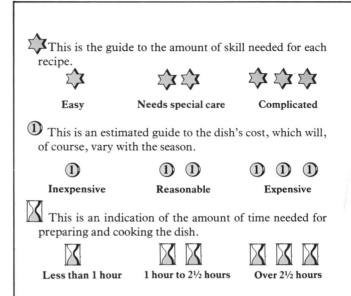

This is the guide to the amount of skill needed for each recipe.

Easy   **Needs special care**   **Complicated**

This is an estimated guide to the dish's cost, which will, of course, vary with the season.

Inexpensive   **Reasonable**   **Expensive**

This is an indication of the amount of time needed for preparing and cooking the dish.

Less than 1 hour   **1 hour to 2½ hours**   **Over 2½ hours**

Front Cover: Meatballs with Hot Mexican Sauce p. 1356

**Published by Marshall Cavendish House
58 Old Compton Street
London W1V 5PA**

This Edition Published 1986

©*Marshall Cavendish Ltd 1986, 1985, 1979, 1978, 1977, 1976, 1975, 1974, 1973, 1972, 58 Old Compton Street, London W1V 5PA*

*Printed and bound by
L.E.G.O. Spa Vicenza*

Cataloguing in Publication Data

*Supercook
1. Cookery
1. Cameron-Smith, Marye
641.5   TX717   79-52319*

*ISBN (for set) 0 85685 534 0
ISBN (this volume) 0 85685 545 6
Library of Congress catalog card number 78-52319*

Recipes in Volume 11

Minnow

The minnow is a small freshwater fish, better known in Britain as the TIDDLER. It is often compared to WHITEBAIT, although it has a slightly bitter flavour. The minnow is often substituted for GUDGEON and is cooked in the same way.

Minorcan Vegetable Soup

Minorcan Vegetable Soup is a soup in which a subtle blend of Spanish and French cuisine is achieved. Serve it on its own followed by a crisp green salad and a selection of cheeses, for an appetizing supper.

4 SERVINGS

3 tablespoons olive oil
4 garlic cloves, chopped
2 large onions, coarsely chopped
2 leeks, white part only, chopped
2 celery stalks, trimmed and chopped
8 oz. tomatoes, blanched, peeled and chopped
1 large red pepper, white pith removed, seeded and cut into strips
2 pints [5 cups] water
1 small cabbage, outer leaves removed and shredded
1 teaspoon dried thyme
1 bay leaf
1 teaspoon salt
½ teaspoon black pepper
4 slices of brown bread
2 garlic cloves, crushed and mixed with 2 tablespoons olive oil

In a large saucepan, heat the oil over moderate heat. When the oil is hot, add the garlic and fry it, stirring constantly, for 2 to 3 minutes. Add the onions, leeks

Minorcan Vegetable Soup has a subtle Mediterranean flavour.

and celery. Fry the mixture, stirring occasionally, for 5 to 7 minutes, or until the onions are soft and translucent but not brown. Add the tomatoes and the red pepper and cook, stirring occasionally, for a further 15 minutes.

Add the water, stirring constantly. Increase the heat to high and bring the mixture to the boil.

Add the cabbage, thyme, bay leaf, salt and pepper. Cover the pan, reduce the heat to low and simmer the soup for 2 hours.

Spread the slices of bread with the garlic and oil mixture. Place the bread in a warmed large soup tureen, or in individual soup bowls. Pour the soup over the bread and serve immediately.

Mint

Mint is a herb belonging to a genus of strong-scented plants of the *labiatae* family. There are at least 25 species and most of them are cultivated for the aromatic oil which they secrete. Its natural habitat is most probably the Mediterranean and Western Asia, but it now grows in most temperate and sub-tropical regions of the world.

It is said that mint was brought to Britain by the Romans who called the herb *mentha* after a mythological naiad who was crushed underfoot by Proserpina, goddess of spring, in a fit of jealous rage. She immediately became a plant which smells sweeter the more it is crushed.

The best known species of mint are:
Spearmint This mint is one of the most commonly grown in home gardens. It is used to flavour meat and savoury dishes, salads, drinks and sauces. The distilled oil is also used to flavour sweets [candies] and toothpaste.
Peppermint This mint is used in herbal teas but is cultivated more especially for its essential oil which is used to flavour liqueurs, sweets [candies] and toothpaste. It is also used as an ingredient in remedies for indigestion.
Applemint This mint has a delicate flavour and is most often used to flavour fruit compôtes.
Bergamint or **orange mint** Also known as eau de cologne mint and lavender mint, this mint is used to flavour ice-cream, fruit sauces and drinks.

Mint Ale

A cool refreshing summer drink, Mint Ale should be served really cold. Squeeze the lemons in advance and chill the juice in the refrigerator before using. The ginger ale should also be chilled for at least 1 hour before using.

ABOUT 2 PINTS

6 large fresh mint sprigs, washed, shaken dry and roughly chopped
8 oz. icing sugar [2 cups confectioners' sugar], sifted
3 tablespoons water
juice of 12 lemons, chilled
1½ pints [3¾ cups] dry ginger ale, chilled
3 fresh mint sprigs (optional)

Combine the chopped mint, sugar and water in a large mixing bowl. Pound the mint into the sugar and water with a wooden spoon until the sugar is dissolved. Set the bowl aside for 2 hours.

Strain the mint mixture through a strainer into a large glass jug. Pour on the lemon juice and ginger ale and stir well

with a long-handled spoon.

Garnish the ale with the mint sprigs, if you are using them, and serve at once.

Mint Chutney

This is a spicy, fresh green chutney from India. It should be served on the day of making but will keep for a day or two if covered and kept in the refrigerator. Serve it with curry or other Indian dishes (it is particularly good with Pakoras). This chutney may also be made with fresh coriander leaves.

8 FLUID OUNCES

2 oz. desiccated coconut [½ cup shredded coconut]
5 fl. oz. [⅝ cup] yogurt
2 oz. fresh mint
2 green chillis
juice of 1 lemon
1 teaspoon salt
½ teaspoon sugar

In a small bowl, combine the coconut with the yogurt. Set aside to soak for 1 hour.

Strip off all the mint leaves from the stalks. Discard all but three of the stalks.

Put the mint leaves and the three stalks, the coconut and the yogurt mixture and all the remaining ingredients in an electric blender. Blend until the mixture is smooth.

Alternatively, pound the ingredients in a mortar with a pestle until smooth. Taste the mixture and add more seasoning if necessary.

Using a spatula, scrape the chutney into a small bowl. Cover the bowl and put it into the refrigerator to chill for 1 hour before serving.

Mint Dressing

A cool, refreshing dressing, this is perfect spooned over cold cooked lamb or on a tomato or potato salad.

ABOUT 2 FLUID OUNCES

3 tablespoons olive oil
1 tablespoon lemon juice
½ teaspoon salt
½ teaspoon black pepper
1 tablespoon finely chopped fresh mint
2 teaspoons sugar

In a small mixing bowl, combine all the ingredients and mix well with a wooden spoon. Alternatively place all the ingredients in a screw-top jar and shake well.

Place the dressing in the refrigerator to chill for 30 minutes before serving.

Mint Julep

This is the classic Kentucky recipe for Mint Julep made with bourbon whiskey. Recipes from other states in the southern United States call for rum or Cognac. A Mint Julep looks very cool and appetizing, and it is, but it is also a very strong drink, so do not be misled by its appearance into thinking it is like a light punch.

1 SERVING

6 small fresh mint leaves
1 teaspoon castor sugar
1 teaspoon cold water
8 fl. oz. [1 cup] shaved ice
4 fl. oz. [½ cup] bourbon whiskey
2 lemon slices
1 fresh mint sprig
¼ teaspoon icing [confectioners'] sugar

Put the mint leaves on the bottom of a large glass or silver mint-julep mug. Add the castor sugar and water. With a bar muddler, crush the mint leaves until they are well bruised. Keep pounding and stirring until the sugar is dissolved. Fill the glass with the shaved ice and pour in the bourbon. With a long handled spoon,

Mint Pastries, filled with fruit, nuts and mint, and a traditional Mint Sauce to serve with roast lamb.

mix the bourbon and the ice together.

Dry the outside of the glass and place it in the coldest part of the refrigerator to chill for at least 1 hour. The glass should be thoroughly frosted and the ice inside should be almost solid.

Remove the glass from the refrigerator using a napkin or kitchen paper towel—this will prevent finger marks from forming on the frost.

Garnish the drink with the lemon slices and plant the mint sprig in the ice. Sprinkle the mint with the icing [confectioners'] sugar and serve with a straw.

Mint and Mushroom Soup

A smooth and delicately flavoured soup, Mint and Mushroom Soup makes a delightful first course for a dinner party, or, served with crusty bread and butter and a salad, a very simple light lunch.

4 SERVINGS

4 large potatoes, coarsely chopped
1 small onion
1½ pints [3¾ cups] chicken stock
    grated rind and juice of 1 lemon
1 tablespoon chopped fresh
    rosemary or 1½ teaspoons dried
    rosemary
½ teaspoon salt

¼ teaspoon black pepper
2 oz. [¼ cup] butter
8 oz. mushrooms, wiped clean
    and sliced
1 tablespoon flour
2 tablespoons finely chopped fresh
    mint
5 fl. oz. double cream [⅝ cup heavy
    cream]

Place the potatoes and the onion in a large saucepan. Pour in the stock. Add the lemon rind and juice, rosemary, salt and pepper. Place the pan over high heat and bring the mixture to the boil. Reduce the heat to low and simmer, stirring occasionally, for 25 minutes, or until the vegetables are tender.

Meanwhile, in a small saucepan, melt the butter over low heat. When the foam subsides, add the mushrooms and toss them in the butter until they are thoroughly coated. Cook them slowly, stirring occasionally, for 10 minutes. Sprinkle over the flour and, with a wooden spoon,

stir it into the mushroom mixture. Remove the pan from the heat and set aside.

With a slotted spoon, remove the potatoes and onion from the stock mixture. Purée them in a food mill, or rub them through a strainer with the back of a wooden spoon. Return the puréed vegetables to the stock mixture.

Add the mushrooms to the stock mixture. Increase the heat to high and bring the soup to the boil, stirring constantly. Stir in the mint. Remove the pan from the heat.

Pour the soup into a large tureen and stir in the cream. Alternatively, serve the soup in individual soup bowls, adding a spoonful of cream to each one.

Mint Pastries

Sweet pastries filled with dried fruit, nuts and mint, Mint Pastries may be served cold for tea or with morning coffee.

8 SQUARES

1 teaspoon butter
8 oz. [2 cups] Biscuit Crust dough
2 oz. [⅓ cup] sultanas or seedless raisins
2 oz. [⅓ cup] currants
2 oz. [⅓ cup] chopped mixed peel
1 oz. [¼ cup] slivered almonds
2 tablespoons chopped fresh mint
1 egg, lightly beaten
1 oz. icing sugar [¼ cup confectioners' sugar]

Preheat the oven to fairly hot 400°F Gas Mark 6, 200°C). Lightly grease a medium-sized baking sheet with the butter. Set aside.

On a lightly floured board or marble slab, roll out the dough to a rectangle about ¼-inch thick. Cut the dough in half and set one half aside. Lift the remaining dough on to the baking sheet. Set aside.

In a medium-sized mixing bowl, combine the sultanas or seedless raisins, currants, peel, almonds and mint. Sprinkle the dough with the mint mixture, leaving a ½-inch border on each side. Using a pastry brush, brush the border with half the beaten egg. Place the reserved dough half on top and press the edges together to seal.

Brush the top with the remaining beaten egg and sprinkle with the icing [confectioners'] sugar. With a sharp knife, mark the top layer of dough into squares.

Place the baking sheet in the oven and bake for 20 to 25 minutes or until the pastry is golden brown and the sugar has almost melted.

Remove the sheet from the oven and let the pastry cool on the baking sheet for 15 minutes. With a sharp knife, cut the pastry into squares. Transfer the squares to a wire rack to cool completely before serving.

Mint Sauce

The traditional British sauce for roast lamb and peas, Mint Sauce should be made with young fresh mint, preferably straight from the garden.

ABOUT 6 FLUID OUNCES

12 tablespoons finely chopped fresh mint

An unusual plum soufflé, Mirabelle Soufflé is a pleasant, light dessert. The juice makes a refreshing drink.

1½ tablespoons sugar
3 fl. oz. [⅜ cup] malt vinegar
1 tablespoon hot water

Pound the mint and sugar together in a mortar with a pestle. Alternatively, mix them in a small bowl with a wooden spoon. Add the vinegar and hot water and stir until the sugar has dissolved. Set the bowl aside and leave it for 1 to 2 hours before serving.

Mirabeau, à la

A garnish which is usually served with grilled [broiled] meat, *à la Mirabeau* (mee-rah-boh) consists of strips of anchovy fillets arranged in a criss-cross fashion over the meat with slices of stoned olives in between. The dish is then topped with ANCHOVY BUTTER and blanched tarragon leaves or watercress.

Mirabelle

The mirabelle is a small round cherry-like plum, golden-yellow in colour, sometimes with red dots. It has a thin skin, is juicy and sweet and has a strong fragrance. It is cultivated in Alsace and Lorraine and in some other parts of France and Germany. In England the mirabelle is called the 'cloth of gold'.

The fruit is most often eaten stewed and in tarts or made into a jam or jelly. A pure white liqueur made from the fruit is also called mirabelle.

Mirabelle Soufflé

An unusual soufflé made with plums, Mirabelle Soufflé must be served as soon as it is taken from the oven. Greengages or Victoria or any other plums may be substituted if you cannot obtain mirabelles.

When you have cooked the plums, pour the juice into a glass or jug and chill in the refrigerator for 1 hour. It makes a very refreshing drink either plain or topped with soda water.

4-6 SERVINGS

2 oz. [¼ cup] plus 1 teaspoon butter
3 tablespoons dry breadcrumbs
12 oz. mirabelle plums, halved and stoned
2 tablespoons cold water
4 oz. [½ cup] sugar
2 oz. [½ cup] flour
10 fl. oz. [1¼ cups] milk, scalded (brought to just below boiling point)
grated rind and juice of 1 lemon
5 egg yolks
6 egg whites

Using the teaspoon of butter, grease the bottom and sides of a 3-pint [2-quart] soufflé dish. Sprinkle the inside of the dish with the breadcrumbs. Set aside.

Place the plums in a medium-sized saucepan with the water and 2 ounces [¼ cup] of the sugar. Cover the pan and place it over moderate heat. Cook the plums for 10 to 15 minutes or until they are soft but still retain their shape. Remove the pan from the heat.

Using a slotted spoon, remove the plum halves from the pan and place them, cut sides down, in the soufflé dish. Set aside.

Preheat the oven to moderate 350°F (Gas Mark 4, 180°C).

In a large saucepan, melt the remaining butter over moderate heat. Remove the pan from the heat and, with a wooden spoon, stir in the flour to make a smooth paste. Gradually add the milk, stirring constantly.

Return the pan to the heat and cook the mixture, stirring constantly, for 2 minutes or until it is thick and smooth.

Remove the pan from the heat and stir in the remaining sugar and the lemon rind and juice. Beat in the egg yolks, one at a time. Set the pan aside to allow the egg yolk mixture to cool slightly.

In a large mixing bowl, beat the egg whites with a wire whisk or rotary beater until they form stiff peaks.

With a metal spoon, gently fold the egg whites into the egg yolk mixture.

Spoon the mixture into the soufflé dish on top of the plums and place the dish in the centre of the oven. Bake for 30 to 35 minutes or until the soufflé has risen and is lightly browned.

Remove the soufflé dish from the oven and serve at once.

Miranda's Salad

This is a very attractive salad which may be served with cold meats or on its own as a light luncheon dish. If fresh pineapple is not available canned pineapple may be used.

6-8 SERVINGS

4 red apples, cored and cut into ½-inch cubes
2 tablespoons lemon juice
4 slices of fresh pineapple
1 head of celery, trimmed and finely chopped
2 lettuces, outer leaves removed, washed and separated into leaves
DRESSING
2 tablespoons chopped fresh parsley
2 tablespoons chopped fresh chives
6 tablespoons olive oil
2 tablespoons lemon juice
½ teaspoon salt
¼ teaspoon black pepper

(Low Cal)

Put the apple cubes in a large mixing bowl and sprinkle the lemon juice over them. Toss the apples with a spoon until they are coated with the lemon juice. Add the pineapple and celery to the bowl.

Add the lettuce and toss the salad until it is well mixed.

In a small mixing bowl combine the parsley, chives, oil, lemon juice, salt and pepper. Using a wooden spoon, mix them together thoroughly. Pour the dressing over the salad.

Place the salad in the refrigerator to chill for 30 minutes before serving.

Mirepoix

A *mirepoix* (meer-reh-pwah) is a mixture of diced vegetables, such as onions, carrots, celery, parsnips and leeks, stewed in butter. Ham or belly of pork, a bay leaf and thyme are sometimes added. It forms the basis of many sauces, notably ESPAGNOLE or BROWN SAUCE.

A mirepoix can also be added to pot roasts or braised meats.

A vegetable mirepoix (without the ham) is often used as a garnish for meat or fish dishes.

Mirlitons
MACAROON-FILLED TARTLETS

A classic French pastry, Mirlitons (meer-leh-tawn) are small cases of flaky pastry filled with a rich macaroon mixture. Serve for afternoon tea, or as an accompaniment to coffee.

12 TARTLETS

PASTRY
6 oz. [1½ cups] flour
⅛ teaspoon salt
2 oz. [¼ cup] butter
4 to 5 tablespoons iced water
2 oz. [¼ cup] vegetable fat
FILLING
3 oz. peach conserve
2 eggs
2 oz. [¼ cup] castor sugar
4 oz. macaroon biscuits [cookies], crushed
½ teaspoon vanilla essence
2 oz. [½ cup] slivered almonds

To make the pastry, sift the flour and salt into a medium-sized mixing bowl. Divide the butter into two pieces and add one piece to the flour. With your fingertips, rub the butter into the flour until it resembles fine breadcrumbs. With a knife, mix in enough of the water to form a firm dough.

Turn the dough out on to a floured board and, with your hands, shape it into a square. Roll out the dough into an oblong and dot two-thirds of it with small pieces of half the vegetable fat. Fold over one-third of the dough and then the other third to make a neat, square parcel. Press down the edges with the rolling pin to seal them.

Turn the dough round so that the sealed ends are facing you and roll out again into an oblong. Dot with pieces of the remaining vegetable fat, fold in three, seal the edges, turn the dough and roll out again. Wrap in greaseproof or waxed paper and chill in the refrigerator for 10 minutes.

Repeat this process with the remaining butter.

Preheat the oven to fairly hot 375°F (Gas Mark 5, 190°C).

Remove the dough from the refrigerator and, on a floured board, roll it out into a circle about ⅛-inch thick. With a 4-inch pastry cutter, cut the dough into circles. Line 12 patty tins with the dough circles. Using a fork, lightly prick the bases of the pastry cases two or three times. Spoon 1 teaspoonful of the peach conserve into each patty tin. Set the tins aside.

In a medium-sized heatproof mixing bowl, combine the eggs and sugar. Place the bowl over a saucepan of simmering water and, using a wire whisk or rotary beater, beat the mixture until it is thick.

Remove the pan from the heat and continue to beat the mixture for 1 minute. Remove the bowl from the pan and stir in the crushed macaroons and vanilla essence.

Spoon the mixture into the pastry cases and sprinkle over the slivered almonds.

Place the patty tins in the oven and bake the mirlitons for 25 to 30 minutes or until the fillings have turned light brown.

Remove the tins from the oven and allow the mirlitons to cool in the tins for 10 minutes. Remove the mirlitons from the tins and set them aside on a wire rack to cool completely before serving.

Miroton de Boeuf is a classic French dish, using leftover cooked beef.

Miroton de Boeuf
BEEF IN ONION AND MUSHROOM SAUCE

Miroton de Boeuf (mee-roh-tohn d'berf) *is a classic French way of using up cold leftover roast beef. It makes an ideal family supper dish.*

4 SERVINGS

2 oz. [¼ cup] butter
1 tablespoon olive oil
8 oz. onions, finely chopped

4 oz. mushrooms, wiped clean and chopped
1 teaspoon flour
5 fl. oz. [⅝ cup] beef stock
2 fl. oz. [¼ cup] white wine
1 bay leaf
1 garlic clove, crushed
1 teaspoon chopped fresh sage or ½ teaspoon dried sage
½ teaspoon salt
¼ teaspoon black pepper
1 lb. cold roast beef, cut into thin slices
5 potatoes, cooked until tender, sliced and kept warm
2 teaspoons lemon juice

In a large heavy frying-pan, melt the butter with the oil over moderate heat. When the foam subsides, add the onions and mushrooms and cook them, stirring occasionally, for 5 to 7 minutes or until the onions are soft and translucent but not brown.

With a wooden spoon, stir in the flour. Add the stock, wine, bay leaf, garlic, sage, salt and pepper and stir well. Increase the heat to high and bring the mixture to the boil. Reduce the heat to low and simmer the mixture for 20 minutes. Add the beef and cook for a further 5 minutes.

Arrange the potato slices around the edge of a warmed large serving dish. With a slotted spoon, remove the slices of beef from the pan and place them in the centre of the dish. Keep warm.

Add the lemon juice to the frying-pan Increase the heat to high and bring the sauce to the boil. Boil for 3 minutes or until it has reduced slightly. Remove the pan from the heat. Remove and discard the bay leaf. Pour the sauce over the meat and serve immediately.

Miso

Miso (mee-soh) is a soya bean paste which is used as a flavouring in soups and for vegetables. The paste is available in Japanese food shops and may be either red, white or dark brown in colour.

Mistress Hill's Cakes

This is an old recipe from the days when all cake recipes seemed to start with 'take 3 pounds of flour'. . . However, this recipe has been cut down to today's proportions, and the cakes resemble biscuits [cookies].

36 CAKES

4 oz. [½ cup] plus 1 teaspoon butter
8 oz. [2 cups] flour, sifted
6 oz. [¾ cup] sugar
2 egg yolks
grated rind of 2 lemons

Using the teaspoon of butter grease two large baking sheets and set aside.

In a medium-sized mixing bowl, combine the flour and sugar. Add the remaining butter and cut it into small pieces with a table knife. Using your fingertips, rub the butter into the flour and sugar until the mixture resembles coarse breadcrumbs.

Add the egg yolks and lemon rind to the flour mixture and stir them in with the table knife. Using your hands, work the mixture to form a smooth dough. Cover the dough and place it in the refrigerator to chill for 30 minutes.

Preheat the oven to warm 325°F (Gas Mark 3, 170°C).

Remove the dough from the refrigerator. Break off small pieces of the dough and roll them between your hands to form 1-inch ball shapes. Place the balls of dough on the baking sheets. Flatten each ball slightly with the prongs of a fork.

Place the baking sheets in the oven and bake the cakes for 15 minutes or until the edges are pale brown.

Remove the baking sheets from the oven and allow the cakes to cool for 5 minutes. Then transfer the cakes to a wire rack to cool completely.

Store the cakes in an airtight tin or serve immediately.

Mistress Hill's Cakes were adapted from a very old recipe, and are flavoured with freshly grated lemon rind. Serve them with tea or coffee.

Mi Tse Ho-Tui

HAM IN HONEY SYRUP

An elegant dish from China, Mi Tse Ho-Tui (mee tz' hoh-tway) is not difficult to prepare and makes an impressive main dish for a dinner party. Serve with sweet potatoes and sautéed courgettes [zucchini].

4-6 SERVINGS

1 x 3 lb. middle leg of gammon, washed, soaked in cold water overnight and drained

HONEY SYRUP SAUCE

2 tablespoons sugar mixed with 4 tablespoons water

2 tablespoons clear honey

2 tablespoons sherry

2 teaspoons cherry brandy

2 teaspoons cornflour [cornstarch] dissolved in 3 tablespoons water

Half fill the lower part of a large steamer with boiling water. Place the gammon in the upper part and place the steamer over moderate heat. Steam the gammon for 2¼ hours.

Remove the steamer from the heat and, using large spoons, remove the gammon from the pan. Set the gammon aside until it is cool enough to handle.

When the gammon is cool enough to handle, with a sharp knife cut it into ¼-inch thick slices. Arrange the slices decoratively on a heatproof serving dish.

To make the sauce, combine all the sauce ingredients in a small saucepan. Place the pan over moderate heat and bring the mixture to the boil, stirring constantly. Remove the pan from the heat and pour the sauce evenly over the gammon slices.

Place the serving dish in the top part of the steamer and return the steamer to moderate heat. Steam the meat and sauce for 3 minutes.

Remove the steamer from the heat. Remove the serving dish from the steamer and serve at once — the dish should be brought to the table wreathed in clouds of steam.

Mixed Grill

A mixed grill is a traditional English dish which is a combination of various grilled [broiled] meats. These include lamb chops, steak, kidneys, bacon and sausages. The dish is garnished with mushrooms and tomatoes and served with fried potatoes. A fried egg is sometimes included.

A succulent Chinese dish, Mi Tse Ho-Tui is surprisingly easy to prepare.

Mixed Seafood Casserole

Mixed Seafood Casserole is a delicious mixture of fish and shellfish with a rich cream and wine sauce. Serve with parsleyed potatoes and a green bean salad and accompany it with a well-chilled bottle of Sancerre white wine.

8 SERVINGS

8 oz. canned crabmeat, cartilage and shell removed

1 egg, lightly beaten

2 tablespoons chopped fresh parsley

½ teaspoon salt

¼ teaspoon black pepper

4 whole sole fillets, skinned and halved

8 oz. Dublin Bay prawns [large Gulf shrimps], shelled

8 oz. shrimps, shelled

8 oz. scallops, quartered

4 fl. oz. [½ cup] fish stock

4 fl. oz. [½ cup] dry white wine

2 fl. oz. [¼ cup] lemon juice

5 fl. oz. double cream [⅝ cup heavy cream]

1 lemon, cut into wedges

Preheat the oven to moderate 350°F (Gas Mark 4, 180°C).

In a small bowl, mash the crabmeat with a fork. Add the egg, parsley, salt and pepper and mix to a smooth paste.

Using a table knife, spread the paste thickly over one side of each of the sole fillets. Roll up the fillets, Swiss [jelly] roll fashion, and place the rolls in a flameproof casserole.

Arrange the prawns [large Gulf shrimps], shrimps and scallops over and around the rolls. Pour in the fish stock, wine and lemon juice.

Place the casserole over moderate heat and bring the liquid to the boil. Cover the casserole and transfer it to the oven. Bake for 20 minutes, or until the sole is tender and flakes easily when tested with a fork.

Remove the casserole from the oven. With tongs, transfer the fish rolls and shellfish to a warmed serving dish. Keep warm while you make the sauce.

Strain the liquid from the casserole into a small saucepan. Bring it to the boil over high heat. Boil for 3 minutes or until the liquid has reduced by about half. Reduce the heat to low and add the cream. Cook the sauce, stirring constantly with a wooden spoon, for 3 to 5 minutes, or until it is hot but not boiling.

Remove the pan from the heat and pour the sauce over the fish and shellfish. Serve immediately, garnished with the lemon wedges.

Low Cal

Mixed Spice

Commercial mixed spice is made from a blend of grated nutmeg, ground cinnamon, ground ginger and ground cloves. However home-made mixed spice can also include ground coriander and crushed cardamom.

Ground allspice can be substituted for mixed spice since its flavour resembles a combination of nutmeg, cinnamon and cloves.

Mkate Wa Mayai

EGG CAKE

Mkate Wa Mayai (oom-kah-tay way my-yigh) is a plain but delicious cake from the coastlands of East Africa. In Swahili the name literally means cake, or bread, with eggs. Serve it warm, cut into slices and spread with Cinnamon Butter, or let it cool completely before serving.

ONE 8-INCH CAKE

1 teaspoon butter

8 oz. [2 cups] plus 1 tablespoon flour

½ teaspoon salt

1 teaspoon baking powder

8 oz. [1 cup] castor sugar

6 egg yolks

1 teaspoon vanilla essence

6 egg whites, stiffly beaten

2 oz. [⅓ cup] currants, soaked in 4 tablespoons sweet sherry for 10 minutes

Preheat the oven to moderate 350°F (Gas Mark 4, 180°C). Using the teaspoon of butter, grease an 8-inch square cake tin. Dust it with the tablespoon of flour, tipping and rotating the tin. Knock out any excess flour. Set aside.

Sift the remaining flour, salt and baking powder into a medium-sized mixing bowl. Set aside.

In a large mixing bowl, beat the sugar and egg yolks together with a wire whisk or rotary beater until the mixture is pale and frothy. Add the vanilla essence and beat for a further 30 seconds.

With a metal spoon, carefully fold in the flour mixture until the ingredients are thoroughly combined. Fold in the beaten egg whites.

Spoon the cake mixture into the prepared tin. Place the tin in the centre of the oven and bake for 15 minutes or until the cake has just set.

Drain the currants and discard the sherry. Sprinkle the currants over the top of the cake and continue baking for a further 1 hour, or until a skewer inserted into the centre of the cake comes out clean.

Moc

Remove the tin from the oven and leave the cake in the tin for 10 minutes before turning it out on to a wire rack to cool.

Mocha

Mocha is a good quality coffee bean grown in Mocha, the southern part of the Yemen. Coffee made with these beans is extremely rich and is generally served in Middle Eastern style, in very small cups.

Mocha is also a term applied to sweet dishes flavoured with coffee and is sometimes used to describe a mixture of coffee and chocolate.

Mocha Cream Pie

A delicious American dessert, Mocha Cream Pie is a rich combination of chocolate, coffee and rum.

ONE 9-INCH PIE

3 oz. dark [semi-sweet] cooking chocolate
4 tablespoons strong black coffee
2 tablespoons rum
16 fl. oz. [2 cups] Crème Pâtissière
1 x 9-inch Flan Case made with rich shortcrust pastry, baked blind and cooled
5 fl. oz. double cream [⅝ cup heavy cream], stiffly whipped

Place the chocolate, coffee and rum in a small saucepan and place the pan over low heat. Melt the chocolate, stirring constantly. As soon as the chocolate has melted, remove the pan from the heat. Set it aside to cool slightly.

In a medium-sized mixing bowl, combine the chocolate mixture and the Crème Pâtissière. Place the bowl in the refrigerator and chill for 2 hours.

Remove the bowl from the refrigerator and spoon the chocolate mixture into the pastry case, spreading it out evenly with a flat-bladed knife.

Decorate with the whipped cream and serve immediately.

Mocha Katy

A creamy rich pudding, Mocha Katy is ideal for serving at a dinner party.

6-8 SERVINGS

12 oz. [1½ cups] sugar
3 fl. oz. [⅜ cup] water
2 tablespoons instant coffee powder
4 eggs
12 oz. [1½ cups] unsalted butter, softened

8 sponge finger biscuits [cookies]
2 fl. oz. [¼ cup] dry sherry
2 fl. oz. [¼ cup] whisky
10 fl. oz. double cream [1¼ cups heavy cream], stiffly whipped
2 oz. [½ cup] slivered almonds, toasted

In a medium-sized saucepan, dissolve the sugar in the water over moderate heat, stirring constantly. Increase the heat to moderately high and bring the syrup to the boil.

Boil the syrup for 5 minutes or until the temperature reaches 240°F on a sugar thermometer or until a small amount of the syrup dropped into cold water forms a soft ball when rolled between the fingers. Remove the pan from the heat. Stir the coffee into the syrup.

In a large mixing bowl, beat the eggs with a wire whisk or rotary beater until they are well mixed. Gradually pour the hot syrup on to the eggs, beating constantly. Continue beating until the mixture is thick and pale.

Beat in the butter, in spoonfuls. Make sure that each spoonful is absorbed before adding the next. Place the bowl in the refrigerator to chill for 3 hours or until the mixture is very thick and cold.

A few minutes before removing the egg and butter mixture from the refrigerator, place the sponge finger biscuits [cookies] in a serving bowl or dish, large enough to take them in one layer. Pour over the sherry and whisky and leave for 5 minutes or until the biscuits [cookies] have absorbed almost all of the liquid.

Remove the egg and butter mixture from the refrigerator and pour it over the biscuits [cookies]. With a spatula or table knife, spread the whipped cream on top. Cover the bowl or dish and put it in the refrigerator to chill until it is required.

Just before serving, sprinkle the almonds on top.

Mock Cream

Mock Cream is made on a base of milk and cornflour [cornstarch]; and its slightly heavy consistency makes it particularly suitable for piping. It may also be used as a filling or topping for sponge cakes.

ABOUT 8 FLUID OUNCES

2 tablespoons cornflour [cornstarch]
8 fl. oz. [1 cup] milk
1 vanilla pod
2 oz. [¼ cup] unsalted butter
2 tablespoons castor sugar

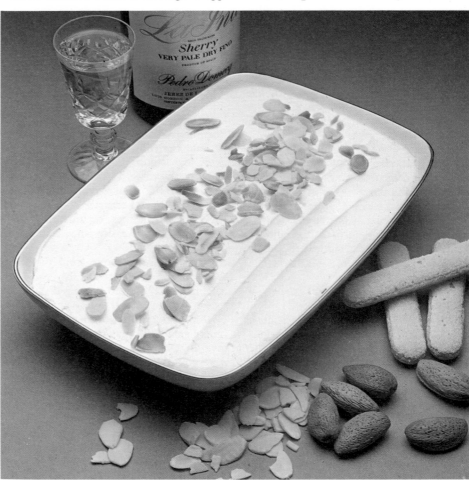

Mock Turtle Soup has a very distinctive and delicious flavour.

Put the cornflour [cornstarch] in a medium-sized saucepan. Gradually add the milk, stirring constantly with a wooden spoon until the mixture is smooth. Add the vanilla pod and set the pan over moderately low heat. Stirring constantly, bring the mixture slowly to the boil.

Cook the mixture, stirring constantly, for 2 to 3 minutes, or until it is thick and smooth. Remove the pan from the heat. Leave the cornflour [cornstarch] and milk mixture to become completely cold. Remove the vanilla pod from the pan, rinse and set aside for future use.

In a medium-sized mixing bowl, cream the butter and sugar together with a wooden spoon until the mixture is smooth. Gradually beat in the cornflour [cornstarch] and milk mixture. Continue beating for 5 to 7 minutes, or until the cream is stiff enough to pipe.

The cream is now ready to use.

Sprinkled with toasted almonds, Mocha Katy is a rich creamy dessert.

Mock Turtle Soup

This soup is a marvellous combination of meats and vegetables, all simmered together and strained to make a very distinctive soup. Although traditionally the meat from the calf's head, squeezed of juices after cooking and cut into squares, or, as suggested in this recipe, forcemeat balls, are eaten with the soup, they may be omitted if preferred. If omitted, reduce the cooking time for the jellied soup to just 15 minutes. Mock Turtle Soup tends to be very fatty, so make sure you skim it well.

8-10 SERVINGS

1 oz. [2 tablespoons] butter
1 tablespoon vegetable oil
8 oz. knuckle of veal, boned and cut into 1-inch pieces
4 oz. lean cooked ham, diced
4 oz. lean beef (shin), diced
1 large onion, quartered
1 carrot, scraped and quartered
1 turnip, peeled and quartered
2 shallots, coarsely chopped
1 celery stalk, trimmed and cut into 2-inch pieces
4 oz. button mushrooms, wiped clean

bouquet garni, consisting of 4 parsley sprigs, 1 thyme spray and 1 bay leaf tied together
2 tablespoons dried marjoram
1 tablespoon dried savory
1 tablespoon dried basil
6 peppercorns
2 teaspoons salt
1 teaspoon black pepper
3 pints [7½ cups] water juice of 1 lemon
1 large orange, peeled and segmented
¼ calf's head, cleaned
16 forcemeat balls, made from Forcemeat of Pork recipe, substituting beef for the pork
2 fl. oz. [¼ cup] Madeira

In a very large flameproof casserole, melt the butter with the oil over moderate heat. When the foam subsides, add the veal, ham and beef and fry, turning the meat pieces frequently, for 5 minutes or until they are brown all over. With a slotted spoon, remove the meat from the casserole and set aside.

Add the onion, carrot, turnip, shallots, celery and mushrooms to the casserole. Fry, stirring occasionally, for 8 to 10 minutes, or until the vegetables begin to soften.

Return the veal, ham and beef to the casserole and add the bouquet garni, marjoram, savory, basil, peppercorns, salt and pepper. Pour in the water and add the lemon juice and orange segments.

Increase the heat to high and bring the mixture to the boil. Simmer for 15 minutes. Remove the casserole from the heat. With a metal spoon, carefully skim any fat off the surface.

Add the calf's head. Return the casserole to the heat and bring the soup to the boil again. Simmer for a further 15 minutes. Remove the casserole from the heat and, with a metal spoon, skim off any fat.

Return the casserole to low heat. Cover and simmer for 2½ to 3 hours, or until all the meat is very tender.

Remove the casserole from the heat. With a slotted spoon and tongs, remove the large pieces of meat, the calf's head and large vegetables from the casserole and discard. Strain the soup into a large soup tureen and discard the vegetables and seasonings in the strainer. Leave the soup to cool completely for 5 to 6 hours or overnight, or until it sets into a jelly and a layer of fat has formed on the top.

When you are ready to serve the soup, remove the fat from the surface with a metal spoon. Spoon the jellied soup into a large saucepan. Set the pan over moderate heat and simmer the soup for 10 minutes.

Add the forcemeat balls and pour in the Madeira. Cover the pan, reduce the heat to moderately low and cook for a further 25 minutes, or until the forcemeat balls are cooked.

Taste the soup for seasoning and add more salt and pepper if necessary.

Transfer the soup and the forcemeat balls to individual serving bowls and serve at once.

Mode, à la

A la Mode (ah lah mohd), literally 'in the current style', is a French term used to describe cuts of meat, for example beef, which are braised in their own juices and sometimes stock or wine.

In the United States, the term is used for pies and cakes to which ice-cream is added as a garnish. Apple Pie à la Mode is a favourite dessert.

Mohrschokoladedessert

CHOCOLATE PUDDING

This delicious pudding is a combination of eggs, almonds and chocolate, served with a rich sauce. For those of you with strong stomachs, serve Mohrschokoladedessert (moor - show - koh - lakd - dehz - zert) *with brandy-flavoured whipped cream!*

6 SERVINGS

4 oz. [½ cup] plus 3 teaspoons butter, softened
4 oz. [½ cup] plus 1 tablespoon castor sugar
3 oz. dark [semi-sweet] cooking chocolate, broken into pieces
6 egg yolks
4 oz. [⅔ cup] ground almonds
6 stale sponge finger biscuits [cookies], crumbled
6 egg whites, stiffly beaten
SAUCE
2 oz. [¼ cup] unsalted butter
4 oz. [½ cup] castor sugar
4 oz. dark [semi-sweet] cooking chocolate, broken into pieces
2 fl. oz. [¼ cup] water
2 fl. oz. [¼ cup] milk
2 tablespoons brandy

Grease a 2-pint [1½-quart] pudding basin with 2 teaspoons of the butter. Sprinkle in 1 tablespoon of the sugar and tip and rotate the basin until the sides and bottom are evenly coated. Knock out any excess sugar and set aside.

In the top part of a double boiler, or a heatproof bowl set over a pan of boiling water, melt the chocolate, stirring occasionally. Remove the pan from the heat and remove the bowl from the pan. Set aside to cool.

In a large mixing bowl, cream 4 ounces [½ cup] of the remaining butter and the remaining sugar together with a wooden spoon until the mixture is light and fluffy. Beat in the egg yolks and the cooled, melted chocolate. With a metal spoon, fold in the ground almonds and then the biscuit [cookie] crumbs.

Carefully fold in the stiffly beaten egg whites. Spoon the mixture into the prepared pudding basin and smooth the top with a spoon.

Fill the lower half of a steamer three-quarters full of water. Place the pan over high heat, with the top part of the steamer in place and covered, and bring the water to the boil. Alternatively, use a large saucepan with a well-fitting lid.

Cut out a circle of greaseproof or waxed paper 4 inches wider than the basin. Using the remaining teaspoon of butter, grease the paper circle. Cut out a circle of aluminium foil the same size as the paper circle and place the two circles together, the buttered side of the paper away from the foil. Holding them firmly together, make a large pleat across the centre. Place the circles, buttered side down, over the pudding basin and tie securely with string.

Place the basin in the top part of the steamer, or in the saucepan. Cover the pan, reduce the heat to moderately low and steam the pudding for 1 hour, adding more boiling water when necessary. While the pudding is steaming, make the sauce.

In a small saucepan, melt the butter with the sugar over moderate heat, stirring constantly until the sugar has dissolved. Remove the pan from the heat and set aside.

In the top part of a double boiler, or a heatproof bowl set over a pan of boiling water, melt the chocolate, stirring occasionally. Add the sugar and butter mixture and stir well. Gradually add the water and milk, stirring constantly. Stir in the brandy. Remove the pan from the heat.

Remove the pudding from the steamer. Discard the paper and foil. Place a serving dish, inverted, over the pudding basin and reverse the two. The pudding should slide out easily.

Pour the sauce over the pudding and serve at once.

Light Molasses Crumb Pie is very popular in the United States. Serve it with a glass of ice-cold milk.

Molasses

Molasses is a dark, very sweet syrup, the residue of the refining process in sugar. There are two types of molasses, one made from sugar beet and one made from sugar cane.

Molasses made from sugar beet is dark and bitter and is used in the distilling of alcohol, particularly rum, and in various industrial processes such as the manufacture of cattle feed. Molasses made from sugar cane is lighter and sweeter and is used in pies, cakes and confectionery.

Molasses is produced in the southern states of the United States and in the West Indies. Molasses may be bought from most health food stores and the larger supermarkets. If it is unobtainable, black treacle is very similar and may be substituted.

Molasses Crumb Pie

Molasses and soda combine to make this a sweet but very light pie. Serve in small wedges with a glass of cold milk.

ONE 9-INCH PIE

1 x 9-inch Flan Case, made from rich shortcrust pastry, baked blind and cooled
4 oz. [1 cup] flour

½ teaspoon salt
2 oz. [¼ cup] butter
1 oz. [2 tablespoons] vegetable fat
2 oz. [⅓ cup] soft brown sugar
1 teaspoon bicarbonate of soda [baking soda]
2 fl. oz. [¼ cup] hot water
2 fl. oz. [¼ cup] molasses or black treacle

Preheat the oven to moderate 350°F (Gas Mark 4, 180°C).

Place the flan case on a baking sheet and set aside.

Sift the flour and salt together into a large mixing bowl. Add the butter and vegetable fat and cut them into small pieces with a table knife. With your fingertips, rub the fat into the flour until the mixture resembles coarse breadcrumbs. Stir in the sugar. Set the topping aside.

In a medium-sized mixing bowl, dissolve the soda in the hot water. Add the molasses or black treacle and stir well until the liquids have combined. Pour the molasses mixture into the prepared flan case. Spoon the topping over the molasses mixture and smooth over with a spoon.

Place the pie in the centre of the oven and bake for 15 to 20 minutes or until the topping is light and golden brown.

Remove the pie from the oven and set aside on a wire rack to cool completely before serving.

Molasses Hazelnut Pie

This is a very rich pie, adapted from a traditional American recipe.

8 SERVINGS

1 x 9-inch Flan Case, made with rich shortcrust pastry, baked blind and cooled
1 oz. [2 tablespoons] butter
2 oz. [¼ cup] sugar
2 eggs
4 fl. oz. [½ cup] molasses or black treacle
¼ teaspoon salt
2 teaspoons grated orange rind
2 fl. oz. [¼ cup] evaporated milk
4 oz. [⅔ cups] hazelnuts, chopped
5 fl. oz. double cream [⅝ cup heavy cream], stiffly whipped

Preheat the oven to very hot 450°F (Gas Mark 8, 230°C). Place the flan case on a baking sheet. Set aside.

In a medium-sized mixing bowl, cream the butter with a wooden spoon until it is soft and creamy. Add the sugar and beat well until the mixture is light and

fluffy. Stir in the eggs and beat well to make a smooth batter.

Stir in the molasses or treacle, salt, orange rind, milk and hazelnuts. Pour the mixture into the flan case and place the flan in the oven. Bake for 10 minutes.

Reduce the oven temperature to warm 325°F (Gas Mark 3, 170°C) and bake the flan for a further 30 minutes or until the filling has set.

Remove the flan from the oven and transfer it to a wire rack to cool completely.

Place the flan on a serving dish and, using a flat-bladed knife, spread the whipped cream over the filling. Serve immediately.

Molasses Sponge Cake

Molasses Sponge Cake, soaked with melted molasses or treacle and rich, dark rum, can be eaten as a dessert with whipped cream, or served cold, cut into slices, as a cake.

ONE 9-INCH CAKE

1 teaspoon butter
6 oz. [1½ cups] plus 1 tablespoon flour
6 eggs, separated
4 oz. [½ cup] castor sugar
6 fl. oz. [¾ cup] molasses or black treacle
2 to 3 tablespoons milk
¼ teaspoon salt
2 tablespoons dark rum

Preheat the oven to moderate 350°F (Gas Mark 4, 180°C). With the butter, grease a 9-inch round cake tin. Sprinkle in the tablespoon of flour and tip and rotate the tin to coat the sides and bottom evenly. Knock out any excess flour and set aside.

In a medium-sized heatproof mixing bowl, beat together the egg yolks and sugar with a wire whisk or rotary beater. Place the bowl over a large saucepan half filled with barely simmering water. Set the pan over low heat and cook the mixture, beating constantly, until it is thick enough to hold a ribbon trail on itself when the whisk is lifted.

Remove the pan from the heat. Lift the bowl out of the pan. Gradually beat in half of the molasses or treacle, beating until the mixture is thoroughly combined. Sift in the remaining flour and beat it in with a wooden spoon until the batter is smooth.

Beat in 2 tablespoons of the milk, adding a little more if necessary to obtain a dropping consistency.

In a medium-sized mixing bowl, beat the egg whites with a wire whisk or rotary beater until they form soft peaks. Add the salt and beat until the mixture forms stiff peaks. With a metal spoon, carefully fold the egg whites into the flour and molasses or treacle mixture.

Spoon the mixture into the prepared tin, smoothing it down with a flat-bladed knife.

Place the tin in the centre of the oven and bake for 40 to 45 minutes or until a skewer inserted into the centre of the cake comes out clean.

Meanwhile, in a small saucepan, combine the remaining molasses or treacle and the rum. Set the pan over moderate heat and bring the mixture to the boil, stirring constantly. Remove the pan from the heat and keep the mixture hot.

Remove the cake from the oven. Set the cake aside to cool in the tin for 5 minutes. Turn the cake out on to a wire rack and, with a skewer, make holes in the cake 1-inch apart and to within 1-inch of the base.

Pour the hot treacle or molasses mixture into the holes in the cake, reserving 2 tablespoons. With a flat-bladed knife, spread the 2 tablespoons of molasses or treacle over the top of the cake. Place the cake on a serving plate and serve immediately, or cool and serve.

Molasses Taffy

Molasses Taffy is a dark toffee, flavoured with rum and made crunchy with a handful of walnuts. It will keep well if wrapped in waxed paper and stored in an airtight tin.

80 SWEETS [CANDIES]

12 oz. [2 cups] soft brown sugar
6 fl. oz. [¾ cup] molasses or black treacle
1 oz. [2 tablespoons] butter
2 tablespoons lemon juice
3 oz. [½ cup] walnuts, coarsely chopped
4 fl. oz. [½ cup] water
½ teaspoon rum essence

Place the sugar, molasses or black treacle, butter, lemon juice, walnuts and water in a large saucepan. Place the pan over moderate heat and stir the mixture with a wooden spoon until the sugar has dissolved.

Increase the heat to moderately high and boil the mixture until it reaches 260°F on a sugar thermometer or until a little dropped into cold water separates into threads as it cools. The threads should bend slightly when touched with the spoon.

Remove the pan from the heat. Allow the bubbles to subside and then stir in the rum essence.

Lightly oil a large marble slab or heatproof surface. Pour the sugar mixture on to the prepared surface and leave it until a thin skin forms and it is cool enough to handle.

Using an oiled palette knife or spatula, release the sugar mixture from the surface and form it into a ball. Divide the ball into four balls. Gradually stretch each ball to make a long rope about ¾-inch thick. Fold the rope in half and, holding one end, twist the rope around three times.

Using oiled scissors, cut the rope into ½-inch lengths. Wrap each piece of the toffee in a piece of waxed paper and store in an airtight tin until ready to be eaten.

Mollina Soup

This is a simple soup from southern Spain which is delicious served as part of a supper menu with crusty bread. If Seville oranges are not available substitute any kind of orange.

4 SERVINGS

2 lb. cod or haddock steaks, 2-inches thick
2 teaspoons salt
4 fl. oz. [½ cup] olive oil
2 garlic cloves
1 medium-sized onion, finely chopped
2 pints [5 cups] fish stock
1 teaspoon grated lemon rind
juice of 3 Seville oranges

Place the fish steaks on a board and sprinkle them with the salt. Set aside for 15 minutes.

In a medium-sized saucepan, heat the oil over moderate heat. Add the garlic and cook, stirring occasionally, for 4 to 6 minutes or until the garlic is golden brown. Using a slotted spoon, remove and discard the garlic.

Add the onion to the pan and cook, stirring occasionally, for 5 to 7 minutes or until it is soft and translucent but not brown. Gradually stir in the stock and lemon rind.

Increase the heat to moderate and bring the liquid to the boil. Add the fish to the pan. Reduce the heat to low and cook the fish for 10 to 15 minutes or until it flakes easily when tested with a fork.

Remove the pan from the heat and stir in the orange juice. Spoon the fish into a heated soup tureen. Pour over the soup and serve immediately.

On a lightly floured surface, roll out the dough to a rectangle ½-inch thick. Cut the dough into 2-inch squares or circles.

Fill a large deep-frying pan one-third full with vegetable oil. Place the pan over moderate heat and heat the oil until it registers 350°F on a deep-fat theromom-eter or until a small cube of stale bread dropped into the oil browns in 55 seconds.

Place the dough pieces, four or five at a time, in the oil, and cook them for 3 minutes or until they are golden brown and crisp. With a slotted spoon, remove the biscuits [cookies] from the oil and drain them on kitchen paper towels. Keep the biscuits [cookies] warm while you fry the remaining dough pieces in the same way.

When all the biscuits [cookies] have been cooked, pile them on a plate and serve immediately.

Monday Soup

Monday Soup will certainly brighten up the start of another week. Serve the soup with crisp croûtons lightly rubbed with a garlic clove.

4-6 SERVINGS

1½ lb. tomatoes, chopped
1 lb. fresh peas, weighed after shelling
1 pint [2½ cups] chicken stock
4 fl. oz. [½ cup] water
1 teaspoon salt
½ teaspoon black pepper
1 teaspoon sugar
1 teaspoon grated lemon rind
½ teaspoon dried basil
½ teaspoon dried marjoram
½ teaspoon grated nutmeg
  juice of 1 lemon
2 tablespoons sour cream

In a large saucepan, bring all the in-gredients except the sour cream to the boil over high heat.

Reduce the heat to low, cover the pan and simmer the soup for 1 hour.

Remove the pan from the heat. Pour the contents of the pan through a strainer into a bowl. Using the back of a wooden spoon rub the vegetables through the strainer. Discard any pulp remaining in the strainer.

Rinse and dry the saucepan. Return the strained soup to the pan. Place the pan over moderate heat and bring the soup to the boil. Taste the soup and add more seasoning if necessary.

Remove the pan from the heat. Ladle the soup into individual soup bowls. Put 1 teaspoon of sour cream in each bowl and serve immediately.

Molasses Sponge Cake is soaked with melted molasses and dark rum.

Mombasa Biscuits [Cookies]

Mombasa Biscuits [Cookies] are little crisp deep-fried biscuits [cookies] eaten all over East Africa. Serve with tea or coffee.

24 BISCUITS [COOKIES]

12 oz. [3 cups] flour
2 teaspoons baking powder
2 tablespoons sugar
½ teaspoon salt
1 egg, lightly beaten
8 fl. oz. [1 cup] water
  sufficient vegetable oil for deep-frying

Sift the flour, baking powder, sugar and salt into a large mixing bowl. Make a well in the centre and pour in the egg and water. Stir gently with a wooden spoon or spatula to mix the egg and water. Grad-ually mix in the flour mixture. When all the liquid has been absorbed, use your hands to knead and mix the dough lightly until it comes away from the sides of the bowl and forms a ball. If the dough is too dry, add a little more water. If it is too wet, add more flour.

Turn the dough out on to a lightly floured surface and knead it until it is smooth and elastic. Wash and dry the bowl and return the dough to it. Cover the bowl and set it aside to rest for at least 30 minutes at room temperature.

Monosodium Glutamate

Monosodium glutamate is the chemical name of a seasoning, Ve-tsin, which is widely used in Chinese cookery. It has no aroma of its own but when used in conjunction with savoury foods it enhances their natural flavour. It is now used extensively in the West, particularly to bring out the flavour of packaged and pre-cooked foods.

Monte's Mackerel

A quick and easy way to prepare mackerel, Monte's Mackerel makes the most of the fish's strong, rich flavour. Serve it with sautéed potatoes and French beans for a delicious family supper.

4 SERVINGS

2 tablespoons olive oil
1 small onion, finely chopped
4 small mackerel, cleaned and skinned
1 tablespoon lemon juice
¼ teaspoon salt
½ teaspoon black pepper
1 teaspoon fennel seeds
2 bay leaves

Preheat the oven to moderate 350°F (Gas Mark 4, 180°C).

In a small frying-pan, heat 1 tablespoon of the oil over moderate heat. When the oil is hot, add the onion and fry, stirring occasionally, for 5 to 7 minutes or until it is soft and translucent but not brown. Remove the pan from the heat. Using a slotted spoon, remove the onion from the pan and set it aside to drain on kitchen paper towels.

Pour the remaining oil into a baking tin. Place the mackerel in the tin and sprinkle them with the fried onion, lemon juice, salt, pepper and fennel seeds. Add the bay leaves and place the tin in the oven. Bake the fish for 45 to 50 minutes or until it flakes easily when tested with a fork.

Remove the baking tin from the oven. Transfer the mackerel to a warmed serving dish and serve immediately.

Montevideo Fish Casserole

A filling spicy supper dish of Latin American origin, Montevideo Fish Casserole may be served hot with a green vegetable and boiled potatoes, or left to cool and served with a salad.

4-6 SERVINGS

2 fl. oz. [¼ cup] olive oil
6 medium-sized onions, chopped
3 garlic cloves, crushed
1 green pepper, white pith removed, seeded and cut into strips
1 red pepper, white pith removed, seeded and cut into strips
1 tablespoon chopped fresh basil or 1½ teaspoons dried basil
1 lb. tomatoes, blanched, peeled and sliced
¼ teaspoon hot chilli powder
¼ teaspoon ground cumin
8 oz. halibut steaks, skinned
2 mackerel fillets, skinned
8 oz. cod steaks, skinned
½ teaspoon salt
¼ teaspoon black pepper
1 tablespoon white wine vinegar

In a large, flameproof casserole, heat the olive oil over moderate heat. When the oil is hot, add the onions and garlic and cook, stirring occasionally, for 5 to 7 minutes, or until the onions are soft and translucent but not brown.

Add the peppers, basil, tomatoes, chilli powder and cumin. Cover the casserole, reduce the heat to low and simmer the mixture for 1½ hours, or until it resembles a thick sauce.

Preheat the oven to warm 325°F (Gas Mark 3, 170°C).

Add the fish, salt and pepper to the casserole and stir well to mix. Place the casserole in the oven and bake for 20 to 30 minutes or until the fish flakes easily when tested with a fork.

Remove the casserole from the oven and stir in the vinegar. Serve immediately, or allow to cool before serving.

Monywa Soup

This delicious soup is almost a meal in itself, with pieces of sole, lightly cooked in butter, added to a mixture of coconut milk and spices. Fresh coconut milk should be used, but the coconut mixture here is an adequate substitute. Serve the soup poured over thin noodles and garnish with raw onions and lemon quarters.

4-6 SERVINGS

8 oz. [1 cup] masoor dhal, washed, soaked in cold water for 30 minutes and drained
1½ pints [3¾ cups] water
2 teaspoons salt
6 sole fillets
1 teaspoon turmeric
2 oz. [¼ cup] butter
2 large onions, finely chopped
1 garlic clove, crushed
½ teaspoon ground ginger
½ teaspoon mild chilli powder
1 teaspoon ground coriander
½ teaspoon black pepper
1 large green pepper, white pith removed, seeded and cut into rings
2 celery stalks, trimmed and cut into 2-inch lengths
4 oz. [½ cup] creamed coconut, dissolved in 16 fl. oz. [2 cups] warm water

Place the dhal in a large saucepan. Add the water and half the salt and place the pan over high heat. When the mixture comes to the boil, skim off any scum with a slotted spoon. Reduce the heat to low, cover the pan and simmer the dhal for 40 minutes, or until all the water has been absorbed.

Remove the pan from the heat and rub the dhal through a fine wire strainer into a large mixing bowl. Set the resulting purée aside.

Sprinkle the sole with the turmeric and the remaining salt and rub them into the fish well.

In a large heavy-bottomed saucepan, melt the butter over moderate heat. When the foam subsides, add the fish to the pan, two or three fillets at a time, and fry for 2 minutes on each side. With a slotted spoon, transfer the fish to a chopping board and, using a sharp knife, cut it into 2-inch pieces. Set aside.

Add the onions, garlic and ginger to the saucepan and fry, stirring occasionally, for 5 to 7 minutes, or until the onions are soft and translucent but not brown. Add the chilli powder, coriander and pepper and fry for a further 4 minutes, stirring frequently. Add the green pepper and celery and gradually pour in the dissolved creamed coconut, stirring constantly.

Add the dhal purée in spoonfuls to the pan, stirring constantly until the mixture is smooth.

Add the fish pieces to the pan. Increase the heat to high and bring to the boil, stirring constantly. Boil for 2 minutes. Reduce the heat to low and cover the pan. Simmer the soup for 10 to 15 minutes or until it is hot and steaming.

Remove the pan from the heat. Spoon the soup into individual serving bowls and serve at once.

Moorfowl

Moorfowl, or sometimes moorgame or moorcock, is a Scottish name for GROUSE.

A spicy soup, made with lightly cooked sole added to coconut milk, Monywa Soup is a meal in itself. Use fresh coconut milk if possible.

Morbrad med Aebler og Svesker is a succulent Danish dish of pork, stuffed with apple and prunes.

Moorhen

The moorhen is a small waterfowl found on inland waters in Great Britain. It is rarely eaten.

Moravian Loaf

This loaf, adapted from a traditional Czechoslovakian recipe, contains mashed potatoes. The bread is very light and may be served, slightly warm, with butter.

ONE 2-POUND LOAF

½ oz. fresh yeast
6 oz. [¾ cup] plus ½ teaspoon sugar
4 fl. oz. [½ cup] lukewarm water
1½ lb. [6 cups] flour
1 teaspoon salt
1 teaspoon ground cinnamon
5 oz. [⅝ cup] plus 1 teaspoon butter
8 oz. potatoes, cooked and mashed
3 tablespoons sugar mixed with 2 teaspoons grated nutmeg and ¼ teaspoon ground mace

Crumble the yeast into a small bowl and mash in the ½ teaspoon of sugar with a kitchen fork. Add 2 fluid ounces [¼ cup] of the water and cream the water and yeast together. Set the bowl aside in a warm, draught-free place for 15 to 20 minutes or until the yeast mixture is puffed up and frothy.

Sift the flour, salt, cinnamon and remaining sugar into a warmed, large mixing bowl. Add 3 ounces [⅜ cup] of the butter. With a table knife, cut the butter into small pieces. Then, with your fingertips, rub the butter into the flour mixture until the mixture resembles coarse breadcrumbs.

Add the potatoes to the flour mixture. Make a well in the centre of the flour and potato mixture and pour in the yeast mixture and the remaining water. Using your fingers or a spatula, gradually draw the flour mixture into the liquids. Continue mixing until all the flour is incorporated and the dough comes away from the sides of the bowl.

Turn the dough out on to a lightly floured board or marble slab and knead it for 8 minutes, reflouring the surface if the dough becomes sticky. The dough should be smooth and elastic.

Rinse, thoroughly dry and lightly grease the large mixing bowl. Shape the dough into a ball and return it to the bowl. Cover the bowl with a clean damp cloth and set it in a warm, draught-free place. Leave it for 2 hours or until the dough has risen and almost doubled in bulk.

Lightly grease a 2-pound loaf tin with the 1 teaspoon of butter. Set aside.

Turn the risen dough out of the bowl on to a floured surface and knead it for about 4 minutes. Shape the dough into an oblong shape and put it into the prepared tin.

In a small saucepan, melt the remaining butter over moderate heat. Remove the pan from the heat. With a pastry brush,

brush the top of the dough with a little of the melted butter. Return the tin to a warm place for 30 minutes or until the dough has risen almost to the top of the tin. Brush the dough again with a little of the remaining melted butter during the rising time.

Preheat the oven to fairly hot 375°F (Gas Mark 5, 190°C).

Using a sharp knife, make three deep cuts in the top of the dough. Sprinkle the sugar and spice mixture into the cuts and pour in the remaining melted butter.

Place the tin in the centre of the oven and bake for 1 hour. If the loaf begins to look too brown, cover the top of the tin with aluminium foil.

Remove the tin from the oven, tip the loaf out of the tin and rap the underside with your knuckles. If the bread sounds hollow, like a drum, it is cooked. If it does not sound hollow, reduce the oven temperature to warm 325°F (Gas Mark 3, 170°C), return the loaf, upside-down, to the oven and bake for a further 4 minutes.

Remove the loaf from the oven and turn out on to a wire rack to cool.

Morbrad med Aebler og Svesker

LOIN OF PORK STUFFED WITH APPLE AND PRUNES

A Danish dish, Morbrad med Aebler og Svesker (mohr-brad meth ay-bler oh svis-ker) makes a filling family meal. Serve it with broccoli and boiled potatoes.

6 SERVINGS

1 x 5 lb. boned loin of pork
1 large cooking apple, peeled, cored and chopped
1 tablespoon lemon juice
½ teaspoon salt
¼ teaspoon black pepper
15 dried prunes, stoned, soaked in water overnight and drained
2 oz. [⅓ cup] walnuts, chopped
2 oz. [¼ cup] butter
3 tablespoons olive oil
6 fl. oz. [¾ cup] red wine
1 tablespoon cornflour [cornstarch] dissolved in 2 tablespoons water
5 fl. oz. double cream [⅝ cup heavy cream]
1 tablespoon cranberry sauce

Ask your butcher to tie the pork loin securely at 1-inch intervals and pierce

it lengthways to make a tunnel approximately 1-inch in diameter right through the meat.

Sprinkle the apple cubes with the lemon juice and set aside. Rub the pork with the salt and pepper. With your fingers, insert the apples, prunes and walnuts alternately into the tunnel in the meat. With the handle of a long wooden spoon, press the stuffing into the meat, packing it tightly.

In a large flameproof casserole, melt the butter with the olive oil over moderate heat. When the foam subsides, place the meat in the casserole and cook, turning it frequently with two large forks, for 10 minutes or until it is lightly and evenly browned on all sides.

Drain off all the fat from the casserole. Pour in the wine and increase the heat to high. Bring the liquid to the boil.

Remove the casserole from the heat, cover it and place it in the oven. Roast the meat for 2½ hours or until the juices that run out are clear when the pork is pierced with the point of a sharp knife.

Remove the casserole from the oven. Transfer the meat to a carving board. Keep warm while you prepare the sauce.

With a metal spoon, remove any fat from the liquid in the casserole. Strain the liquid into a small saucepan. Add the cornflour [cornstarch] mixture. Set the saucepan over moderate heat and cook the sauce, stirring constantly, for 2 to 3 minutes or until it is thick.

Stir in the cream and cranberry sauce and reduce the heat to low. Cook, stirring constantly, for 2 minutes. Remove the pan from the heat and pour the sauce into a warmed sauceboat. Keep warm.

Remove and discard the strings from the meat. Cut it into thick slices. Arrange the slices on a warmed large serving dish and serve immediately, with the sauce.

Morcon

BEEF ROLL WITH TOMATO SAUCE

A succulent and fairly inexpensive meat dish adapted from a traditional Filipino recipe, Morcon (mohr-kohn) makes an excellent dinner party dish since it is easy to carve and some of the preparation may be done in advance.

6 SERVINGS

3 lb. beef skirt [flank], cut crosswise into 2 or 3 pieces and flattened by beating to ¼-inch thick
½ teaspoon salt

Morcon is an economical dish of beef and is ideal to serve at a dinner party, as some of the preparation may be done in advance.

¼ teaspoon black pepper
1 tablespoon lemon juice
1 garlic clove, crushed
4 cooked ham slices
4 hard-boiled eggs, sliced
4 oz. Cheddar cheese, thinly sliced
8 oz. green olives, stoned and chopped
3 fl. oz. [⅜ cup] vegetable oil
1 oz. [2 tablespoons] butter
1 lb. tomatoes, blanched, peeled and chopped
1 tablespoon soy sauce
4 fl. oz. [½ cup] water
1 oz. [2 tablespoons] beurre manié

Lay the beef pieces on a flat surface, overlapping the pieces to make a large oblong. With a mallet or heavy pestle, pound the overlapping edges together to seal. Sprinkle over the salt, pepper and lemon juice. Rub over the garlic.

Place the ham slices over the beef and arrange the egg slices, in lines, over the ham. Top with the cheese slices.

Sprinkle the eggs and cheese with the olives and one-third of the oil. Roll up the meat Swiss [jelly] roll fashion and tie with pieces of string at 1-inch intervals to keep it in shape.

In a large flameproof casserole, melt the butter with the remaining oil over moderate heat. When the foam subsides place the meat roll in the casserole and brown, turning carefully from time to time, for 10 minutes, or until it is lightly and evenly browned.

Reduce the heat to low and add the tomatoes, soy sauce and water. Cover the casserole and simmer for 45 minutes to 1 hour, or until the meat is tender when pierced with the point of a sharp knife, and the juices that run out are faintly rosy.

Remove the casserole from the heat. Using two large spoons, lift out the meat roll and place it on a carving board. Remove and discard the string. Cut the meat into 1-inch slices. Place them on a heated serving dish and keep warm.

Return the casserole to the heat and add the beurre manié, stirring constantly. Bring the sauce to the boil and cook, stirring constantly, for 3 to 5 minutes or until the sauce has thickened.

Remove the pan from the heat and pour the sauce over the sliced meat. Serve immediately.

Morel

One of the best of the edible FUNGI, the morel is distinguishable by its fleshy, pitted cap. The morel grows mainly in woodland clearings and on mountain slopes.

Morels may be cooked whole or, if they are large, halved or quartered. They are usually cooked in butter with a little chopped shallot or garlic.

Morello Cherry

The Morello is a sour cherry with dark red or black flesh and a very acid flavour. Morello cherries are rarely eaten raw but are used extensively in cooking.

Morello Cherry Flan

The rich almond pastry given in this recipe makes a delightful contrast to the bitter-sweet taste of the Morello cherry and cream filling. Serve Morello Cherry Flan as the perfect dessert for a dinner party.

6 SERVINGS

4 oz. [1 cup] flour, sifted
2 oz. [⅓ cup] ground almonds
1 tablespoon sugar

3 oz. [⅜ cup] butter, softened
1 egg yolk
½ teaspoon vanilla essence
1½ lb. canned stoned Morello cherries, drained
6 fl. oz. [¾ cup] Crème Chantilly
1 oz. [¼ cup] flaked almonds, toasted

In a medium-sized mixing bowl, combine the flour, ground almonds and sugar. Make a well in the centre and in it place the butter, egg yolk and vanilla essence. Using your fingertips, incorporate the flour mixture into the butter and egg yolk until a smooth paste is formed. Cover the paste and place it in the refrigerator to chill for 30 minutes.

Preheat the oven to moderate 350°F (Gas Mark 4, 180°C). Place an 8-inch flan tin on a baking sheet.

Remove the paste from the refrigerator and pat it out into a round flat shape. Place the paste between two large pieces of greaseproof or waxed paper and roll it out into a circle about 11-inches in diameter. Peel off one piece of greaseproof or waxed paper and place the paste, paper side up, over the flan tin. Peel off the remaining paper and gently press the paste into the flan tin, trimming the edges with a sharp knife.

Line the flan case with aluminium foil or greaseproof or waxed paper and half fill it with dried beans. Place the baking sheet in the oven and bake the flan case blind for 15 minutes. Remove the foil or paper and the beans and bake for 5 minutes more or until the pastry is firm to the touch. Remove the baking sheet from the oven.

Remove the flan case from the tin and set aside on a wire rack to cool completely.

When the case is cold, place it on a serving dish. Fill the centre with the cherries. With a flat-bladed knife, spread the Crème Chantilly over the cherries, pulling it up into soft peaks.

Sprinkle over the almonds and serve immediately.

Morello Cherry Sauce

Serve Morello Cherry Sauce with puddings or as an accompaniment to vanilla or chocolate ice-cream.

8 SERVINGS

2½ lb. canned stoned Morello cherries, drained
3 lb. [6 cups] sugar
3 fl. oz. [⅜ cup] water
2 tablespoons lemon juice
½ teaspoon ground cinnamon
¼ teaspoon ground ginger

In a large saucepan, heat the cherries, sugar and water over low heat, stirring occasionally until the sugar has dissolved. Increase the heat to moderate and boil the syrup and cherries for 8 minutes or until a teaspoon of the syrup dropped into cold water will form a soft ball.

Remove the pan from the heat and stir in the lemon juice, cinnamon and ginger. Allow the syrup and cherries to cool for 10 minutes before pouring the mixture into a heatproof glass serving dish.

Serve warm or cold.

Morello Cherries with Yogurt

A simple pudding with a very fresh flavour, Morello Cherries with Yogurt may be served for breakfast with cereal sprinkled on top, or as a simple lunch or dinner dessert. If fresh Morello cherries are available do use them instead of the canned variety — the dish will taste even better.

4 SERVINGS

1 lb. canned stoned Morello cherries, drained
3 oz. [½ cup] brown sugar
½ teaspoon ground ginger
½ teaspoon vanilla essence
15 fl. oz. [1⅞ cups] yogurt

In a large saucepan, heat the cherries and sugar over low heat, stirring frequently until the sugar has dissolved. Add the ginger and vanilla essence and stir well. Cover the pan and simmer the mixture for 5 to 8 minutes or until the cherries are very soft but not pulpy. Remove the pan from the heat.

Pour the cherry mixture into a heatproof serving dish and allow to cool for 30 minutes. Then place the dish in the refrigerator to chill for 1 hour.

Remove the dish from the refrigerator and stir in the yogurt. Serve immediately.

Mornay, à la

A French cooking term, *à la Mornay* (ah lah mawr-nay) is used to describe food, usually fish and eggs, which are served with a rich cheese sauce.

Mornay Sauce

This is a savoury cheese sauce for serving with eggs and vegetables. The sauce also goes well with fish, in which case replace the milk in the basic béchamel sauce with fish stock, and with chicken, in which case use chicken stock instead of milk.

16 FLUID OUNCES

12 fl. oz. [1½ cups] béchamel sauce
4 tablespoons single [light] cream
2 oz. [½ cup] Parmesan cheese, grated
2 oz. [½ cup] Gruyère cheese, grated
1 teaspoon prepared mustard
⅛ teaspoon cayenne pepper
¼ teaspoon salt

In a small saucepan, bring the béchamel sauce to the boil over moderate heat, stirring frequently. Remove the pan from the heat.

Add the cream, Parmesan, Gruyère, mustard, cayenne and salt. Return the pan to low heat and cook the sauce, stirring constantly, until the cheese melts. Do not allow the sauce to boil.

Remove the pan from the heat. Pour the sauce into a heated sauceboat and serve immediately.

Moroccan Chicken

Moroccan Chicken is a simple dish of chicken pieces flavoured with garlic, lemon and oregano. Serve on a bed of rice or plain noodles, with a well-seasoned tomato salad.

4-6 SERVINGS

2 fl. oz. [¼ cup] olive oil

1 x 4½ lb. chicken, skinned and cut into serving pieces
1 medium-sized onion, thinly sliced and pushed out into rings
2 garlic cloves, crushed
1 teaspoon salt
½ teaspoon black pepper
½ teaspoon dried oregano
1 bay leaf
finely grated rind and juice of 1 large lemon
10 fl. oz. [1¼ cups] chicken stock
1 teaspoon cornflour [cornstarch] dissolved in 1 tablespoon chicken stock

Low Cal

In a large flameproof casserole, heat the oil over moderate heat. When the oil is hot, add half the chicken pieces and fry, turning them over occasionally with tongs, for 8 to 10 minutes, or until the chicken pieces are well browned on all sides.

With a slotted spoon, remove the chicken pieces from the casserole and set them aside to drain on kitchen paper towels. Fry and drain the remaining pieces in the same way.

Remove the casserole from the heat

Moroccan Chicken is a simple but appetizing dish with lemon and oregano.

and pour off all but 2 tablespoons of the oil.

Add the onion and garlic and return the casserole to the heat. Fry the onion, stirring occasionally, for 6 to 8 minutes, or until it is golden brown. Stir in the salt, pepper, oregano, bay leaf, lemon rind and juice and the chicken stock.

Bring the liquids to the boil, stirring constantly. Return the chicken pieces to the casserole.

Cover the casserole and reduce the heat to low. Simmer for 1½ to 2 hours, or until the chicken pieces are tender.

Remove the casserole from the heat. With a slotted spoon, remove the chicken pieces from the casserole and transfer them to a warmed serving dish. Keep the chicken hot while you finish the sauce.

Strain the liquids in the casserole into a small saucepan. Using the back of a wooden spoon, press down on the vegetables and seasonings in the strainer to extract all the juices. Discard the contents of the strainer.

Stir in the cornflour [cornstarch] mixture. Set the pan over moderate heat and cook the sauce, stirring constantly, until it is thick and smooth.

Remove the pan from the heat. Pour the sauce over the chicken pieces and serve immediately.

Moroccan Lamb and Honey Casserole

Moroccan Lamb and Honey Casserole is a sweet and spicy dish. Serve it with rice and a cucumber and yogurt salad for an unusual tasty meal.

6 SERVINGS

3 lb. boned leg of lamb, cut into 1-inch cubes
1 garlic clove, crushed
1 teaspoon ground saffron
1 teaspoon ground cumin
1-inch piece fresh root ginger, peeled and finely chopped
2 cloves
24 fl. oz. [3 cups] chicken stock
3 tablespoons clear honey
1½ lb. small white onions, peeled

Preheat the oven to moderate 350°F (Gas Mark 4, 180°C).

In a large flameproof casserole, combine the lamb, garlic, saffron, cumin, ginger, cloves, chicken stock and half the honey. Set the casserole over moderately high heat and bring the liquid to the boil, stirring occasionally. Reduce the heat to low, partly cover the casserole and simmer for 30 minutes.

Remove the casserole from the heat. Strain the liquid from the casserole through a fine strainer into a small heavy saucepan. Set the casserole aside. Put the saucepan over high heat and bring the liquid to the boil. Boil rapidly for 5 minutes or until the liquid has reduced by about one-third the original quantity. Remove the pan from the heat and pour the liquid back into the casserole. Stir in the onions and the remaining honey, mixing until the ingredients are thoroughly blended.

Cover the casserole and place it in the oven. Braise for 30 minutes or until the meat and onions are tender when pierced with the point of a sharp knife.

Remove the casserole from the oven and serve immediately.

Moroccan Liver Kebabs

Moroccan Liver Kebabs, with its cumin-scented meat and hot spicy onions, will conjure up wonderful visions of warm Arab nights and succulent North African cooking. Serve with rice and a cool and refreshing salad and accompany with some dry white wine.

4 SERVINGS

1½ lb. lamb's liver, thickly sliced
1 tablespoon lemon juice
1 teaspoon salt
½ teaspoon black pepper
2 fl. oz. [¼ cup] plus 2 tablespoons olive oil
4 tablespoons cumin seeds
3 medium-sized onions, thinly sliced
1 tablespoon canned hot Harissa sauce

(Low Cal)

Preheat the grill [broiler] to moderately high.

Sprinkle the lamb's liver with the lemon juice and set aside for 10 minutes. Pat dry with kitchen paper towels. Rub the salt and pepper into the meat and, using a pastry brush, brush the liver lightly with the 2 tablespoons of oil.

Place the meat on a piece of aluminium foil and place the foil under the grill [broiler]. Grill [broil] the liver for 2 minutes on each side, or until it is partially cooked. Remove the liver from the grill [broiler] and transfer it to a chopping board.

With a sharp knife, cut the liver slices into 2-inch cubes. Place the cumin on a plate and roll the liver cubes in it, one by one. Thread the liver cubes on to skewers, then roll them again in the cumin. Set aside and keep warm.

In a medium-sized frying-pan, heat the remaining olive oil over moderate heat. When the oil is hot, add the onions and cook, stirring occasionally, for 5 to 7 minutes, or until they are soft and translucent but not brown.

Meanwhile, place the skewers under the grill [broiler] and grill [broil] the liver kebabs for 4 to 6 minutes, turning occasionally, or until the liver is tender and cooked through.

Stir the Harissa sauce into the onions

Cumin-scented Moroccan Liver Kebabs are reminiscent of Arab nights.

and mix well. Cook the mixture for a further 1 minute.

Remove the pan from the heat and transfer the onion mixture to a warmed serving dish. When the kebabs are cooked, remove them from the grill [broiler] and place them on the onion mixture.

Serve at once.

Mortadella

Mortadella is a large sausage, usually served thinly sliced as an hors d'oeuvre. It originated in Italy although similar sausages are now produced throughout Europe.

Mortar

A mortar is a thick marble, metal, stoneware or glass bowl in which meats, nuts, herbs, spices, etc. are pounded with a pestle until they form a powder or paste. Wooden mortars and pestles are available, but they are not as effective because the surface is soft.

Mortars vary in size from 2-pint [1½-quart] ones for making forcemeats and pâtés to cup-sized ones in which herbs and spices are crushed.

Morue à l'Americaine

SALT COD WITH RICE AND BRANDY AND WINE SAUCE

Salt cod is a relatively exotic delicacy in the English-speaking world, but around the Mediterranean it is consumed with great relish. The recipe below for Morue à l'Americaine (maw-roo ah lah-mair-ee-kehn) is easy to prepare — and makes a deliciously different dinner dish. Serve with a mixed green salad and a well-chilled Pouilly Fumé or white Burgundy wine.

4 SERVINGS

10 oz. [1⅔ cups] long-grain rice, washed, soaked in cold water for 30 minutes and drained
1 pint [2½ cups] water
1½ teaspoons salt
2 lb. salt cod, soaked in cold water for 24 hours
3 tablespoons olive oil
1 large onion, finely chopped
1 garlic clove, crushed
5 oz. canned tomato purée
½ teaspoon freshly ground black pepper
8 fl. oz. [1 cup] dry white wine
2 fl. oz. [¼ cup] brandy
1 oz. [2 tablespoons] butter

Morue à l'Americaine is a deliciously different fish and rice dish.

Put the rice in a medium-sized saucepan. Pour over the water and add 1 teaspoon of the salt. Place the pan over moderate heat and bring the water to the boil. Cover the pan, reduce the heat to very low and simmer the rice for 15 minutes, or until all the liquid has been absorbed and the rice is tender. Remove the pan from the heat and set aside.

Drain the salt cod and dry it on kitchen paper towels. Skin the cod and chop into 1½-inch pieces. Set aside.

In a large frying-pan, heat the oil over moderate heat. When the oil is hot, add the onion and garlic and cook, stirring occasionally, for 5 to 7 minutes, or until the onion is soft and translucent but not brown. Stir in the tomato purée, the remaining salt and the pepper and cook, stirring occasionally, for 3 minutes. Stir in the wine and bring the mixture to the boil, stirring frequently.

Add the salt cod and brandy to the pan, stirring well to combine all the ingredients. Reduce the heat to low, cover the pan and cook, stirring and turning the salt cod from time to time, for

1423

20 to 25 minutes, or until the fish flakes easily when tested with a fork.

Meanwhile, in a large saucepan, melt the butter over moderate heat. When the foam subsides, add the rice to the pan. Cook, stirring frequently, for 3 to 5 minutes, or until the rice is heated through and is well coated with the butter.

Remove the pan from the heat. Arrange the rice in a ring on a warmed serving platter. Remove the frying-pan from the heat and spoon the fish and sauce into the centre of the rice ring. Serve at once.

Mos-bolletjies
RAISIN BUNS

These South African buns are made by fermenting raisins in yeast which gives them an unusual wine flavour. Serve Mos-bolletjies (moss boll-ee-kees) for tea with lots of butter.

16 BUNS

4 oz. [½ cup] plus 2 teaspoons butter
12 oz. [2 cups] seedless raisins
1 oz. fresh yeast
2 oz. [¼ cup] sugar
1½ pints [3¾ cups] lukewarm water
8 fl. oz. [1 cup] milk
3 lb. [12 cups] flour
1 tablespoon salt
2 teaspoons ground cinnamon
2 teaspoons grated nutmeg
2 eggs, lightly beaten
1 tablespoon vegetable oil

Grease two large baking sheets with the 2 teaspoons of butter. Set aside.

Place half the raisins on a chopping board and chop them coarsely. Set aside.

Crumble the yeast into a small bowl and mash in ½ teaspoon of the sugar with a kitchen fork. Add 5 fluid ounces [⅝ cup] of the water and cream the water and yeast together.

Stir the chopped raisins into the yeast mixture. Cover the bowl and set it aside in a warm, draught-free place for at least 6 hours or overnight.

In a small saucepan, scald the milk (bring to just under boiling point) over moderate heat. Reduce the heat to low and add the remaining butter. When the butter has melted, remove the pan from the heat. Set aside to allow the milk and butter mixture to cool to lukewarm.

Sift the flour, remaining sugar, salt, cinnamon and nutmeg into a warmed, large mixing bowl. Make a well in the centre of the flour mixture and strain in the yeast mixture through a fine strainer. Discard the raisins remaining in the

strainer. Add the milk and butter mixture, the remaining water, the eggs and the remaining raisins.

Using your fingers or a spatula, gradually draw the flour into the liquid. Continue mixing until all the flour is incorporated and the dough comes away from the sides of the bowl.

Turn the dough out on to a floured board or marble slab and knead for about 10 minutes, reflouring the surface if the dough becomes sticky. The dough should be elastic and smooth.

Rinse, thoroughly dry and lightly grease the large mixing bowl. Shape the dough into a ball and return it to the bowl. Dust the top of the dough with a little flour and cover the bowl with a clean, damp cloth. Set the bowl in a warm, draught-free place and leave it for 1 to 1½ hours, or until the dough has risen and almost doubled in bulk.

Turn the risen dough out of the bowl on to a floured surface and knead it for about 4 minutes. Cut the dough into about 16 small pieces and form them into balls. Place the balls close together on the baking sheets. Using a pastry brush, brush the balls lightly with the oil. Leave in a warm place to rise for 1 to 1½ hours or until the balls have risen and almost doubled in bulk.

Preheat the oven to fairly hot 400°F (Gas Mark 6, 200°C).

Place the baking sheets in the centre of the oven and bake for 30 to 40 minutes, or until the buns are golden brown.

Remove the sheets from the oven. With a sharp knife, carefully cut between each bun. Let the buns cool slightly, then transfer them to a wire rack to cool completely before serving

Moscari Psito
ROAST VEAL

A delectable Greek dish of veal flavoured with rosemary, garlic, lemon and orange and cooked in white wine, Moscari Psito (moss-kah-ree psee-toh) may be served with buttered noodles and a crisp green salad. Accompany with a Greek white wine such as Hymettus.

6 SERVINGS

1 x 6 lb. shoulder of veal, boned
1 garlic clove, thinly sliced
1 teaspoon salt
½ teaspoon black pepper
  finely grated rind of 1 lemon
  finely grated rind of 1 medium-sized orange
1 teaspoon dried rosemary
1 oz. [2 tablespoons] butter
1 tablespoon olive oil

2 tablespoons lemon juice
2 tablespoons orange juice
10 fl. oz. [1¼ cups] dry Greek white wine
1 bay leaf, crumbled

Make incisions in the surface of the meat and insert the garlic clove slices. Rub over half of the salt and pepper. Sprinkle over the lemon and orange rinds and the rosemary.

Roll up the veal tightly and secure the roll at 1-inch intervals with trussing thread or string.

In a large flameproof casserole, melt

A Greek veal dish, fragrantly flavoured with rosemary, lemon and orange, Moscari Psito should be served with buttered noodles.

the butter with the oil over moderate heat. When the foam subsides, place the veal in the casserole and cook, turning the meat frequently with two large forks, for 8 to 10 minutes or until it is lightly and evenly browned on all sides. Remove the casserole from the heat and set aside.

In a small mixing bowl, combine the lemon and orange juices, the wine and the bay leaf. Pour the wine mixture over the veal in the casserole.

Return the casserole to the heat and bring the liquid to the boil. Reduce the heat to very low, cover the casserole and braise for 2 hours, or until the veal is tender and the juices run clear when the meat is pierced with the point of a sharp knife. Remove the casserole from the heat.

With two large forks, lift the veal out of the casserole. Remove and discard the trussing thread or string and place the veal on a carving board. Keep the meat hot while you finish the sauce.

With a metal spoon, skim off any fat from the surface of the juices in the casserole. Pour the juices through a fine wire strainer into a medium-sized sauce-pan. Discard the contents of the strainer.

Set the pan over high heat and boil the sauce, stirring occasionally, until it has reduced to half its original quantity.

Remove the pan from the heat. Pour the sauce into a warmed sauceboat and serve immediately, with the meat.

Moselle Wine

Germany produces some of the greatest white wine in the world — as even the French reluctantly concede. And most of that really good German wine is produced in two areas of the country, both named after the rivers along whose banks the vines are cultivated. One of these rivers is the Moselle.

Moselle wine is easily identifiable. It is, first of all, marketed in a recognizable slender green bottle. Almost all of it is made from the Riesling grape and is refreshing, somehow spring-like and young to taste. It is also the lightest, alcoholically, of the major white wines, rarely containing more than 10 per cent alcohol per bottle.

Although vineyards exist along almost the entire length of the river, from the time it enters Germany from Luxembourg and France to where it meets the Rhine at Koblenz, most of the best Moselle wine grapes are grown in what is called the Middle Moselle, a thirty-mile stretch of the river between Trier and Reil, and in a few villages along the banks of the Saar, the Moselle's most important tributory.

Since most German wines take the name of their village of origin (although one or two of the most famous vineyards, such as Scharzhofberger, the most famous of the Saar wines, do not), the important thing to learn if you want to read a Moselle wine label is a little geography. The best known of the wine villages of the Middle Moselle and the places where, consequently, the best wine is produced are Zeltingen, Piesport, Wehlen and — most famous of all — Bernkastel. Bernkastel produces several wines, including the best known wine of the region, Bernkasteler Doktor — so called because a medieval bishop of Trier is reputed to have been cured of a fever by drinking the beverage.

On the Saar, the villages to remember are Wiltingen (the village of origin of Scharzhofberger wine), Ayl and Ockfen.

Few of the wines of the Lower Moselle (the part of the river nearest to Koblenz) are exported, but of the few that are, the wine from the village of Zell (Zeller Schwartze Katz) is worth looking for.

Moselle wine goes beautifully with salads, all light meat, and fish and egg dishes. It should be drunk young.

Mostarda

Mostarda (moss-tahr-dah) is an Italian preserve of fruits made in the town of Cremona in Lombardy. Mostarda usually contains whole cherries, pears, oranges, apricots, figs, plums and slices of melon and pumpkin and is preserved in a sugar syrup flavoured with mustard oil.

Mostarda is usually served with cold meat — particularly pork, ham and tongue.

Mother's Bread Pudding

A traditional British recipe, this moist rich pudding makes a very economical and sustaining dessert. Serve Mother's Bread Pudding with Crème à la Vanille or whipped cream.

6 SERVINGS

2 teaspoons butter
12 oz. stale white bread, torn into small pieces
18 fl. oz. [2¼ cups] warm water
6 oz. [1 cup] sultanas or seedless raisins
4 oz. [⅔ cup] raisins
2 oz. [⅓ cup] currants
4 oz. [⅔ cup] soft brown sugar
2 eggs, lightly beaten
5 fl. oz. [⅝ cup] milk
½ teaspoon grated nutmeg
½ teaspoon ground cinnamon
½ teaspoon ground ginger
1 oz. icing sugar [¼ cup confectioners' sugar]

Preheat the oven to warm 325°F (Gas Mark 3, 170°C).

Grease an 8-inch baking dish with the butter and set aside.

Place the bread pieces in a large mixing bowl. Pour over the water and leave the bread to soak for 2 to 3 hours. Pour off any excess water.

Mash the bread with a fork until it is smooth. Mix in the sultanas or seedless raisins, raisins, currants and brown sugar. Add the eggs, milk, nutmeg, cinnamon and ginger and stir well with a wooden spoon until all the ingredients are thoroughly mixed.

Spoon the mixture into the dish. Place it in the oven and bake for 1 to 1½ hours or until a skewer inserted into the centre of the pudding comes out clean.

Remove the pudding from the oven and sprinkle it with the icing [confectioners'] sugar.

Serve immediately.

Mother's Matzo Balls with Chicken Soup

A rich and nourishing soup, this is easy to make and quite delicious. Mother's Matzo Balls with Chicken Soup is an adaptation of the traditional Jewish chicken soup which is supposedly guaranteed to cure all illnesses!

6-8 SERVINGS

SOUP
4 pints [5 pints] cold water
1 chicken stock cube
2 medium-sized onions, quartered
1 lb. carrots, scraped and coarsely chopped
4 medium-sized tomatoes, blanched, peeled and chopped
3 to 4 parsley sprigs, washed
6 peppercorns
2 teaspoons sugar
1 teaspoon salt
1 x 2 lb. chicken, with the giblets (excluding the liver)

MATZO BALLS
4 oz. [1 cup] matzo meal
1 teaspoon salt
½ teaspoon black pepper
1 tablespoon finely chopped fresh parsley
2 egg whites, stiffly beaten
2 egg yolks, lightly beaten
½ tablespoon vegetable oil
1 tablespoon warm water

First make the soup. In a large saucepan, bring the water to the boil over high heat. Crumble the chicken stock cube into the water and stir well. Add the onions, carrots, tomatoes, parsley, peppercorns, sugar and salt. Bring to the boil again. Add the chicken and giblets.

Cover the pan. Reduce the heat to low and simmer for 1 to 1¼ hours, or until the chicken is very tender when pierced with the point of a sharp knife.

Remove the pan from the heat. Transfer the chicken to a chopping board. Strip the chicken meat from the bones and cut it into small pieces. Set it aside on a plate and keep warm. Discard the bones and skin. Set the soup aside to cool until the fat solidifies on top.

Meanwhile, prepare the matzo balls. In a medium-sized mixing bowl, combine the matzo meal, salt, pepper and chopped parsley. With a metal spoon, gently fold in the egg whites.

In a small bowl, combine the egg yolks, oil and water. Gradually add the egg yolk mixture to the egg white and matzo mixture. Set aside.

With a metal spoon, skim the fat off the surface of the soup. Return the pan to high heat and bring the soup back to the boil. Add the chicken meat and reduce the heat to moderately high.

Drop in walnut-sized balls of the matzo meal mixture. Simmer for 10 to 15 minutes, or until the matzo balls are light and fluffy.

Remove the pan from the heat and serve immediately.

Motley Cake

A pretty, two-coloured cake which is ideal for a tea party or a children's party, Motley

Cake is decorated with pink glacé icing and white fondant flowers.

ONE 9-INCH CAKE

8 oz. [1 cup] plus 1 teaspoon butter
8 oz. [1 cup] sugar
6 eggs, separated
12 oz. [3 cups] flour
1 teaspoon baking powder
½ teaspoon vanilla essence
3 drops red food colouring

ICING
2 drops red food colouring
1 pint [2½ cups] hot Glacé Icing

DECORATION
4 oz. [½ cup] Fondant

Preheat the oven to moderate 350°F (Gas Mark 4, 180°C).

Using the teaspoon of butter, grease a 9-inch round cake tin. Set aside.

In a large mixing bowl, cream the remaining butter and the sugar together with a wooden spoon until the mixture is light and fluffy. Beat in the egg yolks, one at a time, beating constantly until the mixture is smooth.

Sift in the flour and baking powder, a little at a time, beating constantly.

In a large mixing bowl, beat the egg whites with a wire whisk or rotary beater until they form stiff peaks.

With a metal spoon, carefully fold the egg whites into the flour mixture. Divide the batter equally between two medium-sized bowls. Stir the vanilla essence into one and the red food colouring into the other.

Using a tablespoon, drop a spoonful of the white mixture into the cake tin, then a spoonful of the pink mixture. Continue in this way until all the batter is used up. Smooth the batter down lightly with a flat-bladed knife.

Place the cake tin in the centre of the oven and bake for 1½ hours, or until a skewer inserted into the centre of the cake comes out clean.

Remove the cake from the oven and set aside for 15 minutes. Run a knife around the edge of the tin and turn the cake on to a wire cake rack to cool completely.

To make the icing, in a small bowl beat the red food colouring into the glacé icing with a wooden spoon.

When the cake is cold, pour the icing on to the top and, using a flat-bladed knife, spread it over the top and sides of the cake, covering it completely. Set the cake aside while you make the fondant flowers.

Motley Cake is excellent to serve at a children's tea party. The cake inside is two-coloured and gives a very pretty effect when cut.

A tangy, fruity hors d'oeuvre, Moulded Peach Salad makes a very different and refreshing start to a meal.

Shape the fondant into small petal shapes and arrange them, in flower shapes, over the top of the cake. The cake is now ready to serve.

Mould

In cooking, a mould is a hollow receptacle in which food is cooked or chilled so that it retains the shape of the container when turned out.

Mould is also a fungus which grows on the surface of jams, cheeses, preserved fruits and other foods which come into contact with moist air. Mould on jams may be skimmed off since it in no way impairs the flavour. Some cheeses (such as ROQUEFORT) have mould deliberately introduced into them to give them

flavour. Mould on cooked meat, however, means that the meat is stale and should be thrown away.

Moulded Cream Pudding

A wonderfully rich cream dessert made in a ring mould and served with fresh berries, Moulded Cream Pudding is the perfect end to that extra special meal.

4 SERVINGS

1 tablespoon icing [confectioners'] sugar
4 egg yolks
2 oz. [$\frac{1}{4}$ cup] sugar
  grated rind and juice of 1 lemon
$\frac{1}{2}$ oz. gelatine dissolved in 4 table-spoons warm water
15 fl. oz. double cream [1$\frac{7}{8}$ cups heavy cream], stiffly whipped
4 to 6 oz. fresh berries, washed and hulled

Rinse a 1$\frac{1}{2}$-pint [1-quart] ring mould with cold water. Sprinkle the inside with the icing [confectioners'] sugar, knocking out any excess. Set aside.

In a medium-sized mixing bowl, combine the egg yolks and sugar, beating with a wire whisk or rotary beater until the mixture is thick and light in colour. Stir in the lemon rind and juice. Add the dissolved gelatine to the egg and lemon mixture and stir until the ingredients are well mixed.

With a metal spoon fold in the whipped cream. Spoon the mixture into the prepared mould. Place the mould in the refrigerator and chill for 2 hours, or until the pudding has completely set.

To serve, remove the mould from the refrigerator and quickly dip the bottom into hot water. Run a knife around the edge of the mould and turn it out on to a chilled serving dish.

Fill the centre of the ring with the berries and serve immediately.

Moulded Peach Salad

A tangy lemon-flavoured hors d'oeuvre served on a bed of lettuce, Moulded Peach Salad makes an interesting start to a meal.

6 SERVINGS

3 large ripe peaches, peeled, stoned and coarsely chopped
6 oz. fresh pineapple, peeled, cored and chopped into 1-inch cubes
1 pint lemon jelly [2$\frac{1}{2}$ cups lemon gelatin], made with lemon juice instead of water, cool and on the point of setting
1 small lettuce, outer leaves removed, washed and separated into leaves
10 fl. oz. [1$\frac{1}{4}$ cups] sour cream

In a large mixing bowl, combine the peaches, pineapple and the lemon jelly [gelatin]. Spoon the mixture into 6 individual moulds and place the moulds in the refrigerator to chill for 3 hours or until the jelly [gelatin] is set.

Arrange the lettuce on 6 individual serving plates and set aside.

Remove the moulds from the refrigerator. To unmould, quickly dip the bottoms of the moulds in boiling water and run a sharp knife around the edge. Carefully invert the serving plates, holding the lettuce in place, over the moulds and reverse · the two. Shake lightly. The jelly [gelatin] should slide out easily.

Spoon over the sour cream and serve at once.

Moules au Citron
MUSSELS WITH LEMON SAUCE

Moules au Citron (moolz-oh see-trawn) have a fresh tangy flavour and make a delicious hors d'oeuvre or light main course for a summer meal. Serve garnished with lemon wedges and parsley sprigs.

4 SERVINGS

2½ quarts mussels
2 oz. [¼ cup] butter
2 shallots, finely chopped
    bouquet garni consisting of 4
    parsley sprigs, 1 thyme spray
    and 1 bay leaf tied together
½ teaspoon salt
½ teaspoon black pepper
¼ teaspoon grated nutmeg
    juice of 4 lemons
1 tablespoon flour

Wash the mussels in cold water and, with a stiff brush, scrub them to remove any mud on their shells. Discard any mussels which are not tightly shut or do not close if sharply tapped, and any that float or have broken shells. With a sharp knife, scrape off the tufts of hair, or beards, which protrude from between the closed shell halves. Place the mussels in a large bowl of cold water and soak them for 1 hour. Drain the mussels in a colander and set aside.

In a large saucepan, melt half the butter over moderate heat. When the foam subsides, add the shallots, bouquet garni, salt, pepper and nutmeg. Cook, stirring occasionally, for 2 to 3 minutes, or until the shallots are soft and translucent but not brown. Stir in the lemon juice.

Increase the heat to moderately high and add the mussels to the pan. Cook the mussels, shaking the saucepan constantly, for 3 minutes or until the shells open.

Remove the pan from the heat. Transfer the mussels and cooking liquid to a large strainer set over a large bowl. Reserve the strained liquid. Set the mussels aside and keep warm while you prepare the sauce.

In a small saucepan, melt the remaining butter over moderate heat. Remove the pan from the heat and, with a wooden spoon, stir in the flour to make a smooth paste. Gradually add the reserved strained cooking liquid, stirring constantly. Return the pan to low heat and, stirring constantly, cook the sauce for 3 to 4 minutes or until it is thick and smooth. Remove the pan from the heat.

Arrange the mussels decoratively in a large warmed serving dish and pour the sauce over them. Serve immediately.

Moules Marinière
MUSSELS MARINERS' STYLE

Moules Marinière (moolz mah-ree-nyay) make an excellent first course, served in deep soup bowls with a fork to eat the mussels and a soup spoon for the juices. Provide plenty of French bread to dip into the juice, some well-chilled Muscadet to drink and you have a truly French dish.

4 SERVINGS

3 quarts mussels
2 oz. [¼ cup] butter
1 small onion, finely chopped
1 garlic clove, crushed
1 celery stalk, trimmed and finely
    chopped
    bouquet garni consisting of 4
    parsley sprigs, 1 thyme spray
    and 1 bay leaf tied together
16 fl. oz. [2 cups] dry white wine
½ teaspoon salt
¼ teaspoon black pepper
2 tablespoons chopped
    fresh parsley

Low Cal

Wash the mussels in cold water and, with a stiff brush, scrub them to remove any mud on their shells. Discard any mussels which are not tightly shut or do not close if sharply tapped, and any that float or have broken shells.

With a sharp knife, scrape off the tufts of hair, or beards, which protrude from

A relatively inexpensive dish, Moules au Citron, is especially good served with a cold dry white wine.

between the closed shell halves. Place the mussels in a large bowl of cold water and soak them for 1 hour. Drain the mussels in a colander and set aside.

In a large saucepan, melt the butter over moderate heat. When the foam subsides, add the onion and garlic and fry, stirring occasionally, for 5 to 7 minutes or until the onion is soft and translucent but not brown. Add the celery, bouquet garni, wine, salt and pepper and bring the mixture to the boil. Reduce the heat to low, add the mussels and simmer, shaking the pan occasionally, for 5 to 10 minutes, or until the shells open. With a slotted spoon, transfer the mussels to a warmed serving dish. Remove and discard the empty shell halves from the mussels. Set the mussels aside and keep warm.

Strain the mussel cooking liquid into a bowl, then return it to the saucepan. Place the pan over high heat and bring it to the boil. Boil for 2 minutes. Pour the liquid over the mussels, sprinkle over the parsley and serve.

Moussaka
Moussaka (moo-sah-kah) is a savoury dish which originated in the Balkans, but is now one of the best known of all Greek

dishes and is also made with variations in Turkey and in some Middle Eastern countries. The dish traditionally contains mutton and aubergines [eggplant], but it has been widely adapted.

Moussaka I

A basic version of the more traditional Moussaka (moo-sah-kah) *made with mutton, or lamb, tomatoes and aubergines [eggplant] and topped with a creamy sauce, this dish makes a filling lunch or dinner. Serve with a crisp green salad*

4 SERVINGS

- 1 lb. aubergines [eggplant], sliced
- 1 tablespoon plus 1 teaspoon salt
- 1 oz. [2 tablespoons] butter
- 1 medium-sized onion, finely chopped
- 1 large garlic clove, crushed
- 1 lb. lean lamb or mutton, minced [ground]
- 4 medium-sized tomatoes, coarsely chopped
- 2 tablespoons tomato purée
- ¾ teaspoon dried thyme
- ½ teaspoon black pepper
- 3 tablespoons flour
- 4 fl. oz. [½ cup] vegetable oil
- 10 fl. oz. [1¼ cups] béchamel sauce
- 2 egg yolks
- 1 oz. [¼ cup] kefalotiri or Parmesan cheese, finely grated

Preheat the oven to fairly hot 375°F (Gas Mark 5, 190°C).

Place the aubergine [eggplant] slices in a colander and sprinkle over the tablespoon of salt. Set aside to dégorge for 30 minutes.

Meanwhile, in a medium-sized frying-pan, melt the butter over moderate heat. When the foam subsides, add the onion and garlic and fry, stirring occasionally, for 5 to 7 minutes, or until the onion is soft and translucent but not brown.

Add the meat, and fry, stirring frequently, for 8 minutes or until it is thoroughly browned.

Add the tomatoes, tomato purée, thyme, pepper and the remaining salt and cook, stirring occasionally, for 4 minutes. Remove the pan from the heat and set aside.

Dry the aubergine [eggplant] slices with kitchen paper towels. Place the flour on a plate and dip the aubergine [eggplant] slices in the flour, coating them thoroughly and shaking off any excess. Set aside.

In a medium-sized frying-pan, heat 2 fluid ounces [¼ cup] of the oil over moderate heat. When the oil is hot, add about one-half of the aubergine [eggplant] slices and fry them for 3 to 4 minutes on each side, or until they are lightly and evenly browned.

With a fish slice or spatula, remove the aubergine [eggplant] slices from the pan and set them aside to drain on kitchen paper towels. Fry the remaining slices in the same way, adding more oil to the pan as necessary.

Arrange half of the aubergine [eggplant] slices on the bottom of a deep sided large baking dish. Spoon over the lamb or mutton mixture and cover with the remaining aubergine [eggplant] slices. Set aside.

In a small mixing bowl, beat together the béchamel sauce and egg yolks. Pour the mixture over the aubergine [eggplant] slices in the dish, to cover them completely. Sprinkle over the kefalotiri or Parmesan cheese.

Place the dish in the centre of the oven and bake for 35 to 40 minutes, or until the top is lightly browned.

Remove the dish from the oven and serve immediately.

Moussaka II

An unusual dish, possibly of Romanian origin, Moussaka II may be accompanied by hot tomato sauce and Croquettes de Pommes de Terre. The aubergine [eggplant] skins which line the mould are edible, though some people prefer to remove them after cooking.

4 SERVINGS

2 teaspoons vegetable oil
3 medium-sized aubergines [eggplant], halved lengthways
1 tablespoon plus 1 teaspoon salt
2 fl. oz. [¼ cup] cold water
1 tablespoon lemon juice
1 oz. [2 tablespoons] butter
1 medium-sized onion, finely chopped
1 large garlic clove, crushed
1 large green pepper, white pith removed, seeded and finely chopped
8 oz. small button mushrooms, wiped clean and sliced
1 lb. lean mutton or lamb, minced [ground]
2 tablespoons tomato purée
1 tablespoon pine nuts
1 tablespoon finely chopped fresh dill, or 1½ teaspoons dried dill
1 tablespoon paprika
½ teaspoon black pepper
1 tablespoon flour
2 eggs, well beaten

(Low Cal)

Using the vegetable oil, grease a 2-pint [1½-quart] soufflé dish or mould and set it aside.

With the point of a sharp knife, deeply score the flesh of the aubergines [eggplant], leaving the skins intact.

Sprinkle over the tablespoon of salt and lay the aubergines [eggplant] in a colander, cut sides down. Set aside to dégorge for 30 minutes. Dry with kitchen paper towels and set aside.

In a large saucepan, bring the water and lemon juice to the boil over moderate heat. Reduce the heat to very low and place the aubergine [eggplant] halves in the pan, cut sides down, in one layer if possible.

Cover the pan and cook for 15 to 20 minutes, or until the flesh is very tender when pierced with the point of a sharp knife.

Remove the pan from the heat. Remove the aubergines [eggplant] from the pan and set them aside until they are cool

A good way to use up left-over lamb, Moussaka I makes a tasty and economical family meal.

enough to handle.

With a sharp-edged metal spoon, scoop the flesh out of the aubergine [eggplant] halves, keeping the skins intact. Place the flesh on a board and chop it. Set aside.

Line the bottom and sides of the prepared dish or mould with the aubergine [eggplant] skins, pressing down well. Set aside.

Preheat the oven to moderate 350°F (Gas Mark 4, 180°C).

In a medium-sized saucepan, melt the butter over moderate heat. When the foam subsides, add the onion, garlic and green pepper. Cook, stirring occasionally, for 6 to 8 minutes, or until the onion is golden brown.

Add the mushrooms and aubergine [eggplant] flesh and cook, stirring frequently, for 3 to 4 minutes, or until the mushrooms are just tender.

Stir in the minced [ground] mutton or lamb, the tomato purée, pine nuts, dill, paprika, pepper and the remaining salt. Cook, stirring frequently, for 4 minutes.

Remove the pan from the heat and set the mixture aside to cool to lukewarm. With a wooden spoon, beat in the flour and eggs and combine thoroughly. Spoon the mixture into the prepared dish and smooth it down with the back of the spoon. Cover the dish tightly with aluminium foil and place it in a roasting tin half-filled with hot water.

Place the tin in the centre of the oven and bake for 1 hour.

Remove the tin from the oven. Lift the dish out of the tin.

Hold a warmed serving plate, inverted, over the dish and reverse the two. The moussaka should come out easily.

Serve immediately.

Moussaka with Fish

An Israeli recipe, Moussaka with Fish can be made with most types of fish, using either a mixture of fish, or just one kind. Serve with buttered noodles and a green vegetable for a warming and filling meal.

4 SERVINGS

2 large aubergines [eggplant]
1 tablespoon plus 1 teaspoon salt
6 fl. oz. [¾ cup] vegetable oil
1 oz. [2 tablespoons] butter
2 small onions, finely chopped
8 oz. cod fillets, cooked, skinned and flaked
1 lb. halibut steaks, cooked, skinned and flaked
14 oz. canned peeled tomatoes, chopped
¼ teaspoon cayenne pepper

¼ teaspoon dried thyme
1 teaspoon dried dill
½ teaspoon black pepper
1 tablespoon paprika
4 oz. [1 cup] Cheddar cheese, finely grated

SAUCE
1 oz. [2 tablespoons] butter
2 tablespoons flour
5 fl. oz. single cream [⅝ cup light cream]
10 fl. oz. [1¼ cups] milk
4 egg yolks
1 tablespoon lemon juice

Cut the aubergines [eggplant] into slices. Place them in a colander and sprinkle with the tablespoon of salt. Set the aubergines [eggplant] aside for 30 minutes to dégorge. Dry the aubergine [eggplant] slices with kitchen paper towels. Set aside.

Preheat the oven to fairly hot 375°F (Gas Mark 5, 190°C).

In a medium-sized frying-pan, heat 2 fluid ounces [¼ cup] of the oil over moderate heat. When the oil is hot, add about one-third of the aubergine [eggplant] slices and fry them for 3 to 4 minutes on each side, or until they are golden brown. With a fish slice or spatula, remove the aubergine [eggplant]·slices from the pan and set them aside to drain on kitchen paper. Fry the remaining slices in the same way, adding more oil to the pan as necessary. Set aside.

In a medium-sized saucepan, melt the butter over moderate heat. When the foam subsides, add the onions and cook, stirring occasionally, for 5 to 7 minutes, or until they are soft and translucent but not brown.

Stir in the flaked fish, the tomatoes with the can juice, the cayenne, thyme, dill, pepper, paprika and the remaining salt. Cook, stirring frequently, for 3 minutes. Remove the pan from the heat and set aside.

Arrange one-third of the aubergine [eggplant] slices on the bottom of a medium-sized baking dish. Spoon over half the fish and tomato mixture and sprinkle over half the cheese. Cover with another third of the aubergine [eggplant] slices and spoon over the remaining fish and tomato mixture. Sprinkle over the remaining cheese and cover with the remaining aubergine [eggplant] slices. Set aside.

To make the sauce, in a medium-sized saucepan, melt the butter over moderate heat. Remove the pan from the heat and, with a wooden spoon, stir in the flour to make a smooth paste. Gradually stir in the cream and milk, being careful to avoid lumps.

Return the pan to the heat and cook the sauce, stirring constantly, for 3 to 4 minutes, or until it is very thick and smooth. Remove the pan from the heat and set aside to cool to lukewarm. When the sauce has cooled, beat in the egg yolks. Stir in the lemon juice.

Pour the sauce over the aubergine [eggplant] slices to cover them completely. Place the dish in the centre of the oven and bake for 35 to 40 minutes, or until the top is golden brown.

Remove the dish from the oven and serve immediately.

Moussaka Greek-Style

A Greek version of Moussaka, flavoured with mizithra or ricotta cheese, Moussaka Greek-Style can be served hot or cold. This dish improves in flavour if it is made a day in advance and reheated, or served cold. Accompany the Moussaka with a spicy sauce and a tomato or mixed salad.

4 SERVINGS

3 medium-sized aubergines [eggplant]
1 tablespoon plus 1 teaspoon salt
2 oz. [½ cup] flour
6 fl. oz. [¾ cup] vegetable oil
1 oz. [2 tablespoons] butter
4 small shallots, finely chopped
1 lb. lean lamb, finely minced [ground]
2 medium-sized tomatoes, blanched, peeled, seeded and coarsely chopped
1 tablespoon finely chopped fresh chives
2 fl. oz. [¼ cup] red wine
1 teaspoon lemon juice
¼ teaspoon dried sage
¼ teaspoon black pepper
½ teaspoon mixed spice or ground allspice
2 oz. [1 cup] fresh white bread-crumbs
SAUCE
6 oz. mizithra or ricotta cheese
3 egg yolks
12 fl. oz. single cream [1½ cups light cream]
¼ teaspoon salt
¼ teaspoon grated nutmeg
2 oz. [½ cup] kefalotiri or Parmesan cheese, finely grated

Cut the aubergines [eggplant] into slices. Place them in a colander and sprinkle each slice with salt. Set the aubergines [eggplant] aside for 30 minutes to drain off bitter juices. Rinse and dry the aubergine slices with kitchen paper towels.

Place the flour on a plate. Dip the

Zorba's delight — Moussaka Greek-Style should be served with Retsina.

aubergine [eggplant] slices in the flour, coating them thoroughly and shaking off any excess.

In a medium-sized frying-pan, heat 2 fluid ounces [¼ cup] of the oil over moderate heat. When the oil is hot, add about one-third of the aubergine [eggplant] slices and fry them for 3 to 4 minutes on each side, or until they are golden brown.

With a fish slice or spatula, remove the aubergine [eggplant] slices from the pan and set them aside to drain on kitchen paper towels. Fry the remaining slices in the same way, adding more oil to the pan as necessary. Set aside.

Preheat the oven to fairly hot 375°F (Gas Mark 5, 190°C).

In a medium-sized frying-pan, melt the butter over moderate heat. When the foam subsides, add the shallots and fry, stirring occasionally, for 3 to 5 minutes, or until they are soft and translucent but not brown.

Stir in the minced [ground] lamb and cook, stirring frequently, for 8 minutes, or until the meat is well browned. Stir in the tomatoes, chives, wine, lemon juice, sage, pepper, mixed spice or allspice and the remaining salt. Cook, stirring occasionally, for 4 minutes.

Remove the pan from the heat. With a wooden spoon, stir in the breadcrumbs. Set aside.

To make the sauce, in a medium-sized heatproof mixing bowl, mash the mizithra or ricotta cheese with a fork until it is smooth. Beat in the egg yolks to form a smooth paste. Gradually stir in the cream, and add the salt, nutmeg and grated kefalotiri or Parmesan cheese.

Arrange one-third of the aubergine [eggplant] slices on the bottom of a medium-sized baking dish. Spread over half of the meat mixture and cover with another third of the aubergine [eggplant] slices. Spread over the remaining meat mixture and cover with the remaining aubergine [eggplant] slices. Pour over the sauce to cover the aubergine [eggplant] slices completely.

Place the dish in the centre of the oven and bake for 45 to 50 minutes, or until the top is golden brown. Remove the dish from the oven and serve immediately, or cool and serve.

Mousse

Mousse (mooss) is a culinary term derived from the French word meaning frothy or foamy. Mousses may be sweet or savoury, hot or cold (although they are usually served cold), and may be made in several ways.

Most commonly, a flavoured cream, milk or purée base is thickened with egg yolks and stiffly beaten egg whites are folded in, although in the case of a very thick purée such as chestnut only stiffly whipped cream and egg whites are normally added.

Baked mousses containing egg yolks and whites resemble a soufflé in appearance and are generally eaten, hot or cold, as a first course.

Sweet mousses containing eggs, or a fruit purée base with cream, may be frozen to resemble ice-cream, or may be served cold as a dessert.

A simple dessert, Mousse aux Abricots will impress your guests both with its appearance and delicate flavour.

Mousse aux Abricots

APRICOT MOUSSE

A delectable chilled apricot mousse flavoured with brandy, lemon juice, brown sugar and cinnamon, Mousse aux Abricots (mooss-oh-zah-bree-koh) may be served on its own, or sprinkled with toasted almonds or hazelnuts and served with a bowl of chilled Crème Chantilly. Fresh apricots should be used if possible for the flavour from the kernels.

4 SERVINGS

1 lb. fresh apricots, washed, halved, stoned and stones reserved or 8 oz. dried apricots, soaked overnight, drained and chopped
2 oz. [⅓ cup] soft brown sugar
¼ teaspoon ground cinnamon
2 fl. oz. [¼ cup] water
1 teaspoon arrowroot dissolved in 1 tablespoon lemon juice
2 tablespoons apricot brandy
5 fl. oz. double cream [⅝ cup heavy cream], whipped until thick
3 egg whites

Mou

On a hard surface, using a hammer, crack open the apricot stones, if you are using fresh apricots. Discard the stones and peel the skin off the kernels. Discard the skins. Coarsely chop the kernels and set them aside.

In a medium-sized saucepan, combine the apricot halves or dried apricots, the sugar, cinnamon and water.

Set the pan over moderate heat and bring the mixture to the boil, stirring until the sugar has dissolved. Reduce the heat to very low, cover the pan and simmer, stirring occasionally, for 30 minutes, or until the apricots are very tender and beginning to pulp.

Remove the pan from the heat. Pour the mixture into a fine wire strainer held over a medium-sized mixing bowl. Using the back of a wooden spoon, rub the apricots through the strainer until only a dry pulp is left in the strainer. Discard the pulp.

Stir the arrowroot mixture into the apricot purée. Pour the mixture back into the pan and return the pan to the heat. Cook the purée, stirring constantly, until it has thickened.

Remove the pan from the heat and set the mixture aside to cool completely.

When the mixture has cooled, stir in the chopped kernels, if you are using them, the brandy and the cream and combine the mixture thoroughly. Set aside.

In a medium-sized mixing bowl, beat the egg whites with a wire whisk or rotary beater until they form stiff peaks. With a metal spoon, carefully fold the egg whites into the apricot mixture.

Spoon the mixture into a medium-sized chilled glass serving dish. Chill the mousse in the refrigerator for 2 hours before serving.

Mousse aux Abricots et aux Mûres

APRICOT MOUSSE WITH BLACKBERRIES

A very colourful and superb dessert, Mousse aux Abricots et aux Mûres (mooss oh-zah-bree-koh ay oh mure) is remarkably easy to prepare, although you do need a blender. It is ideal for an easily made dinner party dessert as you need not soak the apricots overnight. If you like, you may make the mousse the day before and then chill it in the refrigerator.

6 SERVINGS

12 oz. dried apricots
1 teaspoon lemon juice
2 oz. [¼ cup] sugar
4 egg whites
8 oz. blackberries

4 tablespoons icing [confectioners'] sugar

Place the apricots in a medium-sized saucepan and pour over enough water to cover them. Add the lemon juice and place the pan over moderate heat. Bring the water to the boil, stirring occasionally.

Reduce the heat to low and simmer the apricots for 10 to 15 minutes, or until they are tender.

Remove the pan from the heat and set the apricots aside to cool slightly.

When the apricots are cool, blend them to a purée in an electric blender. If necessary, add additional water so that the blender blades will not stick.

Transfer the apricot purée to a large mixing bowl and stir in the sugar. Taste and add more sugar if you like. Set aside.

In a medium-sized mixing bowl, beat the egg whites with a wire whisk or rotary beater until they form stiff peaks. With a metal spoon, carefully fold the egg whites into the apricot mixture.

Spoon the mousse mixture into 6 glass serving dishes. Place the dishes in the refrigerator and chill for at least 2 hours.

In a small mixing bowl, combine the blackberries and icing [confectioners']

sugar. Place the bowl in the refrigerator to chill until you are ready to serve the mousse.

Just before serving, top each mousse with a spoonful of blackberries.

Mousse au Chocolat

CHOCOLATE MOUSSE

Mousse au Chocolat (mooss oh shoh-koh-lah) is a rich French confection, flavoured with dark chocolate, brandy and coffee, ideal to serve as a dinner party dessert. The mousse is best made a day before serving and chilled in the refrigerator. For a more decorative effect, pipe whipped cream over the mousse just before serving.

6 SERVINGS

8 oz. dark [semi-sweet] cooking chocolate, broken into small pieces
3 tablespoons strong black coffee
1½ oz. [3 tablespoons] unsalted butter, cut into small pieces
4 eggs, separated
2 tablespoons brandy

In a medium-sized heatproof mixing bowl, combine the chocolate and coffee. Place the bowl in a large saucepan half-filled with hot water.

Set the pan over moderately low heat and cook the mixture, stirring constantly with a wooden spoon, until the chocolate has melted and the mixture is smooth.

Beat in the butter, a few pieces at a time, and continue beating until it is thoroughly blended into the chocolate mixture.

Add the egg yolks and cook, beating constantly with a wire whisk or rotary beater, for 5 minutes or until the mixture has thickened and is smooth. Do not let the mixture come to the boil or the eggs will scramble.

Remove the pan from the heat. Lift the bowl out of the pan and stir in the brandy.

Light and airy desserts, such as Mousse aux Framboises and Mousse au Chocolat, are perfect to serve at the end of a dinner party.

Set the mixture aside for 30 minutes to cool completely.

Meanwhile, in a medium-sized mixing bowl, beat the egg whites with a wire whisk or rotary beater until they form stiff peaks.

With a metal spoon, carefully fold the egg whites into the cooled chocolate mixture.

Spoon the mixture into 6 individual serving glasses or bowls. Place the glasses or bowls in the refrigerator and chill for at least 4 hours or overnight.

Mousse aux Framboises
RASPBERRY MOUSSE

☆   ①

Mousse aux Framboises (mooss oh frahm-bwahz) is a delectable cold raspberry cream mousse. Serve with whipped cream for an extra-special dessert.

6 SERVINGS

1 teaspoon vegetable oil
2 oz. [¼ cup] castor sugar

2 fl. oz. [¼ cup] fresh orange juice
1 lb. fresh raspberries
12 fl. oz. double cream [1½ cups heavy cream]
4 eggs, separated
½ oz. gelatine dissolved in 4 tablespoons warm water

With the teaspoon of oil, grease a 3-pint [2-quart] mould or soufflé dish. Set aside.

In a medium-sized saucepan, dissolve the sugar in the orange juice over low heat, stirring occasionally. Increase the heat to high and boil the mixture for 1 minute.

Reduce the heat to low and add the raspberries to the pan, stirring to coat them thoroughly with the syrup. Cover the pan and simmer for 10 minutes, stirring occasionally, or until the raspberries are beginning to pulp.

Remove the pan from the heat. Pour the mixture into a fine wire strainer held over a medium-sized mixing bowl. Using

the back of a wooden spoon, rub the raspberries through the strainer, until only a dry pulp is left. Discard the pulp in the strainer. Set the purée aside.

In a medium-sized heatproof mixing bowl, beat the cream and egg yolks together with a wire whisk or rotary beater.

Place the bowl in a pan half-filled with hot water and set the pan over low heat. Cook the custard, whisking constantly, until it is thick and smooth. Do not allow the custard to boil or the eggs will scramble.

Remove the pan from the heat. Lift the bowl out of the pan. Beat the custard into the raspberry purée. Beat in the dissolved gelatine and set the mixture aside to cool to room temperature, stirring occasionally.

Meanwhile, in a medium-sized mixing bowl, beat the egg whites with a wire whisk or rotary beater until they form stiff peaks.

Using a metal spoon, carefully fold the egg whites into the raspberry mixture.

Pour the mixture into the prepared mould or dish and place it in the refrigerator to chill for 4 hours, or until the mousse has completely set.

Remove the mousse from the refrigerator. Run a sharp knife around the edge of the mousse and quickly dip the bottom of the mould or dish in boiling water.

Place a serving dish, inverted, over the mould or dish and reverse the two, giving a sharp shake. The mousse should slide out easily. Serve at once.

Mousse à l'Orange et au Chocolat
ORANGE AND CHOCOLATE MOUSSE

Mousse à l'Orange et au Chocolat (Moss ah loh-ranj ay oh shoh-koh-lah) is a well-known dessert, with many variations. This version is made with the zest of oranges, orange-flavoured liqueur, chocolate, cream and eggs. As the mousse is so rich, it should be served after a light meal.

4 SERVINGS

2 firm, bright-skinned oranges
4 large sugar cubes
10 fl. oz. single cream [1¼ cups light cream]
1 small vanilla pod
4 eggs, separated
6 oz. dark [semi-sweet] cooking chocolate, melted
2 tablespoons orange-flavoured liqueur

Rub each orange all over with the sugar cubes to extract all the zest from the rind. Place the sugar in a small mixing bowl

and crush the cubes with a wooden spoon. Set aside. Reserve the oranges for future use.

In a small saucepan, scald the cream (bring to just under boiling point) with the vanilla pod over moderate heat. Remove the pan from the heat. Remove and discard the vanilla pod.

Gradually add the hot cream to the sugar cubes, stirring constantly, and continue stirring until the sugar has completely dissolved. Set aside.

In a medium-sized heatproof mixing bowl, beat the egg yolks with a wire whisk or rotary beater until they are pale and frothy. Gradually beat in the sugar and cream mixture and combine thoroughly.

Place the bowl in a large saucepan half-filled with hot water. Set the pan over low heat and cook the mixture, stirring constantly with a wooden spoon, for 5 to 6 minutes, or until it is thick enough to coat the spoon. Do not let the mixture boil or the eggs will scramble.

Remove the pan from the heat. Gradually beat in the melted chocolate. Stir in the orange-flavoured liqueur. Lift the bowl out of the pan and set it aside to cool completely.

In a medium-sized mixing bowl, beat the egg whites with a wire whisk or rotary beater until they form stiff peaks. With a metal spoon, carefully fold the egg whites into the orange and chocolate mixture.

Spoon the mousse into a chilled glass serving dish and chill in the refrigerator for at least 2 hours before serving.

Mousse à l'Orange Glacée
FROZEN ORANGE MOUSSE

A refreshing frozen orange mousse, Mousse à l'Orange Glacée (mooss ah loh-rahnj gla-say) must be made the day before serving, as it is frozen overnight. After freezing, the mousse may be spooned into chilled glasses and served on its own, or with a fresh fruit salad or whipped cream.

4 SERVINGS

6 sugar cubes
2 firm, bright-skinned oranges
10 fl. oz. [1¼ cups] fresh orange juice
4 fl. oz. double cream [½ cup heavy cream]
3 tablespoons orange-flavoured liqueur
¼ oz. gelatine dissolved in 2 tablespoons warm water
2 egg whites

Set the refrigerator to its coldest setting.

Rub the sugar cubes all over the oranges to extract all the zest from the rind. Reserve the oranges for future use.

Place the sugar cubes and the orange juice in a small saucepan. Set the pan over low heat and cook, stirring frequently, until the sugar has dissolved. Increase the heat to moderately high and boil the mixture for 4 minutes, stirring occasionally.

Remove the pan from the heat. Stir in the cream, orange-flavoured liqueur and the dissolved gelatine. Combine the mixture thoroughly and pour it into a 1½-pint [1-quart] freezer tray. Place the freezer tray in the frozen food storage compartment of the refrigerator and chill for 20 minutes.

Meanwhile, in a small mixing bowl, beat the egg whites with a wire whisk or rotary beater until they form stiff peaks.

Remove the orange mixture from the refrigerator and whisk it into the egg whites. Spoon the mixture back into the freezer tray and return it to the storage compartment. Freeze the mixture for 1 hour.

Remove the mixture from the refrigerator and turn it out into a medium-sized mixing bowl. Using a wire whisk or rotary beater, beat the mixture for 1 minute, or until it is smooth.

Spoon the mixture back into the freezer tray and return it to the storage compartment. Freeze the mixture for 4 hours, whisking it every hour.

Freeze the mixture overnight before serving.

Mousse de Saumon
MOULDED SALMON MOUSSE

A superbly decorative moulded salmon mousse, Mousse de Saumon (mooss d' soh-mawn) makes an elegant centrepiece for a cold formal buffet, or, served in small quantities, a first course for a dinner party. The dish takes time and effort to prepare, but the impressive result makes it well worth the effort.

The only accompaniments necessary are boiled new potatoes, tossed in butter and sprinkled with parsley, or hot crusty bread and butter and, to drink, a good chilled white wine such as Pouilly Fumé.

6-8 SERVINGS

2 small shallots, thinly sliced
1 lemon, thinly sliced
1 teaspoon salt
4 black peppercorns, very coarsely crushed
1 large bay leaf, crumbled
1½ lb. salmon steaks
8 fl. oz. [1 cup] dry white wine
10 fl. oz. [1¼ cups] aspic
8 fl. oz. [1 cup] béchamel sauce, cold
½ oz. gelatine dissolved in 4 tablespoons warm water

¼ teaspoon cayenne pepper
2 teaspoons tomato purée
2 tablespoons Madeira
2 tablespoons lemon juice
8 fl. oz. double cream [1 cup heavy cream], whipped until thick but not stiff

GARNISH

6 large, flat lettuce leaves, washed and shaken dry
8 fl. oz. [1 cup] mayonnaise
6 hard-boiled eggs, thinly sliced
6 very small [cherry] tomatoes, thinly sliced
11 black olives, stoned

First, poach the salmon steaks. Cover the bottom of a large, heavy saucepan with the shallots and half the lemon slices. Sprinkle over half the salt, peppercorns and crumbled bay leaf. Arrange the salmon steaks, in one layer if possible, in the saucepan. Sprinkle over the remaining salt, peppercorns and bay leaf, and cover with the remaining lemon slices. Pour over the wine.

Set the pan over moderate heat and bring the liquid to the boil. Reduce the heat to low, cover the pan and simmer for 10 to 15 minutes, or until the salmon flakes easily when tested with a fork. Remove the pan from the heat.

With a slotted spoon, transfer the fish to a wooden board. Discard all the vegetables, flavourings and cooking liquid, or use as a base for fish stock.

Mousse de Saumon is a very elegant dish, guaranteed to impress.

With a sharp knife, skin and bone the fish and cut it into chunks. Mince [grind] the fish in a food mill, or blend in an electric blender. Set the salmon aside.

Pour 7 fluid ounces [⅞ cup] of the aspic into a 2-pint [1½-quart] fish-shaped mould. Tip and rotate the mould over a large shallow bowl filled with crushed ice until the aspic has set evenly over the bottom and sides of the mould. Place the mould in the refrigerator and chill for 30 minutes.

Meanwhile, in a medium-sized mixing bowl, combine the salmon and béchamel sauce. Stir in the dissolved gelatine and blend it in thoroughly. Beat in the cayenne pepper, tomato purée, Madeira, lemon juice and cream. Taste the mixture and add salt and pepper if necessary.

Remove the mould from the refrigerator. Spoon the salmon mixture into the mould, smoothing it down with a flat-bladed knife.

Place the mould in the refrigerator and chill for 2 hours, or until the mousse is just set.

Remove the mould from the refrigerator. Pour over the remaining aspic, smoothing it evenly over the top of the mousse with a flat-bladed knife so that the mousse is completely covered.

Return the mould to the refrigerator and chill for 4 hours.

Completely cover the base of a chilled large oval serving platter with the lettuce leaves, overlapping the leaves in the centre. Set the platter aside.

Fill a small forcing bag, fitted with a medium-sized star-shaped nozzle, with the mayonnaise and set aside.

Remove the mould from the refrigerator. Run a sharp knife around the edge of the mousse to loosen the sides. Quickly dip the bottom of the mould into boiling water. Holding the lettuce leaves in place with one hand, invert the serving platter and place it over the mould. Check that

the lettuce leaves are still in place and reverse the mould and platter, giving a sharp shake. The mousse should slide out easily.

Pipe decorative swirls of the mayonnaise around the edge of the mousse. Place the egg slices, side by side, around the edge of the dish. Place a tomato slice on every other egg slice. Place an olive in the centre of each tomato slice.

Place the dish in the refrigerator and chill for 30 minutes before serving.

Mousseline

Mousseline (moo-sell-een) is a term used to describe various preparations to which cream has been added. For instance, in French haute cuisine small moulds of minced [ground] poultry, fish, shellfish or game to which cream is added are called mousselines. When cream is added to HOLLANDAISE SAUCE the resulting compound is called MOUSSELINE SAUCE.

The word mousseline is also often used in confectionery to denote a cake or dessert containing a large amount of eggs or cream.

Mousseline au Chocolat can be served with coffee or as a dessert.

Mousseline au Chocolat

RICH CHOCOLATE CAKE

A rich but light chocolate cake, Mousseline au Chocolat (moo-sell-een oh shoh-koh-lah) is sandwiched together with mint-flavoured cream which is also piped on top.

ONE 8-INCH CAKE

2 teaspoons butter
1 lb. [2 cups] plus 2 tablespoons castor sugar
2 oz. cornflour [$\frac{1}{2}$ cup cornstarch]
2 oz. [$\frac{1}{2}$ cup] flour
$\frac{1}{2}$ teaspoon salt
2 oz. [$\frac{1}{2}$ cup] cocoa powder
8 eggs, separated
1 teaspoon vanilla essence

FILLING
8 fl. oz. double cream [1 cup heavy cream]
1 tablespoon mint-flavoured liqueur
2 drops green food colouring (optional)

Preheat the oven to moderate 350°F (Gas Mark 4, 180°C). With the butter, grease two deep 8-inch sandwich tins. Lightly dust each tin with 1 tablespoon of sugar, knocking out any excess. Set aside.

Sift the cornflour [cornstarch], flour,

salt and cocoa powder into a medium-sized mixing bowl. Set aside.

In a large mixing bowl, beat the remaining sugar and the egg yolks together with a wooden spoon until the mixture is pale and frothy. Stir in the vanilla essence. With a metal spoon, carefully fold in the flour and cocoa mixture until the ingredients are well combined.

In a large mixing bowl, beat the egg whites with a wire whisk or rotary beater until they form stiff peaks. With a metal spoon, carefully fold the egg whites into the flour mixture.

Spoon the cake mixture into each of the prepared cake tins. Place the tins in the centre of the oven and bake for 40 to 45 minutes, or until the cakes spring back when lightly pressed with a fingertip.

Remove the tins from the oven and set the cakes aside to cool for 10 minutes before turning them out on to a wire rack to cool completely.

To make the filling, in a medium-sized mixing bowl beat the cream with a wire whisk or rotary beater until it forms stiff peaks. Add the mint-flavoured liqueur and food colouring, if you are using it. Mix well to blend them into the cream and distribute the colouring evenly.

Place one of the cakes on a decorative serving platter. Spread the top of the cake

An inexpensive and filling dish, Mouton Farci is the perfect dish for a family meal. This dish should be garnished with onions and carrots.

with half of the cream filling. Place the other cake on top. Pipe the remaining cream in a decorative pattern over the top of the cake.

Serve at once.

Mousseline Sauce

   ①

Mousseline (moo-sell-een) *Sauce may be served with freshly cooked vegetables and cold fish dishes. Make the Hollandaise Sauce according to the basic recipe.*

10 FLUID OUNCES

2 fl. oz. double cream [¼ cup heavy cream]
8 fl. oz. [1 cup] hot Hollandaise Sauce

In a medium-sized mixing bowl, beat the cream with a wire whisk or rotary beater until it thickens slightly.

Using a large spoon fold the Hollandaise Sauce into the cream. Pour the sauce into a warmed sauceboat and serve.

Mouton Farci
STUFFED LOIN OF MUTTON

 ①

Mouton Farci (moo-tohn fahr-see) *is an economical dish for a family supper. Serve it with sautéed potatoes and buttered turnips. If mutton is not available lamb may be used.*

6-8 SERVINGS

4 oz. sausage meat
3 oz. [1½ cups] fresh breadcrumbs
½ teaspoon salt
¼ teaspoon black pepper
1 tablespoon chopped fresh parsley
2 teaspoons chopped fresh dill or 1 teaspoon dried dill
2 teaspoons chopped fresh tarragon or 1 teaspoon dried tarragon
1 garlic clove, crushed
1 egg yolk, lightly beaten
1 tablespoon butter
1 medium-sized onion, chopped
1 x 3 lb. boned loin of mutton, trimmed of excess fat
2 tablespoons vegetable oil
3 carrots, scraped and halved lengthways
10 pickling [pearl] onions
1 pint [2½ cups] chicken stock

Preheat the oven to warm 325°F (Gas Mark 3, 170°C).

In a large mixing bowl, combine the sausage meat, breadcrumbs, salt, pepper, parsley, dill, tarragon, garlic and egg yolk. Mix well to combine all the ingredients thoroughly. Set aside.

In a small frying-pan, melt the butter over moderate heat. When the foam subsides, add the onion and fry, stirring occasionally, for 5 to 7 minutes or until it is soft and translucent but not brown.

Remove the pan from the heat. With a slotted spoon, transfer the onion to the mixing bowl and stir it into the sausage meat mixture.

Lay the mutton out on a flat surface. Spread the sausage meat stuffing evenly over the meat. Carefully roll up the meat, Swiss [jelly] roll style, and tie with string at 1-inch intervals.

In a large flameproof casserole, heat the oil over moderate heat. When the oil is hot, place the rolled mutton in the casserole and brown it, turning occasionally with tongs, for 10 to 15 minutes or until it is evenly browned all over.

Add the carrots and pickling [pearl] onions, shaking the casserole gently to coat the vegetables with the oil. Cook for a further 3 minutes.

Remove the casserole from the heat and pour off and discard the pan liquid. Pour in the chicken stock.

Return the casserole to moderately high heat and bring the stock to the boil.

Remove the casserole from the heat, cover and place it in the bottom of the oven. Braise for 2 to 2½ hours or until the meat is tender when pierced with the point of a sharp knife.

Remove the casserole from the oven. With tongs, transfer the meat roll to a warmed serving dish. With a slotted spoon transfer the vegetables to the serving dish and arrange them decoratively around the meat. Skim off any fat from the cooking juices and strain them into a warmed sauceboat.

Serve immediately.

Mozzarella

Mozzarella is an unripened, soft white cheese, originally made from buffalo's milk although cow's milk is now usually used instead. It is round in shape, weighing between 8 and 10 ounces.

Mozzarella is an essential ingredient in many pasta dishes.

Mozzarella in Carozza
DEEP-FRIED CHEESE SANDWICHES

Mozzarella in Carozza (moht-zah-rell-ah in kah-roht-zah), *literally 'mozzarella in a carriage', is a simple dish of fried cheese sandwiches from Southern Italy. It makes a tasty supper or snack which may be served with a light vegetable or salad.*

6-8 SERVINGS

1 lb. Mozzarella cheese, cut into ¼-inch slices
26 small thin slices white bread, crusts removed
4 eggs
6 fl. oz. [¾ cup] milk
4 oz. [1 cup] seasoned flour, made with 4 oz. [1 cup] flour, 1 teaspoon salt and ½ teaspoon black pepper sufficient vegetable oil for deep-frying

Place a slice of cheese on one of the bread slices and cover with a second slice of bread. Continue making sandwiches in this way until all the bread and cheese have been used up.

In a large dish, beat the eggs and milk together with a fork. Lay the cheese sandwiches in the egg mixture and leave to soak for 20 minutes, basting frequently, or until all the egg mixture has been absorbed. Remove the sandwiches from the dish and pinch the edges of the bread together to completely enclose the cheese.

Place the seasoned flour on a plate. Dip the sandwiches in the flour, one by one, thoroughly coating them on both sides. Shake off any excess flour and set aside.

Fill a large deep-frying pan one-third full of vegetable oil. Place the pan over

A delicious Italian dish, Mozzarella Chicken would be a superb main course for a family meal.

moderately high heat and heat the oil until it reaches 375°F on a deep-fat thermometer, or until a small cube of stale bread dropped into the oil turns golden in 40 seconds.

Carefully drop the sandwiches into the oil, a few at a time, and fry for 1 minute or until they are pale brown and crisp. With a slotted spoon, remove the sandwiches from the pan and drain them on kitchen paper towels. Keep warm while you fry the remaining sandwiches in the same way.

Serve hot.

Mozzarella Chicken

Delightfully different, Mozzarella Chicken makes a delicious family dinner dish. Serve it with plain boiled rice and a crisp salad.

6 SERVINGS

2 tablespoons vegetable oil
1 medium-sized onion, finely chopped
14 oz. canned peeled tomatoes
2 tablespoons tomato purée
1 teaspoon dried oregano
1 teaspoon salt
½ teaspoon black pepper
6 streaky bacon slices, rinds removed
1 oz. [2 tablespoons] butter
1 teaspoon finely chopped fresh tarragon or ¼ teaspoon dried tarragon
6 chicken breasts, skinned and boned
4 oz. Mozzarella cheese, cut into slices

In a medium-sized saucepan, heat the oil over moderate heat. When the oil is hot, add the onion and fry, stirring occasionally, for 5 to 7 minutes, or until it is soft and translucent but not brown.

Add the tomatoes with the can juice, the tomato purée, oregano, salt and pepper. Stir well and bring the liquid to the boil over high heat. Reduce the heat to very low and simmer the tomato sauce for 20 minutes, stirring occasionally.

Meanwhile, in a large frying-pan, fry the bacon over moderate heat for 5 minutes or until it is crisp and has rendered most of its fat. With a slotted spoon, remove the bacon from the pan and set aside to drain on kitchen paper towels. Keep warm.

Add the butter to the bacon fat in the frying-pan. When the foam subsides, stir in the tarragon. Add the chicken breasts and fry, turning occasionally, for 15 to 20 minutes, or until they are tender when pierced with the point of a sharp knife.

Preheat the grill [broiler] to high.

Remove the frying-pan from the heat. With a slotted spoon, transfer the chicken breasts to a warmed flameproof serving dish. Place a slice of bacon over each breast and pour over the tomato sauce.

Place the slices of cheese over the top and place the dish under the grill [broiler]. Grill [broil] for 4 to 5 minutes or until the cheese has melted and is lightly browned.

Remove the dish from the heat and serve at once, straight from the dish.

Mozzarella Crespoltini
CHEESE AND SPINACH CREPES

Mozzarella Crespoltini (moht-zah-rell-ah kres-pohl-tee-nee) are crêpes stuffed with cream cheese and spinach, with a layer of mozzarella melted over the top. It makes a delicious supper dish and needs only a crisp salad as an accompaniment.

4 SERVINGS

8 oz. [2 cups] savoury Crêpe Batter
1 tablespoon plus 1 teaspoon butter

Versatile Mozzarella Crespoltini may be served as a main course or, in smaller quantities, as an appetizer.

6 oz. cream cheese
6 oz. cooked spinach, drained
½ teaspoon salt
¼ teaspoon black pepper
1 egg, lightly beaten
3 oz. [¾ cup] Parmesan cheese, grated
15 fl. oz. [1⅞ cups] béchamel sauce
3 oz. Mozzarella cheese, cut into thin slices

Fry the crêpes according to the instructions in the basic recipe and keep them warm.

Preheat the oven to fairly hot 375°F (Gas Mark 5, 190°C).

With the teaspoon of butter, lightly grease a large, shallow ovenproof dish and set aside.

In a medium-sized mixing bowl, combine the cream cheese, spinach, salt, pepper, egg and 1 ounce [¼ cup] of the Parmesan cheese. Spoon equal amounts of the mixture on to each crêpe, spreading it out evenly with a flat-bladed knife. Carefully roll up each crêpe and place them, seam side down, in the dish.

Pour over the béchamel sauce. Arrange the Mozzarella slices on top of the crêpes

and sprinkle over the remaining Parmesan cheese. Cut the remaining butter into small pieces and dot over the mixture. Place the dish in the oven and bake for 25 to 30 minutes or until the top is golden brown and beginning to crisp.

Remove the dish from the oven and serve at once.

Muffin

The muffin has various meanings in different countries.

In North America, it is a breakfast cake made with flour, milk and butter with baking powder used as a raising agent rather than yeast. It is baked in a special pan called a muffin pan.

In Great Britain, on the other hand, the muffin is a teacake made with yeast. It is cooked in a special ring called a muffin ring on top of the stove on a girdle or heavy baking sheet. It is cooked on both sides — unlike the CRUMPET which is made in the same way but is only cooked on one side. To add to the confusion, a popular crumpet-like breakfast cake in the United States is called an English muffin!

Muffins with Apples

These fruit muffins, traditional American favourites, are equally delicious eaten warm

A delightful way to begin your day, Muffins with Apples make a tasty change from toast at breakfast-time.

or cold and are usually served at breakfast. In this particular recipe we use apples but almost any kind of fruit can be substituted.

12 MUFFINS

2 oz. [¼ cup] plus 1 tablespoon butter, melted
8 oz. [2 cups] flour
½ teaspoon salt
2 teaspoons baking powder
2 oz. [¼ cup] sugar
½ teaspoon ground cinnamon
¼ teaspoon grated nutmeg
¼ teaspoon mixed spice or ground allspice
2 eggs, lightly beaten
5 fl. oz. [⅝ cup] buttermilk
1 tablespoon lemon juice
2 medium-sized eating apples, peeled, cored and grated

Preheat the oven to very hot 450°F (Gas Mark 8, 230°C). With the tablespoon of butter, generously grease a 12-muffin pan and set aside.

Sift the flour, salt, baking powder, sugar, cinnamon, nutmeg and mixed spice or ground allspice into a large mixing bowl. Set aside.

In a medium-sized mixing bowl, beat the eggs with a wire whisk or rotary beater until they are pale yellow in colour

and fall in a steady ribbon from the whisk. Add the remaining butter, the buttermilk and lemon juice to the eggs and stir well.

Stir the egg mixture into the flour mixture as quickly as possible. Do not over-mix as the ingredients should be just combined. Fold in the grated apples.

Spoon the batter into the prepared muffin pan. Place the pan in the centre of the oven and bake for 15 to 20 minutes or until a skewer inserted into the centres of the muffins comes out clean.

Remove the muffins from the oven. Cool in the pan for about 4 minutes and then turn them out on to a plate, if you are serving them warm.

Muffins with Cheese

Muffins with Cheese make a delightfully different breakfast or brunch addition, served warm, split open and buttered. Place a tomato slice on each muffin for added flavour.

12 MUFFINS

2 oz. [¼ cup] plus 1 tablespoon butter, melted
8 oz. [2 cups] flour
2 teaspoons baking powder
½ teaspoon salt
⅛ teaspoon black pepper
2 eggs
5 fl. oz. [⅝ cup] milk
2 oz. [½ cup] Cheddar cheese, grated

Preheat the oven to very hot 450°F (Gas Mark 8, 230°C). With the tablespoon of butter, generously grease a 12-muffin pan and set aside.

Sift the flour, baking powder, salt and pepper into a large mixing bowl. Set aside.

In a medium-sized mixing bowl, beat the eggs with a wire whisk or rotary beater until they are pale yellow in colour and fall in a steady ribbon from the whisk. Add the remaining butter and the milk to the eggs and stir well.

Stir the egg mixture into the flour mixture as quickly as possible. Do not over-mix as the ingredients should be just combined. Stir in the grated cheese.

Spoon the batter into the prepared muffin pan. Place the pan in the centre of the oven and bake for 15 to 20 minutes or until a skewer inserted into the centres of the muffins comes out clean.

Remove the muffins from the oven. Cool in the pan for about 4 minutes and then turn them out on to a plate, if you are serving them warm.

Muffins with Herbs

Lightly flavoured with herbs and a hint of orange, Muffins with Herbs make an unusual breakfast treat. Serve warm, with butter.

36 MUFFINS

4 oz. [½ cup] plus 2 tablespoons butter, melted
14 oz. [3½ cups] flour
1 teaspoon salt
4 teaspoons baking powder
2 tablespoons very finely chopped fresh parsley
½ teaspoon dried marjoram
½ teaspoon ground coriander
¼ teaspoon mixed spice or ground allspice
⅛ teaspoon black pepper
grated rind of 1 orange
4 eggs
10 fl. oz. [1¼ cups] buttermilk

Preheat the oven to very hot 450°F (Gas Mark 8, 230°C). With the 2 tablespoons of butter, generously grease three 12-muffin pans and set them aside.

Sift the flour, salt and baking powder into a large mixing bowl. Stir in the parsley, marjoram, coriander, mixed spice or ground allspice, black pepper and orange rind. Set aside.

In a medium-sized mixing bowl, beat the eggs with a wire whisk or rotary beater until they are pale yellow in colour and fall in a steady ribbon from the whisk. Add the remaining butter and the buttermilk to the eggs and stir well.

Stir the egg mixture into the flour mix-ture as quickly as possible. Do not over-mix as the ingredients should be just combined.

Spoon the batter into the prepared muffin pans. Place the pans in the centre of the oven and bake for 15 to 20 minutes or until a skewer inserted into the centres of the muffins comes out clean.

Remove the muffins from the oven. Cool in the pans for about 4 minutes and then turn them out on to a plate. Serve warm.

Muhalabia
CHILLED GROUND RICE PUDDING

Muhalabia (muh-hahl-ahb-bee-yah) is a custard-like pudding from the Middle East with a very delicate flavour. It may be made in advance and chilled until it is required.

6 SERVINGS

4 oz. [½ cup] ground rice
2 tablespoons sugar
2 pints [5 cups] milk
½ teaspoon vanilla essence
3 tablespoons orange-flower water
¼ teaspoon grated nutmeg

Just for a change, try light and aromatic Muffins with Herbs.

In a medium-sized mixing bowl, combine the rice, sugar and 4 tablespoons of the milk together to make a smooth paste. Set aside.

In a medium-sized saucepan, scald the remaining milk over moderate heat (bring to just below boiling point). Remove the pan from the heat and pour the milk on to the rice mixture, stirring constantly.

Return the milk mixture to the saucepan. Place it over moderate heat and bring to the boil, stirring constantly. As soon as the mixture boils, remove the pan from the heat.

Stir in the vanilla essence, orange-flower water and nutmeg. Pour the mixture into a large serving bowl and allow it to cool, stirring occasionally. Place the bowl in the refrigerator and chill for 1 hour, or until the pudding has cooled completely, before serving.

Mulberry

The mulberry is the fruit of the mulberry tree which is thought to be native to Western Asia. In appearance it is similar to the blackberry and ranges from red to dark purple in colour. The mulberry has a brief season from August to the beginning of September and should be picked only when it is fully ripe. It is only produced commercially for canning, since it does not travel well.

Mulberries may be eaten raw with cream and sugar, but more usually they are used with apples in pies, jams and jellies.

Mulberry and Apple Pie

Mulberry and Apple Pie, with spices, brown sugar, mulberries and apples and a crunchy

shortbread and almond topping, may be served hot or cold, with chilled whipped cream.

4-6 SERVINGS

2 oz. [¼ cup] plus 1 teaspoon unsalted butter
10 oz. [2½ cups] coarsely crushed shortbread biscuits [cookies]
2 oz. [⅓ cup] ground almonds
2 oz. [¼ cup] castor sugar
1 large egg, well beaten with 2 tablespoons double [heavy] cream

FILLING

1 tablespoon arrowroot
⅛ teaspoon ground allspice
¼ teaspoon ground cloves
24 oz. canned mulberries, drained and 10 fl. oz. [1¼ cups] of the can juice reserved
2 large cooking apples, peeled, cored, thinly sliced, cooked until nearly tender and drained
1½ oz. [¼ cup] soft brown sugar

Preheat the oven to fairly hot 375°F (Gas Mark 5, 190°C).

With the teaspoon of butter, grease a medium-sized deep pie dish or soufflé dish and set it aside.

In a medium-sized saucepan, melt the remaining butter over moderate heat. Remove the pan from the heat. Add the shortbread crumbs to the pan and stir well with a wooden spoon to coat the crumbs thoroughly with the butter. Beat in the ground almonds, sugar and the egg and cream mixture. Combine the mixture thoroughly.

Spoon one-third of the mixture into the prepared pie dish. With your fingers, press the mixture down until it evenly covers the bottom of the dish. Set aside.

In a small saucepan, dissolve the arrowroot with the allspice and cloves in the reserved mulberry juice.

Set the pan over moderate heat and cook the mixture, stirring constantly, for 3 to 4 minutes, or until it is thick and smooth.

Remove the pan from the heat. Stir in the mulberries. Set aside.

Arrange half the apple slices in a layer on the bottom of the pie dish. Sprinkle over half the brown sugar. Spoon over half of the mulberry mixture, smoothing it over the apple slices with the back of the spoon. Cover with the remaining apple slices and sprinkle over the remaining sugar. Spoon over the remaining mulberry mixture and smooth it down with the back of the spoon.

Cover the filling with the remaining biscuit [cookie] mixture and carefully smooth it evenly over the filling with a flat-bladed knife.

Place the pie in the centre of the oven

and bake for 30 to 40 minutes, or until the top is golden brown.

Remove the pie from the oven and serve immediately, or cool and serve, straight from the dish.

Mulberry Jelly

Mulberries are low in pectin and this jelly, which contains only a small portion of apple to assist setting, has a very light set.

ABOUT 3 POUNDS

1 lb. mulberries, stalks removed
1 large cooking apple, chopped
4 fl. oz. [½ cup] water
1½ to 2 lb. [3 to 4 cups] sugar

In a medium-sized saucepan, bring the mulberries, apple and water to the boil over moderate heat. Cover the pan, reduce the heat to low and cook the fruit for 20 minutes or until it is soft and pulpy. Remove the pan from the heat.

Scald a jelly bag or a large square of double-thick cheesecloth with boiling water. Hang the bag or cheesecloth on a frame or tie the ends to the legs of an upturned stool. Place a preserving pan underneath.

Pour the fruit mixture into the bag or cheesecloth and leave it to drain. Do not squeeze the bag to hurry the process as this will make the jelly cloudy. Measure the quantity of juice. For each 1 pint [2½ cups] of juice you will need 1 pound [2 cups] of sugar.

Add the sugar to the juice. Place the pan over moderate heat and stir until the sugar has dissolved. Increase the heat to moderately high and bring the mixture to the boil. Boil briskly, without stirring, for about 10 minutes, or until the jelly has reached setting point.

To test if the jelly has reached setting point, remove the pan from the heat and spoon a little of the jelly on to a cold saucer. Cool it quickly. If the surface is lightly set and wrinkles slightly when pushed with your finger, it is ready. If setting point has not been reached, return the pan to the heat and continue boiling, testing frequently.

With a metal spoon, skim the scum off the surface of the jelly. Ladle the jelly into hot, clean, dry jam jars, leaving ½-inch space at the top of each jar. Wipe the jars with a damp cloth. Cover them with jam covers and secure with rubber bands. Label the jars and store them in a cool, dark, dry place.

A delicious dessert, Mulberry and Apple Pie can be eaten hot or cold.

Mulled Wine

A perfect drink for winter parties or for convivial evenings at home, Mulled Wine cheers up the cheapest 'plonk' or vin ordinaire and makes of it something special. This recipe is a basic one, but almost any spice of your choice may be added, and some mulled wine enthusiasts say that the addition of a little brandy gives the drink that much more of a 'kick'.

1¼ PINTS

26 fl. oz. [3¾ cups], or 1 bottle, dry red wine
   juice and thinly pared rind of 1 lemon
½ teaspoon grated nutmeg
2-inch cinnamon stick
3 tablespoons sugar
1 lemon, thinly sliced

Pour the wine into a medium-sized saucepan and add the juice and rind of the lemon, the nutmeg, cinnamon stick and sugar. Place the pan over moderately high heat and bring the mixture to the boil,

stirring occasionally to dissolve the sugar. Boil the mixture for 2 minutes.

Remove the pan from the heat and remove and discard the lemon rind and cinnamon stick. Pour the wine mixture into a large jug and garnish with the lemon slices. Serve hot.

Mullet Andalucian-Style

Fish with a Spanish flavour, Mullet Andalucian-Style is a delicately flavoured dish combining pine nuts, tomatoes and green peppers. Serve Mullet Andalucian-Style with sautéed potatoes and a crisp green salad.

6 SERVINGS

6 medium-sized red mullets, cleaned and with eyes removed
   juice of 1 lemon
3 oz. [½ cup] ground pine nuts
2 garlic cloves, crushed
1 onion, chopped

Mullet Andalucian-Style is both delicious to eat and beautiful to present. Serve this dish with a chilled white wine, such as Spanish Chablis.

---

4 tablespoons chopped fresh parsley
1 teaspoon salt
½ teaspoon black pepper
3 tablespoons olive oil
1 medium-sized green pepper, white pith removed, seeded and cut into ¼-inch strips
6 medium-sized tomatoes, blanched, peeled, seeded and sliced
1 oz. [2 tablespoons] butter, cut into small pieces
6 black olives

Place the red mullets in a large shallow bowl. Pour over the lemon juice and set aside to marinate at room temperature for 15 minutes.

Preheat the oven to moderate 350°F

Low Cal

(Gas Mark 4, 180°C). In a medium-sized mixing bowl, combine the pine nuts, garlic, onion, parsley, salt and pepper together with a wooden spoon. Gradually add the olive oil, beating constantly until the mixture is well blended. Set aside.

Remove the fish from the marinade, discarding the marinating liquid. Pat the fish dry with kitchen paper towels. Place the fish, in one layer, in a large shallow baking dish.

Spread the nut and herb mixture over the fish, making sure each fish is evenly coated. Arrange the green pepper strips over the fish and cover with the tomatoes. Dot over the butter and place the dish in the centre of the oven.

Bake the fish for 25 minutes, or until the flesh flakes easily when tested with a fork. Remove the dish from the oven and transfer the fish and vegetables to a warmed serving dish. Place the olives in the uppermost eye socket of each fish and serve immediately.

Mullet with Bacon and Peas

An unusual combination of fish with the savoury flavour of bacon, Mullet with Bacon and Peas makes an attractive and colourful dish. Serve with creamed potatoes and grilled [broiled] tomatoes.

6 SERVINGS

6 streaky bacon slices, finely chopped
1 medium-sized onion, finely chopped
3 oz. [$\frac{3}{4}$ cup] seasoned flour, made with 3 oz. [$\frac{3}{4}$ cup] flour, $\frac{1}{2}$ teaspoon salt and $\frac{1}{4}$ teaspoon black pepper
6 medium-sized red mullets, cleaned
4 oz. [$\frac{1}{2}$ cup] butter
1 tablespoon soft brown sugar
1 lb. fresh peas, weighed after shelling
1 teaspoon salt
$\frac{1}{2}$ teaspoon black pepper
$\frac{1}{2}$ teaspoon chopped fresh thyme or $\frac{1}{4}$ teaspoon dried thyme
10 fl. oz. [1$\frac{1}{4}$ cups] chicken stock
4 fl. oz. [$\frac{1}{2}$ cup] dry white wine
1 tablespoon cornflour [cornstarch] dissolved in 2 tablespoons water

In a medium-sized frying-pan, fry the bacon over moderately high heat, stirring occasionally, for 5 minutes or until it is crisp and has rendered most of its fat. With a slotted spoon, transfer the bacon to a plate and keep warm.

Reduce the heat to moderate and add the onion to the frying-pan. Fry, stirring occasionally, for 5 to 7 minutes, or until it

is soft and translucent but not brown. Remove the pan from the heat and, with a slotted spoon, transfer the onion to the plate with the bacon.

Place the seasoned flour in a large shallow dish. Dip the fish in the flour mixture, shaking off any excess. Set aside.

Add half of the butter to the fat in the frying-pan and return it to moderate heat. When the foam subsides, add the fish, three at a time, and fry them for 5 minutes on each side, or until the flesh flakes easily when tested with a fork. Transfer the fish to a warmed serving dish and keep warm while you fry the remaining fish in the same way, using the remaining butter. Keep warm while you prepare the sauce.

Reduce the heat to low and add the onion, bacon and brown sugar to the pan. Cook, stirring constantly, for 3 minutes, or until the sugar has dissolved.

Add the peas, salt, pepper, thyme, chicken stock and wine. Increase the heat to high and bring the mixture to the boil, stirring occasionally. Reduce the heat to low and simmer for 10 minutes, or until the peas are tender. Remove the pan from the heat.

Stir in the dissolved cornflour [cornstarch] and return the pan to the heat. Cook the sauce, stirring constantly, for 2 minutes or until it thickens.

Remove the pan from the heat and spoon the sauce over the fish. Serve immediately.

Mullet Baked in Rock Salt

A delectable dish with a special fragrant flavour, Mullet Baked in Rock Salt is Spanish in origin. Serve with green beans and an apple and onion salad.

4 SERVINGS

12 oz. [2 cups] rock salt
1 x 4 lb. grey mullet, cleaned but with the head left on
1 teaspoon chopped fresh chives
1 teaspoon chopped fresh tarragon or $\frac{1}{2}$ teaspoon dried tarragon
1 rosemary sprig
juice of 1 lemon

Preheat the oven to warm 325°F (Gas Mark 3, 170°C).

Cover the bottom of a large, deep ovenproof dish with approximately one-third of the rock salt. Place the fish on the salt. Sprinkle over the chives and tarragon and place the rosemary sprig on top. Sprinkle over the lemon juice. Pour in the remaining rock salt to surround and cover the fish completely. With the back of a wooden spoon pat down the salt.

Place the dish in the oven and bake the

fish for 50 minutes.

Remove the dish from the oven. Using a rolling pin or pestle, break the hardened crust of the salt. With a sharp knife, prise the salt off and discard. Serve the fish at once, from the dish.

Mullet with Fennel and Wine

An easy-to-prepare dish, Mullet with Fennel and Wine is delicate and makes a colourful presentation for a dinner party. Serve with boiled new potatoes and broccoli.

4 SERVINGS

1 x 4 lb. grey mullet, cleaned, but with head and tail left on
juice of 2 lemons
2 oz. [$\frac{1}{4}$ cup] plus 1 teaspoon butter, cut into small pieces
1 teaspoon salt
$\frac{1}{2}$ teaspoon black pepper
2 garlic cloves, crushed
2 medium-sized lemons, thinly sliced
3 large tomatoes, thinly sliced
4 fennel sprigs or 1$\frac{1}{2}$ teaspoons dried fennel seeds
2 thyme sprays or 1 teaspoon dried thyme
10 fl. oz. [1$\frac{1}{4}$ cups] dry white wine

Place the fish in a large shallow dish and sprinkle over the lemon juice. Set aside to marinate at room temperature for 15 minutes.

Preheat the oven to moderate 350°F (Gas Mark 4, 180°C). Lightly grease a large baking dish with the teaspoon of butter. Set aside.

Remove the fish from the dish and pat it dry with kitchen paper towels. Rub the fish all over with the salt, pepper and crushed garlic. Place it in the prepared baking dish. Discard the marinade.

Place a layer of lemon slices in the stomach cavity of the fish, then cover with a layer of tomato slices. Place two fennel sprigs and one thyme spray on top of the tomato and dot with half of the remaining butter.

Make similar layers of the remaining lemon, tomato, herbs and butter on top of the fish. Tie two pieces of string around the fish to close the cavity and keep the stuffing in place.

Pour the wine over the fish and place the dish in the centre of the oven. Bake the fish for 45 minutes, or until the flesh flakes easily when tested with a fork.

Remove the dish from the oven. With slotted spoons, carefully transfer the fish to a serving dish. Remove and discard the string. Strain the juices in the dish over the fish and serve immediately.

Mullet Polynesian-Style

An exotic dish perfect for a dinner party, Mullet Polynesian-Style is easy to prepare and quite delicious. Serve on a bed of saffron rice and accompany with an orange salad.

4 SERVINGS

1 x 4 lb. grey mullet, cleaned and filleted
1 teaspoon salt
½ teaspoon black pepper
½-inch piece fresh root ginger, peeled and finely chopped
1 teaspoon garam masala
2 oz. [¼ cup] plus 1 teaspoon butter
1 medium-sized onion, finely chopped
1 medium-sized pineapple, peeled, cored and thinly sliced or 1½ lb. canned pineapple rings, drained
2 oz. [½ cup] flaked almonds
4 bananas, cut into 4 slices lengthways
2 oz. [¼ cup] sesame seeds, blanched
2 oz. [¼ cup] creamed coconut dissolved in 8 fl. oz. [1 cup] water

Preheat the oven to moderate 350°F (Gas Mark 4, 180°C). Sprinkle the mullet fillets with the salt, pepper, ginger and garam masala and set aside.

In a large saucepan, melt 2 ounces [¼ cup] of the butter over moderate heat. When the foam subsides, add the onion and cook, stirring occasionally, for 5 to 7 minutes, or until it is soft and translucent but not brown.

Add the fillets to the pan and cook for 5 minutes on each side. Remove the pan from the heat and set aside.

Grease a large shallow baking dish with the remaining teaspoon of butter. Arrange half of the pineapple slices in the baking dish.

Place the fish fillets, skin sides down, on top of the pineapple. Cover the fish with the onion and the remaining pineapple slices and sprinkle over the almonds. Arrange the banana slices on top and sprinkle over the sesame seeds. Pour over the dissolved coconut. Cover the dish and place it in the centre of the oven. Bake the fish for 20 minutes.

Uncover the dish and continue baking for a further 15 minutes, basting occasionally, or until the fish flakes easily when tested with a fork.

Remove the dish from the oven and serve immediately.

A colourful and flavourful dish, Mullet Polynesian-Style combines the exotic spices of the east with the sweetness of tropical fruit.

Mulligatawny Soup
CURRIED SOUP

A corruption of a Southern Indian word meaning pepper water, Mulligatawny (mull-ig-ah-tawn-nee) Soup is a spicy soup which is usually accompanied by cooked rice and garnished with lemon quarters. The soup may be made with chicken, mutton, beef or vegetables.

6 SERVINGS

5 pints [6¼ pints] water
1½ teaspoons salt
1 x 3 lb. chicken, cut into 6 pieces and giblets reserved (excluding the liver)
2-inch piece fresh root ginger, peeled and bruised
2 bay leaves
1½-inch slice creamed coconut
1½ oz. [3 tablespoons] butter
2 medium-sized onions, finely chopped
2 garlic cloves, crushed
½ teaspoon hot chilli powder
1 tablespoon ground coriander
1 teaspoon ground cumin
½ teaspoon black pepper
4 tablespoons ground almonds
1½ tablespoons gram or chick-pea flour

In a large saucepan, bring the water, 1 teaspoon of the salt, the chicken pieces, giblets, ginger and bay leaves to the boil over high heat. Cover the pan, reduce the heat to low and simmer for 45 minutes or until the chicken is very tender when pierced with the point of a sharp knife. With a slotted spoon or tongs, transfer the chicken pieces to a chopping board and set aside to cool.

Increase the heat to moderately high and boil the stock in the pan for 15 minutes or until it is reduced to about 3 pints [7½ cups]. Remove the pan from the heat and pour the stock through a strainer into a large bowl. Discard the ginger, bay leaves and giblets. Stir in the creamed coconut and, when it has dissolved, set this stock mixture aside.

When the chicken pieces are cool enough to handle, cut all the meat off the bone and dice it. Discard the bones and set the diced meat aside on a plate.

Rinse out the pan in which the chicken was cooked and dry it. Add the butter to the pan and melt it over moderate heat. When the foam subsides, add the onions and fry, stirring occasionally, for 8 to 10 minutes or until they are golden brown.

Add the garlic, chilli powder, coriander, cumin, pepper and the remaining salt and fry, stirring frequently, for 5 minutes.

Stir in the ground almonds and the

gram or chick-pea flour and cook, stirring constantly, for 1 minute. Gradually add the stock and coconut mixture, stirring constantly. When the soup comes to the boil, stir in the diced chicken. Reduce the heat to low and cook, stirring occasionally, for 15 minutes. Taste the soup and add more salt and pepper if necessary.

Remove the pan from the heat and ladle the soup into individual soup bowls. Serve immediately.

Mung Bean

The mung bean, or green gram as it is sometimes called, is probably native to India, although it is now cultivated in the tropical areas of Asia, Africa and America. It is a pod bean, each pod usually containing about 15 green, brown or mottled seeds, and it is usually eaten as a pulse or ground into fine meal.

In parts of China and the United States the seeds of the mung bean are sometimes germinated to produce bean sprouts.

Munster

Munster is a French semi-hard cheese produced mostly in Alsace (it takes its name from a small town near Strasbourg) and the Vosges. It is round in shape and has a brick-red rind. It is usually flavoured with caraway or anise seeds, although one popular variety is made with cumin.

Murg Bhuna
FRIED CHICKEN

Indian-style fried chicken, Murg Bhuna (moorgh bhoo-nah) is a simple, lightly spiced dish. Serve it with chappatis or naan, onion and tomato salad and iced lager.

4 SERVINGS

1 x 4 lb. chicken, skinned and cut into serving pieces
2 fl. oz. [¼ cup] yogurt
½ teaspoon turmeric
3 garlic cloves, crushed
½ teaspoon hot chilli powder
1 teaspoon paprika
3 tablespoons lemon juice
2 oz. [¼ cup] butter
½ teaspoon cardamom seeds, crushed
½ teaspoon salt
12 spring onions [scallions], finely chopped

Prick the chicken pieces all over with a fork and place them in a large mixing bowl.

In a small mixing bowl, mix together

the yogurt, turmeric, two-thirds of the garlic, the chilli powder, paprika and half the lemon juice. Pour this mixture over the chicken pieces and, with your fingers, rub it all over them. Cover the bowl and set it aside for 4 hours.

In a frying-pan, melt half the butter over moderate heat. When the foam subsides, add the chicken pieces and fry, turning them frequently, for 15 minutes, or until they are well browned all over. Add the cardamom seeds and the salt.

Reduce the heat to low, cover the pan, and continue cooking for a further 10 to 15 minutes or until the chicken is tender.

Uncover the pan and continue cooking for 10 minutes to allow most of the liquid to evaporate.

Meanwhile, in a small frying-pan, melt the remaining butter over moderate heat. When the foam subsides, reduce the heat to low and add the remaining garlic. Stirring constantly, fry the garlic for 1 to 2 minutes or until it is beginning to brown. Add the spring onions [scallions] and continue frying, stirring occasionally, for 4 to 6 minutes or until they are golden.

Remove the frying-pan from the heat and spoon the onions, garlic and butter over the chicken. Sprinkle the remaining lemon juice over the top and continue frying until there is very little liquid left in the pan.

Remove the pan from the heat and transfer the chicken mixture to a heated serving dish. Serve immediately.

Murg Kashmiri

CHICKEN WITH ALMONDS AND RAISINS

Delightfully aromatic, Murg Kashmiri (moorgh kash-mee-ree) is an Indian dish of roasted chicken basted with a mixture of cream, saffron, almonds and raisins.

4 SERVINGS

1 x 4 lb. chicken, skinned
  juice of $\frac{1}{2}$ lemon
1 tablespoon coriander seeds
1 teaspoon black peppercorns
1 teaspoon cardamom seeds
6 cloves
1$\frac{1}{2}$-inch piece fresh root ginger, peeled and very finely chopped
1 teaspoon salt
$\frac{1}{2}$ teaspoon hot chilli powder
3 oz. [$\frac{3}{8}$ cup] butter
2 medium-sized onions, very finely chopped
10 fl. oz. double cream [1$\frac{1}{4}$ cups heavy cream]
$\frac{1}{4}$ teaspoon saffron threads soaked in 2 tablespoons hot water
2 oz. [$\frac{1}{2}$ cup] slivered almonds
2 oz. [$\frac{1}{3}$ cup] raisins

Preheat the oven to fairly hot 400°F (Gas Mark 6, 200°C).

With a fork prick the chicken all over. Rub the lemon juice all over the chicken and set aside.

Using a mortar and pestle or an electric grinder, crush the coriander seeds, peppercorns, cardamom seeds and cloves. Sift the crushed spices through a fine wire strainer into a small mixing bowl. Discard the husks in the strainer. Mix in the ginger, salt and chilli powder.

Using a small wooden spoon, cream in half of the butter to make a smooth paste. Rub the paste all over the chicken. Put the chicken into a medium-sized flameproof casserole. Place the casserole in the oven and roast the chicken for 15 minutes.

Meanwhile, in a small saucepan, melt the remaining butter over moderate heat. When the foam subsides, add the onions and fry them, stirring occasionally, for 8 to 10 minutes or until they are golden brown. Remove the pan from the heat and stir in the cream, saffron and water mixture, the almonds and raisins.

Reduce the oven temperature to moderate 350°F (Gas Mark 4, 180°C). Continue roasting the chicken, basting it every 10 minutes with the cream and almond mixture, for 1 hour or until the chicken is tender, and the juices run clear when the thigh is pierced with the point of a sharp knife.

Remove the casserole from the oven. Using a large fork and a spoon lift the chicken out of the casserole and place it on a carving board. Carve the chicken into serving pieces. Arrange the chicken pieces in a warmed serving dish and keep hot while you finish the sauce.

Using a metal spoon, skim off and discard most of the fat on the surface of the sauce.

Set the casserole over moderate heat and cook the sauce for 2 minutes, stirring constantly and scraping the bottom of the pan to dislodge the sediments.

Remove the casserole from the heat. Pour the sauce over the chicken pieces and serve immediately.

Murgi Dahi

CHICKEN COOKED IN YOGURT

Chicken cooked in yogurt, Murgi Dahi (moor-gee dah-hee) is a strongly flavoured dish from India. Serve it as part of an Indian meal with bread rather than with rice.

4-6 SERVINGS

8 chicken pieces, skinned
8 fl. oz. [1 cup] yogurt
6 garlic cloves
2 green chillis

1$\frac{1}{2}$-inch piece fresh root ginger, peeled and chopped
1 teaspoon cumin seeds
1 red or green pepper, white pith removed, seeded and coarsely chopped
1 teaspoon paprika
1 teaspoon salt
1$\frac{1}{2}$ oz. [3 tablespoons] butter
2 tablespoons finely chopped coriander leaves
  juice of $\frac{1}{4}$ lemon

Prick the chicken pieces all over with a fork. Place them in a dish or bowl and set aside.

In an electric blender, blend the yogurt, garlic, chillis, ginger, cumin seeds, red or green pepper, paprika and salt together until the mixture is smooth. Alternatively, finely mince or chop the garlic, chillis and red or green pepper and mix them with the spices and the yogurt.

Pour the yogurt marinade over the chicken pieces and, with your fingers, rub

Murg Kashmiri is a rich Indian dish and will be greatly appreciated by those who enjoy unusual food.

Preheat the oven to moderate 350°F (Gas Mark 4, 180°C).

In a large frying-pan, heat the oil over moderate heat. When the oil is hot, add the chicken pieces to the pan, a few at a time, and fry, turning frequently, for 5 to 8 minutes, or until they are lightly browned all over. With tongs or a slotted spoon, transfer the chicken pieces to a large ovenproof casserole. Set aside while you brown the remaining chicken pieces in the same way.

Add the onions to the pan, and cook, stirring occasionally, for 5 to 7 minutes or until they are soft and translucent but not brown. Remove the pan from the heat and, with a slotted spoon, transfer the onions to the casserole.

In a small bowl, mix together the turmeric, cumin, coriander and lemon juice. Pour the spice mixture and the chicken stock over the chicken in the casserole. Sprinkle over the salt and pepper.

Cover the casserole and place it in the oven. Bake for 1½ hours or until the chicken is very tender when pierced with the point of a sharp knife.

Remove the casserole from the oven and serve immediately.

Mush

Mush is a highly nutritious porridge, usually made from Indian corn or MAIZE.

In the United States, where it originated, it is traditionally served with maple syrup, molasses or dark treacle.

Mushrooms

Mushroom is the name now generally used to describe any kind of edible FUNGI although, botanically speaking, many inedible, highly toxic varieties of umbrella-shaped fungi are also termed mushrooms.

The most common edible mushrooms are field mushrooms, which grow wild in pasture land and have a white cap and pale gills, and horse mushrooms, which are similar in appearance to the field mushrooms but much larger.

Most of the mushrooms used today are produced on a commercial scale in mushroom farms. When the mushrooms are picked they are sorted into three grades: button mushrooms (small, unopened), used in salads, sauces, for pickling and garnishing; cup mushrooms (slightly opened), often sliced or chopped, used in stews, soups and stuffings; and flat mushrooms (completely opened), ideal for serving as a vegetable accompaniment and, coarsely or finely chopped, in stews, soups, etc.

Both the caps and stalks of the mush-

it all over them. Cover the dish and set it aside for 4 hours.

Put the chicken pieces and the marinade into a large saucepan. Put the saucepan over moderately high heat and bring the mixture to the boil. When the sauce has been bubbling for 2 minutes, reduce the heat to moderate and cook the chicken, stirring occasionally, for 35 to 40 minutes or until it is tender and the sauce in the pan is very thick. Remove the pan from the heat.

In a large frying-pan, melt the butter over moderate heat. When the foam subsides add the chicken pieces. Reduce the heat to moderately low and fry the chicken pieces very gently, turning them over in the butter so that they are well coated, for 3 minutes. Spoon over the sauce and scrapings left in the saucepan. Sprinkle over the coriander leaves and the lemon juice. Cover the pan and cook for a further 5 minutes.

Spoon the chicken and the sauce on to a heated serving dish. Serve immediately.

Murray Chicken

A popular dish in the southern states of the United States, Murray Chicken may be served with creamy mashed potatoes and green beans.

4-6 SERVINGS

2 fl. oz. [¼ cup] vegetable oil
1 x 3½ lb. chicken, cut into 8
   serving pieces
2 medium-sized onions, sliced
1 teaspoon turmeric
¼ teaspoon ground cumin
¼ teaspoon ground coriander
2 tablespoons lemon juice
15 fl. oz. [1⅞ cups] hot home-made
   chicken stock
½ teaspoon salt
½ teaspoon black pepper

room are used in cooking. Mushrooms may be grilled [broiled], fried or eaten raw.

To grill [broil] mushrooms, wipe them clean and trim the stalks. Brush the mushrooms with a little melted butter and place them under a grill [broiler] preheated to moderately high. Grill [broil] them, basting occasionally with melted butter, for 5 minutes. Remove the mushrooms from the grill [broiler] and serve immediately.

To fry mushrooms, wipe them clean and trim the stalks. In a frying-pan, melt a little butter (about 1 ounce [2 tablespoons] to every 4 ounces of mushrooms) over moderate heat. When the foam subsides, add the mushrooms and cook them, stirring occasionally, for 3 minutes. Remove the mushrooms from the heat and serve.

Dried mushrooms are also sometimes used in cooking, especially in Chinese and Middle Eastern cooking. There are two main types — European and Chinese. Both require a preliminary soaking in cold water for 30 minutes before they can be used.

Mushroom and Asparagus Mayonnaise

A delightful salad that may be served on a bed of lettuce, Mushroom and Asparagus Mayonnaise makes an excellent accompaniment to cold roast meat.

4-6 SERVINGS

8 oz. button mushrooms, wiped clean and thinly sliced
1 lb. asparagus, cooked and sliced into 1-inch pieces
8 fl. oz. [1 cup] mayonnaise
1 tablespoon finely chopped fresh chives
2 hard-boiled eggs, thinly sliced
DRESSING
6 tablespoons olive oil
2 tablespoons white wine vinegar
½ teaspoon salt
¼ teaspoon black pepper

First prepare the dressing. In a medium-sized mixing bowl, combine all the dressing ingredients, beating with a fork until they are well blended. Add the sliced mushrooms and set aside to marinate for 30 minutes.

Add the sliced asparagus, mayonnaise and chives to the mushroom mixture and mix well, being careful not to mash the asparagus.

Transfer the mixture to a large serving dish. Garnish with the egg slices and serve immediately.

Mushroom and Bacon Salad

Mushroom and Bacon Salad may be served as part of an hors d'oeuvre, as an accompaniment to grilled [broiled] meat or as part of a large mixed salad.

4 SERVINGS

8 oz. button mushrooms, wiped clean and thinly sliced
4 streaky bacon slices, rinds removed
1 celery stalk, trimmed and finely chopped
1 tablespoon chopped fresh parsley
1 tablespoon chopped fresh chives
DRESSING
6 tablespoons olive oil
2 tablespoons white wine vinegar
½ teaspoon salt
¼ teaspoon black pepper

First make the dressing. In a medium-sized mixing bowl, combine all the dressing ingredients, beating with a fork until they are well blended. Add the sliced mushrooms and set aside to marinate for 30 minutes.

Meanwhile, preheat the grill [broiler] to high.

Place the bacon slices on a rack in the grill [broiler] pan and grill [broil] the bacon, turning once, for 5 minutes, or until it is crisp. Remove the bacon from the grill [broiler] and set aside to drain and cool on kitchen paper towels.

Crumble the bacon into the mushroom mixture and add the celery, parsley and chives. Mix well. Transfer to a serving dish and serve immediately.

Mushrooms and Celery on Toast

For Sunday brunch or a quick snack, try Mushrooms and Celery on Toast. It is easy to make, inexpensive and filling.

2 SERVINGS

1 oz. [2 tablespoons] butter
2 celery stalks, trimmed and finely chopped
1 small onion, finely chopped
6 oz. mushrooms, wiped clean and sliced
½ teaspoon salt
¼ teaspoon black pepper
1 tablespoon chopped fresh parsley
5 fl. oz. double cream [⅝ cup heavy cream]
2 large thick slices of hot buttered toast

In a medium-sized frying-pan, melt the butter over moderate heat. When the

foam subsides, add the chopped celery and onion and fry, stirring occasionally, for 5 to 7 minutes or until the onion is soft and translucent but not brown.

Add the mushrooms and cook for a further 3 minutes, stirring frequently. Stir in the salt, pepper, parsley and cream and cook, stirring occasionally, for 2 to 3 minutes or until the mixture is hot but not boiling.

Remove the pan from the heat. Spoon the mushroom mixture on to the toast slices and serve immediately.

Mushrooms with Cucumber

A simple vegetable dish with a Japanese flavour, Mushrooms with Cucumber is an excellent accompaniment to grilled [broiled] meats. It may also, of course, be served as part of a traditional Japanese meal.

4 SERVINGS

6 oz. button mushrooms, wiped clean
1 small cucumber, sliced
2 tablespoons salt
2 tablespoons vegetable oil
3 tablespoons soy sauce
1 tablespoon sugar
2 tablespoons slivered almonds, toasted

Place the mushrooms and cucumber in a colander and sprinkle with the salt. Set aside to dégorge for 30 minutes.

Rinse the mushrooms and cucumber under cold running water and pat dry with kitchen paper towels.

In a large frying-pan, heat the oil over moderate heat. When the oil is hot, add the mushrooms and cucumber and, stirring frequently, cook for 2 to 3 minutes, or until they are tender but firm. Stir in the soy sauce and sugar and cook for a further 2 minutes, stirring constantly to coat the vegetables with the sauce.

Remove the pan from the heat. Using a slotted spoon, transfer the mushrooms and cucumber to a warmed serving dish. Sprinkle over the toasted almonds. Serve at once.

Mushroom and Ham Crêpes

An easy-to-make and quite delicious dish, Mushroom and Ham Crêpes make a perfect snack lunch. Serve with a tossed green salad and a chilled white wine.

4-6 SERVINGS

8 oz. [2 cups] savoury Crêpe Batter
2 oz. [¼ cup] plus 1 teaspoon butter
2 medium-sized onions, chopped

2 shallots, finely chopped
1 garlic clove, crushed
12 oz. button mushrooms, wiped
    clean and sliced
$\frac{1}{2}$ teaspoon dried thyme
$\frac{1}{2}$ teaspoon salt
$\frac{1}{4}$ teaspoon freshly ground black
    pepper
1 bay leaf
4 oz. lean smoked ham, chopped
    into 1-inch pieces
4 fl. oz. double cream [$\frac{1}{2}$ cup heavy
    cream]
8 fl. oz. [1 cup] béchamel sauce
2 oz. [$\frac{1}{2}$ cup] **Cheddar cheese,**
    grated

Fry the crêpes according to the instructions in the basic recipe and keep them warm.

In a large frying-pan, melt 2 ounces [$\frac{1}{4}$ cup] of the butter over moderate heat. When the foam subsides, add the onions, shallots and garlic and cook, stirring occasionally, for 5 to 7 minutes, or until the onions are soft and translucent but not brown.

Add the mushrooms, thyme, salt, pepper and bay leaf to the pan and stir well to mix. Cook, stirring occasionally,

for 3 minutes. Stir in the ham and cook, stirring occasionally, for 3 minutes or until the ham is heated through.

Remove the pan from the heat and stir in the cream, mixing well. Remove and discard the bay leaf.

Preheat the oven to moderate 350°F (Gas Mark 4, 180°C). Lightly grease a medium-sized baking dish with the remaining teaspoon of butter.

Lay one crêpe out flat in the prepared dish. Spoon about 2 tablespoons of the filling on to the crêpe. Continue making layers of crêpes and filling until the ingredients are used up, ending with a crêpe.

Pour over the béchamel sauce and sprinkle over the grated cheese. Place the dish in the oven and bake for 30 minutes or until the top is brown.

Remove the dish from the oven and serve at once.

Mushrooms Hungarian-Style

Serve Mushrooms Hungarian-Style on toast as a snack, or as an accompaniment to grilled [broiled] *meat or chicken.*

Mushroom and Ham Crêpes make an economical and filling supper dish.

4-6 SERVINGS

2 oz. [$\frac{1}{4}$ cup] butter
1 small onion, finely chopped
1 lb. mushrooms, wiped clean and
    thinly sliced
$\frac{1}{2}$ teaspoon salt
$\frac{1}{4}$ teaspoon black pepper
1 teaspoon paprika
10 fl. oz. [1$\frac{1}{4}$ cups] sour cream
1 tablespoon finely chopped fresh
    parsley

In a large frying-pan, melt the butter over moderate heat. When the foam subsides, add the onion and fry, stirring occasionally, for 5 to 7 minutes, or until it is soft and translucent but not brown.

Stir in the mushrooms, and cook the mixture, stirring occasionally, for a further 3 minutes.

Add the salt, pepper, paprika and sour cream, and, stirring constantly with a wooden spoon, cook for 2 to 3 minutes, or until the mixture is hot but not boiling.

Remove the pan from the heat. Stir in the parsley and serve immediately.

1453

Mushroom Ketchup is inexpensive and easy to make, and may be stored for weeks in airtight bottles.

8 fl. oz. [1 cup] yogurt
2 tablespoons finely chopped fresh mint
½ teaspoon salt
¼ teaspoon white pepper

Place the potatoes, peas and mushrooms in a large salad bowl.

In a medium-sized mixing bowl, mix the yogurt, mint, salt and pepper together with a wooden spoon. Pour the dressing over the vegetables. Using two large spoons, toss the salad until the vegetables are thoroughly coated with the dressing.

Place the bowl in the refrigerator and chill for 1 hour before serving.

Mushroom Pie

A nourishing and sustaining dish, Mushroom Pie is very simple to make and is a delightful meal served with green vegetables.

4-6 SERVINGS

PASTRY
6 oz. [1½ cups] flour
⅛ teaspoon salt
5 oz. [⅝ cup] butter, cut into walnut-sized pieces
3 to 4 tablespoons iced water
1 egg, lightly beaten

FILLING
1 oz. [2 tablespoons] butter
2 medium-sized onions, finely chopped
1½ lb. button mushrooms, wiped clean
1 tablespoon butter, melted
1 teaspoon salt
¼ teaspoon black pepper
5 fl. oz. double cream [⅝ cup heavy cream]
¼ teaspoon cayenne pepper
½ teaspoon dried oregano
4 hard-boiled eggs, sliced

First make the pastry. Sift the flour and salt into a medium-sized mixing bowl. Add the butter and the iced water. With a knife, mix quickly to a firm dough which should be lumpy.

On a lightly floured surface, roll out the dough into an oblong shape. Fold it in three and turn it so that the open edges face you. Roll out again into an oblong shape and proceed as before. Repeat this once again to make three folds and turns in all. Wrap the dough in greaseproof or waxed paper and put it in the refrigerator to chill for 30 minutes.

Mushroom Ketchup

An adaptation of a traditional recipe, Mushroom Ketchup is delicious eaten with informal savoury dishes, especially hamburgers.

ABOUT 1½ PINTS

3 lb. button mushrooms, wiped clean, trimmed and coarsely chopped
4 oz. [½ cup] salt
1 small onion, finely chopped
2 teaspoons pickling spices
6 black peppercorns, crushed
1 teaspoon ground mace
¼ teaspoon mixed spice or ground allspice
juice of 2 lemons
3 fl. oz. [⅜ cup] brandy

Place one-quarter of the mushrooms in a large ovenproof casserole and sprinkle with one-quarter of the salt. Continue making layers of mushrooms and salt, ending with a layer of salt. Cover the casserole and set the mushrooms aside to dégorge for 24 hours, stirring occasionally.

Preheat the oven to cool 300°F (Gas Mark 2, 150°C).

Uncover the casserole and stir in the onion. Cover the casserole, place it in the oven and bake for 30 minutes. Remove the casserole from the oven.

Purée the mushrooms in a food mill or blender until the mixture is thick and smooth. Pour the purée into a medium-sized saucepan and add the pickling spices, peppercorns, mace, mixed spice or ground allspice and lemon juice. Set the pan over moderately high heat and, stirring constantly, bring slowly to the boil. Continue to boil for 3 to 5 minutes or until the purée has reduced slightly.

Remove the pan from the heat and set aside to cool completely. When the mixture is cold, stir in the brandy.

The ketchup is now ready to be used or stored in bottles.

Mushroom and Mint Salad

This delightfully simple salad is an ideal accompaniment to grilled [broiled] fish, and is very nutritious.

4-6 SERVINGS

1 lb. new potatoes, cooked, diced and cooled
4 oz. frozen peas, cooked, drained and cooled
6 oz. button mushrooms, wiped clean and sliced

A filling and nutritious dish, Mushroom Pie is perfect as a main course for a lacto-vegetarian meal.

Preheat the oven to fairly hot 400°F (Gas Mark 6, 200°C).

Meanwhile, make the filling. In a large frying-pan, melt the 1 ounce [2 tablespoons] of butter over moderate heat. When the foam subsides, add the onions and fry, stirring occasionally, for 5 to 7 minutes or until they are soft and translucent but not brown. Remove the pan from the heat. Using a slotted spoon, transfer the onions to a deep pie dish.

Arrange the mushrooms on top of the onions and, with a pastry brush, coat them with the melted butter. Season with ½ teaspoon of the salt and ⅛ teaspoon of the pepper. Pour over the cream and sprinkle over the remaining salt and pepper, the cayenne and oregano. Top with the slices of hard-boiled egg.

Remove the dough from the refrigerator. If it looks streaky, roll it out into an oblong shape and fold it in three again. On a floured surface, roll out the dough to 1-inch larger than the top of the pie dish. With a knife, trim the edges and cut out a ½-inch strip around the dough. Dampen the rim of the dish with water

and press the dough strip on top of the rim. With a pastry brush dipped in water, lightly moisten the strip.

Using the rolling pin, lift the dough on to the dish. With a knife, trim the dough and, with your fingers, crimp the edges to seal them to the strip already on the dish. With a sharp knife, cut a fairly large cross in the centre of the dough. With a pastry brush, coat the surface of the dough with the beaten egg.

Roll out the dough trimmings and use them to make a decoration for the top of the pie.

Place the pie in the oven and bake for 30 minutes or until the pastry is golden brown. Remove the pie from the oven and serve immediately.

Mushroom Purée

A spectacularly tasty accompaniment to almost any meat dish, Mushroom Purée is well worth the time and effort required to make it. It may also be served as a snack, on toast or with crusty French bread.

6 SERVINGS

2½ oz. [¼ cup plus 1 tablespoon] **butter**
2 lb. **mushrooms, wiped clean and sliced**

3 fl. oz. [⅜ cup] **water**
2 teaspoons **salt**
2 tablespoons **lemon juice**
1 teaspoon **grated nutmeg**
½ teaspoon **black pepper**
2 tablespoons **flour**
3 fl. oz. [⅜ cup] **milk**
1 tablespoon **chopped fresh parsley**
4 to 6 **Croûtons**

In a medium-sized frying-pan, melt 1½ ounces [3 tablespoons] of the butter over moderate heat. When the foam subsides, add the mushrooms and mix well. Pour in the water and add 1 teaspoon of the salt, the lemon juice, nutmeg and black pepper. Bring the mixture to the boil, stirring frequently. Simmer, stirring occasionally, for 8 minutes.

Remove the pan from the heat and strain the mushrooms and cooking liquid into a large mixing bowl. Reserve the cooking liquid and set aside.

Purée the mushrooms in a blender or food mill, or, alternatively, mash them with a fork. Set aside.

Add the remaining butter to the frying-pan and melt it over moderate heat. Remove the pan from the heat and, with a wooden spoon, stir in the flour to make a smooth paste. Gradually add the reserved cooking liquid and the milk,

Mushroom Rolls make unusual appetizers, served hot or cold.

stirring constantly. Return the pan to the heat. Simmer the mixture, stirring constantly, for 2 minutes or until it is thick and smooth.

Stir the puréed mushrooms into the sauce and cook, stirring, for 2 minutes. Add the remaining salt if required.

Remove the pan from the heat and transfer the purée to a warmed serving dish. Sprinkle over the parsley and arrange the croûtons decoratively around the purée. Serve at once.

Mushroom Rolls

Serve these savoury rolls as a first course with a fresh watercress salad tossed in French Dressing. Mushroom Rolls may also be served as party snacks.

20 ROLLS

5 oz. [⅝ cup] butter
1 medium-sized onion, coarsely chopped
8 oz. mushrooms, wiped clean and coarsely chopped
¼ teaspoon black pepper
1 tablespoon fresh lemon juice

2 oz. [1 cup] fresh breadcrumbs, soaked in 2 fl. oz. [¼ cup] chicken stock
1 tablespoon finely chopped fresh parsley
20 lean bacon slices, rinds removed

In a large saucepan, melt 4 ounces [½ cup] of the butter over low heat. When the foam subsides, add the onion and mushrooms. Gently simmer, stirring occasionally, for 5 minutes or until the mushrooms are soft. Remove the pan from the heat.

Preheat the grill [broiler] to high.

Using a slotted spoon, transfer the mushrooms and onion to a large mixing bowl. Add the pepper, lemon juice, breadcrumb mixture and parsley. With a potato masher or fork, mash the ingredients together until they form a paste.

Lay the bacon slices out flat. Spread each slice with a little of the paste. Roll up the bacon slices and thread them on to skewers (about four rolls to each skewer). Place the skewers on the grill [broiler] rack.

In a small saucepan, melt the remaining butter over moderate heat. Remove the pan from the heat and brush the melted butter over the rolls. Place the rolls under the grill [broiler] and grill [broil], turning frequently, for 6 to 8 minutes, or until the bacon is crisp.

Remove the skewers from the grill [broiler] and slide the rolls off the skewers on to a warmed serving dish. Serve at once.

Mushroom Sandwich Filling

A delicious filling for sandwiches, Mushroom Sandwich Filling is very easy and quick to make and will keep for 2 to 3 days in the refrigerator. For a tasty snack, spread the filling on slices of lightly toasted brown bread and put under the grill [broiler] to melt the filling.

1 POUND

1 lb. cream cheese
1 teaspoon salt
½ teaspoon black pepper
2 hard-boiled eggs, finely chopped
2 pickled cucumbers, very finely chopped
2 tablespoons chopped fresh chives
2 oz. mushrooms, wiped clean and finely chopped

In a large mixing bowl, mash all the ingredients together with a wooden spoon until they are well combined. Cover the bowl with aluminium foil and place it in the refrigerator.

Use as required.

Mushroom Sauce

An easy-to-make sauce, Mushroom Sauce may be served with fish, meat or vegetables. It is also delicious when added to stews or casseroles.

ABOUT 8 FLUID OUNCES

1 oz. [2 tablespoons] butter
4 oz. mushrooms, wiped clean, stalks removed and sliced
¼ teaspoon salt
⅛ teaspoon black pepper
2 tablespoons flour
12 fl. oz. [1½ cups] chicken stock
1 tablespoon Marsala

In a large saucepan, melt the butter over moderate heat. When the foam subsides, add the mushrooms to the pan. Season with the salt and pepper and fry, stirring occasionally, for 3 to 5 minutes or until the mushrooms are lightly browned.

Remove the pan from the heat. With a slotted spoon, remove the mushrooms from the pan and keep warm.

With a wooden spoon stir the flour into the fat in the saucepan. Gradually add the stock, stirring constantly.

Return the pan to moderately high heat and, stirring constantly, cook the sauce for 2 minutes, or until it is thick. Remove the pan from the heat and stir in the Marsala. Return the mushrooms to the sauce and stir well to coat them thoroughly.

Pour the sauce into a warmed sauceboat and serve at once.

Mushroom Soup I

This easy-to-make Mushroom Soup, flavoured with oregano and cayenne pepper, tastes delicious served with croûtons, or hot, crusty rolls and butter. Although it is preferable to use home-made chicken stock, you can use stock made from a chicken stock cube if you wish.

4-6 SERVINGS

1 oz. [2 tablespoons] butter
1 small onion, finely chopped
3 tablespoons flour
1 teaspoon salt
½ teaspoon black pepper
¼ teaspoon dried oregano
⅛ teaspoon cayenne pepper
1½ pints [3¾ cups] home-made chicken stock
1 lb. mushrooms, stalks removed, wiped clean and sliced
1 bay leaf
5 fl. oz. double cream [⅝ cup heavy cream]

In a large saucepan, melt the butter over moderate heat. When the foam subsides, add the onion and fry, stirring occasion-

Creamy Mushroom Soup I, flavoured with oregano and cayenne pepper, is delicious served with hot croûtons.

ally, for 5 to 7 minutes, or until the onion is soft and translucent but not brown.

Remove the pan from the heat. With a wooden spoon, stir in the flour, salt, pepper, oregano and cayenne to make a smooth paste. Gradually stir in the chicken stock, being careful to avoid lumps. Stir in the mushrooms and bay leaf.

Return the pan to the heat and bring the soup to the boil, stirring constantly. Reduce the heat to low, cover the pan and simmer for 30 minutes.

Uncover the pan and stir in the cream. Cook the soup, stirring constantly, for 2 to 3 minutes or until it is hot.

Remove the pan from the heat. Remove and discard the bay leaf. Pour the soup into a warmed soup tureen or individual soup bowls and serve immediately.

Mushroom Soup II

A thick, hearty soup, Mushroom Soup II is perfect for a light winter lunch, served with crusty bread and butter. Single [light] cream may be substituted to make a richer soup.

6-8 SERVINGS

4 streaky bacon slices, rinds
removed and finely diced
1 tablespoon butter
1 large onion, finely chopped
4 medium-sized potatoes, diced
1 teaspoon salt
½ teaspoon black pepper
1 tablespoon paprika
2 tablespoons flour
2 pints [5 cups] home-made chicken
stock
10 fl. oz. [1¼ cups] milk
1 large bay leaf
2 tablespoons finely chopped fresh
chervil or 1 tablespoon dried
chervil
12 oz. mushrooms, wiped clean and
sliced
5 fl. oz. [⅝ cup] sour cream
1 tablespoon chopped fresh chives

In a large saucepan, fry the bacon, stirring
occasionally, over moderately high heat
for 5 minutes or until it is crisp and has
rendered most of its fat.

With a slotted spoon, remove the bacon
from the pan and set it aside on kitchen
paper towels. Keep hot.

Reduce the heat to moderate and add
the butter to the pan. When the butter has
melted and the foam subsides, add the
onion. Fry, stirring occasionally, for 5 to
7 minutes, or until it is soft and translucent but not brown.

Add the diced potatoes and fry, stirring
frequently, for 4 to 5 minutes, or until
they are golden brown.

Remove the pan from the heat. Sprinkle
over the salt, pepper, paprika and flour.
Stir to coat the vegetables evenly with the
flour mixture.

Gradually pour in the chicken stock,
stirring constantly. Stir in the milk, bay
leaf, chervil and mushrooms.

Return the pan to the heat and bring
the soup to the boil, stirring constantly.
Reduce the heat to low, cover the pan and
simmer for 30 minutes.

Remove the pan from the heat. Pour
the soup through a fine wire strainer held
over a large mixing bowl. Using the back
of a wooden spoon, rub the vegetables
through the strainer until only a dry pulp
is left. Discard the pulp in the strainer.

Alternatively, remove the bay leaf and
blend the soup in an electric blender.

Pour the soup back into the saucepan
and stir in the sour cream. Place the pan
over low heat and cook the soup, stirring
constantly, for 3 to 4 minutes, or until it
is hot.

Remove the pan from the heat. Pour
the soup into a warmed soup tureen or
individual soup bowls. Sprinkle over the
chives and diced bacon and serve.

Mushrooms with Tarragon Mayonnaise

*A delicious salad to serve with cold meats,
Mushrooms with Tarragon Mayonnaise is
an excellent and quickly made dish for a
light luncheon or supper.*

4 SERVINGS

6 fl. oz. [¾ cup] mayonnaise
1 tablespoon tomato ketchup
1 tablespoon fresh lemon juice
2 teaspoons chopped fresh tarragon
or ¾ teaspoon dried tarragon
1 teaspoon salt
½ teaspoon white pepper
6 oz. mushrooms, wiped clean and
sliced
2 celery stalks, trimmed and cut
into ¼-inch lengths
½ small cucumber, peeled and diced
2 tablespoons chopped cashew nuts
2 tablespoons chopped fresh chives

Place the mayonnaise in a serving bowl
large enough to hold all the ingredients.
Mix in the tomato ketchup, lemon juice,
tarragon, salt and pepper.

Add the mushrooms, celery, cucumber
and nuts. Stir well until all the ingredients
are thoroughly combined and the vegetables and nuts are coated with the
mayonnaise mixture. Sprinkle over the
chives.

Place the bowl in the refrigerator and
chill for 1 hour before serving.

Mushrooms in Vine Leaves

*Mushrooms in Vine Leaves, cooked in white
wine, make an excellent and unusual hors
d'oeuvre. Fresh vine leaves are not easily
obtainable so canned ones may be used
instead. Serve garnished with tomatoes and
lemon wedges.*

4 SERVINGS

8 oz. button mushrooms, wiped
clean and coarsely chopped
4 tablespoons fresh lemon juice
1 tablespoon finely chopped fresh
parsley
2 teaspoons finely chopped fresh
tarragon or ¾ teaspoon dried
tarragon
½ teaspoon salt
12 to 16 large vine leaves, rinsed in
hot water and patted dry
8 fl. oz. [1 cup] dry white
wine
½ teaspoon black pepper

Low Cal

Place the mushrooms and lemon juice in
a small mixing bowl and, using two large
spoons, toss the mushrooms so that they

are coated with the lemon juice. Sprinkle
over the parsley, tarragon and salt, tossing
the mushrooms to coat them thoroughly.

Put the vine leaves, shiny sides down,
on a board. Place one to two teaspoons of
the mushroom mixture on each leaf near
the stem. Roll up the leaves, tucking the
sides in to form little parcels.

Place the vine rolls, seam sides down,
in a large flameproof casserole. Pour on
the wine and cover the casserole. Place it
over low heat and simmer the vine rolls
for 20 minutes.

Using a slotted spoon, transfer the vine
rolls to a warmed serving dish and sprinkle
with the black pepper. Serve at once.

Mussel

The mussel is a bivalvular (two-shelled)
edible mollusc with a greenish-black shell
and orange flesh. It is found in coastal
waters, mainly in the more temperate
regions of the world, and is in season from
September to March.

Both wild and cultivated mussels are

eaten, although there are vast differences in quality between the two. Wild mussels — generally found attached to stones and rocks — tend to be hard and leathery and are virtually inedible; cultivated mussels — bred on wooden hurdles — are small, tender and rather plump and have a delicate flavour.

Mussels should be alive when they are bought and care *must* be taken to ensure that they come from a reliable source — severe food poisoning and diseases can be caused by eating mussels taken from polluted waters.

Mussels may be eaten raw (with a squeeze of lemon), steamed (the most usual way of cooking them), pickled, smoked, or fried. They are also sometimes used as a garnish for fish dishes.

Mussels are prepared for cooking in the same way as CLAMS. Wash them thoroughly in cold water and, with a stiff brush, scrub them to remove any mud on their shells. Discard any mussels which are not tightly shut or do not close if sharply tapped, and any that float or have broken shells. With a sharp knife, scrape off the tufts of hair, or beards, which protrude from between the closed shell halves. Place the mussels in a large bowl of cold water and soak them for 1 hour. Drain the mussels in a colander and set aside.

To steam mussels, pour enough water into a large saucepan to make a ½-inch layer. Add a pinch of bicarbonate of soda [baking soda] (this will effectively destroy any poisons secreted in the mussel flesh) and, if you wish to flavour the mussels, add a bouquet garni and a little salt and pepper. Cover the pan and place it over high heat. Steam the mussels for 6 to 10 minutes, or until they are all open. If any of the mussels are still closed, discard them.

Using a slotted spoon, remove the mussels from the pan and transfer them to a large dish. Remove and discard one

---

Perfect for a family supper, Mussels Baked with Basil and Tomato Sauce may be served with a crisp green salad.

shell from each mussel and transfer the mussels to individual serving dishes. Strain the cooking liquid through a fine strainer and serve this separately, if you wish.

The mussels are now ready to be served, or added to soups or stews. If you wish to use mussels in a stew or soup, add them at the end of the cooking time — like all shellfish, if mussels are over-cooked they will become rubbery.

Mussels Baked with Basil and Tomato Sauce

A delightful dish for a family supper, Mussels Baked with Basil and Tomato Sauce is easy to prepare and fairly economical. It may be served with buttered noodles and a crisp green salad. If fresh mussels are unobtainable, 1¼ pounds of canned and drained mussels may be substituted.

4 SERVINGS

1 tablespoon plus 1 teaspoon butter
3 tablespoons olive oil
1 large onion, finely chopped
3 garlic cloves, crushed
1½ lb. canned peeled tomatoes, chopped
½ teaspoon salt
¼ teaspoon black pepper
3 tablespoons chopped fresh basil, or 1½ tablespoons dried basil
3 quarts mussels, scrubbed, steamed and removed from their shells
2 tablespoons fresh breadcrumbs
2 oz. [½ cup] Parmesan cheese, grated

(Low Cal)

Preheat the oven to moderate 350°F (Gas Mark 4, 180°C).

With the teaspoon of butter, lightly grease a medium-sized baking dish.

In a medium-sized saucepan, melt the remaining butter with the olive oil over moderate heat. When the foam subsides, add the onion and garlic and cook, stirring occasionally, for 5 to 7 minutes, or until the onion is soft and translucent but not brown.

Stir in the tomatoes with the can juice, the salt, pepper and basil. Reduce the heat to low and simmer the sauce, stirring occasionally, for 15 minutes. Remove the pan from the heat and stir in the mussels. Pour the mixture into the prepared dish.

In a small bowl combine the breadcrumbs and grated cheese, mixing until they are well blended. Sprinkle the mixture over the mussel mixture.

Place the dish in the centre of the oven and bake for 20 minutes, or until the top is golden brown and bubbling. Remove the dish from the oven and serve.

Mussel and Beef Pie

A traditional English recipe, Mussel and Beef Pie makes a wonderfully nourishing and sustaining meal. Serve with creamed potatoes, baby carrots and beer.

6 SERVINGS

2 oz. [¼ cup] butter
2 tablespoons vegetable oil
2 lb. lean stewing beef, cut into 1-inch cubes
1 large onion, finely chopped
2 medium-sized potatoes, peeled and diced
8 oz. mushrooms, wiped clean and sliced
8 fl. oz. [1 cup] dark beer
½ teaspoon dried thyme
½ teaspoon salt
¼ teaspoon black pepper
1 quart mussels, scrubbed, steamed and removed from their shells

PASTRY

6 oz. [1½ cups] flour
¼ teaspoon salt
4 oz. [½ cup] butter
3 to 4 tablespoons iced water
1 egg, lightly beaten

First make the pastry. Sift the flour and salt into a medium-sized mixing bowl. Cut the butter into small, walnut-sized pieces and add them to the flour. Pour in the iced water and mix quickly into a dough, which should be lumpy.

On a floured surface, roll out the dough into an oblong shape. Fold it in three and turn it so that the open edges face you. Roll again into an oblong shape and fold and turn as before. Repeat this once again to make three folds and turns in all. Put the dough into the refrigerator and chill while you make the filling.

Preheat the oven to fairly hot 400°F (Gas Mark 6, 200°C).

Meanwhile, prepare the filling. In a large frying-pan, melt the butter with the oil over moderate heat. When the foam subsides, add the beef cubes, a few at a time, and cook, stirring and turning occasionally, for 8 to 10 minutes or until they are evenly browned. With a slotted spoon, transfer the cubes to a plate and keep warm while you brown the remaining meat in the same way.

Add the onion and potatoes to the pan and cook, stirring occasionally, for 5 to 7 minutes or until the onion is soft and translucent but not brown. Stir in the mushrooms and cook the mixture for a further 3 minutes.

Pour over the beer and add the thyme, salt and pepper, mixing well to blend. Increase the heat to high and bring the mixture to the boil. Reduce the heat to moderate and return the beef cubes to the pan, stirring well to mix. Simmer the mixture for 15 minutes.

Stir in the mussels and remove the pan from the heat. Pour the mixture into a 9-inch pie dish and set aside.

Remove the dough from the refrigerator. If it looks streaky, roll it out into an oblong shape and fold it in three once again. Roll it out to a piece 1-inch larger than the top of the pie dish. With a sharp knife, cut a ½-inch strip around the dough. Dampen the rim of the dish with water and press the dough strip on to the rim. With a pastry brush dipped in water, lightly moisten the strip.

Using the rolling pin, lift the dough on to the dish. With a knife, trim the dough and, with your fingers, crimp the edges to seal them to the strip already on the dish. With a sharp knife, cut a fairly large cross in the centre of the dough. With a pastry brush, coat the surface of the dough with the beaten egg.

Place the pie in the oven and bake for 45 to 50 minutes or until the pastry is golden brown.

Remove the pie from the oven and serve at once.

Mussel Chowder

An adaptation of the traditional New England Clam Chowder, Mussel Chowder makes a delicious and rich meal. Serve with warm crusty bread and butter. If fresh mussels are unobtainable, 1 pound of canned and drained mussels may be substituted, omitting the mussel cooking liquid.

4-6 SERVINGS

3 oz. salt pork, diced
2 oz. [¼ cup] butter
2 medium-sized onions, finely chopped
3 medium-sized potatoes, peeled and chopped
16 fl. oz. [2 cups] chicken stock
2 quarts mussels, scrubbed, steamed, removed from their shells and 5 fl. oz. [⅝ cup] of the cooking liquid reserved
½ teaspoon salt
¼ teaspoon black pepper
¼ teaspoon cayenne pepper
10 fl. oz. double cream [1¼ cups heavy cream]
1 tablespoon chopped fresh parsley

In a large saucepan, fry the salt pork over moderate heat for 8 to 10 minutes or until there is a film of fat covering the bottom of the pan and the salt pork cubes resemble small croûtons. With a slotted spoon, transfer the salt pork to kitchen paper towels to drain. Set aside and keep warm.

Add the butter to the pan. When the foam subsides, add the onions and potatoes and cook, stirring occasionally, for 5 to 7 minutes or until the onions are soft and translucent but not brown. Pour over the chicken stock and bring to the boil, stirring occasionally.

Reduce the heat to low, cover the pan and simmer for 5 minutes or until the potatoes are tender but still firm.

Add the mussels with their cooking liquid, the salt, pepper, cayenne and reserved salt pork, stirring to mix well. Increase the heat to high and bring the chowder to the boil. Remove the pan from the heat and gradually stir in the cream.

Pour the chowder into a heated soup tureen, sprinkle over the parsley and serve at once.

Mussels Fried in Batter

An unusual dish, Mussels Fried in Batter makes a delicious first course for a dinner party. Or serve with a crisp green salad and French-fried potatoes for a light but sustaining lunch.

4 SERVINGS

sufficient vegetable oil for deep-frying
2 quarts mussels, scrubbed, steamed and removed from their shells
8 fl. oz. [1 cup] Fritter Batter III
6 parsley sprigs
2 lemons, cut into wedges

Fill a large deep-frying pan one-third full of vegetable oil. Place the pan over moderately high heat and heat the oil until it reaches 375°F on a deep-fat thermometer, or until a small cube of stale bread dropped into the oil turns golden brown in 40 seconds.

Using tongs, dip the mussels first in the batter, then drop them carefully into the oil. Fry them, a few at a time, for 3 to 4 minutes, or until they are crisp and golden brown. With a slotted spoon, transfer the mussels to kitchen paper towels to drain. Keep them warm while you coat and fry the remaining mussels in the same way.

Arrange the mussels on a warmed serving dish and garnish with the parsley sprigs and lemon wedges. Serve immediately.

Two traditional dishes made with mussels — American Mussel Chowder and English Mussel and Beef Pie.

Mussels with Garlic Butter

A relatively inexpensive first course, Mussels with Garlic Butter is easy to prepare. Serve with warm French bread.

4 SERVINGS

2 quarts mussels, scrubbed, steamed and top shells removed
4 oz. [½ cup] Beurre d'Ail (garlic butter), cut into small pieces

Preheat the grill [broiler] to moderately high.

Arrange the mussels, on their half shells, in a shallow flameproof dish. Dot the mussel flesh with the garlic butter.

Place the dish under the grill [broiler] and grill [broil] for 5 to 8 minutes, or until the butter has melted and the top is slightly browned.

Remove the dish from the grill [broiler] and serve the mussels immediately.

Mussel Salad

A piquant dish, Mussel Salad may be served as an hors d'oeuvre or as part of a buffet. Serve with warm French bread and some well-chilled Muscadet wine.

4-6 SERVINGS

6 tablespoons olive oil
2 tablespoons white wine vinegar
1 teaspoon lemon juice
1 garlic clove, crushed
1 tablespoon finely chopped shallots
½ teaspoon salt
½ teaspoon black pepper
1 celery stalk, trimmed and finely chopped
1 teaspoon finely chopped fresh sage or ½ teaspoon dried sage
1 teaspoon chopped fresh basil or ½ teaspoon dried basil
3 quarts mussels, scrubbed, steamed and removed from their shells
1 tablespoon chopped fresh parsley

Low Cal

In a large serving dish, combine all the ingredients, except the mussels and parsley, beating with a fork until they are well blended. Stir in the mussels, mixing to coat them well. Set aside to marinate at room temperature for 20 minutes, stirring occasionally.

Sprinkle over the parsley and serve.

Mustard in all the forms in which you can buy it — from the seeds to the prepared types.

Mustard

Mustard, a member of the *cruciferae* family of plants, originated in the Mediterranean and the Middle East, but is now widely cultivated elsewhere in Europe and in the United States. It has been used almost since the beginning of recorded time — both its culinary and medicinal properties are mentioned in early Greek and Roman writings.

There are three main varieties of mustard: white mustard, which has yellowish-orange seeds; black mustard, which has reddish-black seeds; and the less common wild mustard, which produces rather oily seeds which are not used on their own but are sometimes mixed with the other varieties.

Although mustard is cultivated primarily for its seeds, its leaves, which are known as mustard greens, are also used. Medicinal properties were once attributed to mustard greens, but they are now mainly used as a vegetable, raw or cooked. The larger leaves are generally boiled before use to reduce their very sharp, hot flavour.

Mustard seeds are ground to produce a powder and an oil. Pure mustard oil is edible, but it is mainly used in the manufacture of soap, leather and woollen goods and other industrial processes. In World War I, the oil extracted from black mustard was a prime ingredient of mustard gas.

Mustard used as a condiment is made from a mixture of black, white and sometimes wild mustard seeds, and their oils. The seeds are ground and sold as a fine powder, usually with the addition of a ground cereal such as wheat flour to absorb the natural oils and act as a preservative. The powder may be mixed with water or milk to form a paste before use, or added in small quantities in powdered form as a flavouring, for example, in MAYONNAISE.

Ready-made mustard, generally sold in sealed jars, is made mainly from a mixture of ground black, white and sometimes wild mustard seeds (although some countries such as France have mustards made purely from black seeds), mixed to a paste with salt, spices and vinegar or wine.

Mustard may be used to flavour meat, fish, cheese and vegetables and to season soups and sauces.

¼ oz. gelatine dissolved in 2
tablespoons warm tarragon
vinegar

10 fl. oz. double cream [1¼ cups
heavy cream], whipped until thick
but not stiff

8 fl. oz. [1 cup] béchamel sauce,
cold

1 teaspoon vegetable oil

6 black olives, stoned and sliced

4 small hard-boiled eggs, sliced

FILLING

2 medium-sized firm tomatoes,
chopped

2 small shallots, very thinly sliced

8 oz. prawns or shrimps, shelled

1 large red eating apple, cored
and diced

4 oz. canned pineapple rings,
drained and chopped

2 teaspoons finely chopped fresh
sage leaves or 1 teaspoon dried
sage

¼ teaspoon black pepper

2 tablespoons lemon juice

In a medium-sized mixing bowl, beat the
mustard, salt, pepper, the gelatine mixture, cream and béchamel sauce together
with a wooden spoon until the mixture is
smooth and evenly coloured.

Place the bowl in the refrigerator to
chill for 45 minutes, or until the mixture
is just beginning to set.

Remove the mixture from the refrigerator and beat it with a wire whisk or
rotary beater for 3 to 5 minutes, or until
it is completely smooth. Set aside.

With the vegetable oil, grease a 1-pint
[1½-pint] ring mould. Lay the olive slices,
side by side, on the bottom of the mould
and spoon over half the mustard and
cream mixture. Return the mould to the
refrigerator for 30 minutes, or until the
mixture is beginning to set.

Remove the mould from the refrigerator. Lay the hard-boiled egg slices, side
by side, over the nearly set mixture and
spoon over the remaining mustard and
cream mixture, smoothing it down with
the back of a spoon.

Place the mould in the refrigerator to
chill for 2 hours, or until the mixture has
set completely.

Meanwhile, prepare the filling. Place
the tomatoes, shallots, prawns or shrimps,
apple, pineapple and sage in a medium-
sized mixing bowl. Sprinkle over the
pepper and lemon juice. Using two large
spoons, toss the ingredients well. Set
aside.

Remove the mould from the refrigerator. Run a sharp knife around the edge
of the mould to loosen the sides. Quickly
dip the bottom of the mould in boiling
water. Hold a serving plate, inverted,

Mustard and Cress

Mustard and cress, garden CRESS and
mustard seedlings, is generally sold growing in small punnets. It is cut from the
punnet with a pair of scissors or a sharp
knife, leaving the earth and seeds behind.
It should be thoroughly washed and
shaken dry before use.

Mustard and cress is usually used raw
in salads or sandwiches, or as a garnish to
fish or meat. It may also be cooked in
soups and sauces.

Mustard Mould with Prawns or Shrimps and Fruit

*A tangy mould, Mustard Mould with
Prawns or Shrimps and Fruit makes a
refreshing first course, or a decorative
centrepiece for a cold buffet. Any fresh
vegetables or fruit may be used — for
example, chopped celery, diced peaches,
shredded green and red peppers, etc.*

6 SERVINGS

2 tablespoons prepared French
mustard

½ teaspoon salt

¼ teaspoon black pepper

over the mould and reverse the two, giving the mould a sharp shake — it should slide out easily.

Pile the fruit and shellfish mixture in the centre of the ring, arranging any extra filling around the sides of the mould. Chill the mould in the refrigerator for 30 minutes before serving.

Mustard Sauce

This delicious hot Mustard Sauce may be served with meat, game, poultry, fish or eggs. The sauce is particularly good served with roast hare.

ABOUT 10 FLUID OUNCES

1 tablespoon butter
1 garlic clove, crushed
1½ tablespoons flour
½ teaspoon salt
¼ teaspoon black pepper
10 fl. oz. single cream [1¼ cups light cream]
1 tablespoon prepared French or German mustard
1 teaspoon lemon juice

In a medium-sized saucepan, melt the butter over moderate heat. When the foam subsides, add the garlic clove and cook, stirring occasionally, for 4 minutes.

Remove the pan from the heat. With a

Mutton Chops Stuffed with Mushrooms and Celery makes a tasty dish!

wooden spoon, stir in the flour, salt and pepper to make a smooth paste. Gradually stir in the cream, being careful to avoid lumps. Stir in the mustard and combine the mixture thoroughly.

Set the pan over moderately low heat and cook the sauce, stirring constantly and never letting it come to the boil, for 3 to 4 minutes, or until it has thickened and is smooth.

Remove the pan from the heat and stir in the lemon juice. Pour the sauce into a warmed sauceboat and serve immediately.

Mutton

Mutton is the flesh of a sheep over 1 year of age. The meat of sheep under 1 year is sold as lamb.

Good mutton is bright red in colour, close grained and firm in texture. The fat is firm and white.

In France, where mutton is very popular, salt meadow mutton is the most highly praised. It comes from sheep reared on the coast where aromatic plants grow. In England the Southdown cross-breed is thought to produce the best mutton.

Mutton, being older than lamb, should be cooked for a little longer. From 5 to 10 minutes to the pound longer than lamb is usual. So if you cannot obtain mutton and have to substitute lamb in any recipe, reduce the cooking time accordingly.

Like most other meat, mutton is cut differently in Britain, the United States and Europe, but as a general guide, the

---

These tasty little Mutton Pies may be served hot, or cold for picnics.

---

cuts and methods of cooking are as follows: the **leg** is roasted, boiled or cut into pieces and used in stews, kebabs and curries; the **shoulder** is roasted and also cut up for curries and stews; the **loin** is roasted or casseroled, and loin **chops** are fried or grilled [broiled]; the **neck**, **scrag** and **breast** are stewed.

Mutton Chops Stuffed with Mushrooms and Celery

A simple way to turn mutton chops into something special is to fill them with a savoury stuffing. Mutton Chops Stuffed with Mushrooms and Celery makes a tasty supper dish served with new potatoes.

4-6 SERVINGS

6 large mutton chops
1 oz. [2 tablespoons] butter
1 medium-sized onion, finely diced
1 celery stalk, trimmed and finely diced
2 oz. mushrooms, wiped clean and finely diced
1 oz. [½ cup] fresh white breadcrumbs
1 tablespoon chopped fresh tarragon
½ teaspoon salt
¼ teaspoon black pepper
1 egg yolk

With a sharp pointed knife, make a slit in the meaty part of each chop to make a pocket. Set the chops aside.

Preheat the grill [broiler] to high.

In a small saucepan, melt the butter over moderate heat. When the foam subsides, add the onion and cook, stirring occasionally, for 5 to 7 minutes or until it is soft and translucent but not brown. Add the celery, mushrooms, breadcrumbs, tarragon, salt and pepper and mix well with a wooden spoon. Add the egg yolk and stir to mix. Remove the pan from the heat.

Using a teaspoon, stuff the chops with the stuffing. Then sew up the chops with a trussing needle and string to secure them.

Place the chops on the rack in the grill [broiler] pan and grill [broil] them for 7 to 10 minutes. Turn the chops over and grill [broil] them for a further 7 to 10 minutes or until they are thoroughly cooked.

Remove the chops from the heat and untie the string. Arrange the chops on a heated serving dish and serve immediately.

Mutton Pies

  ①

Delicious little pies filled with mutton and vegetables, Mutton Pies make ideal picnic food. Or serve them cold for lunch, accompanied by a mixed green salad.

15 PIES

- 1 lb. boned mutton, cut from the leg and left in one piece
- 1½ teaspoons salt
  bouquet garni, consisting of 4 parsley sprigs, 1 thyme spray and 1 bay leaf tied together
- 2 medium-sized onions
- 1 tablespoon butter
- 1 medium-sized onion, finely chopped
- 1 carrot, scraped and finely chopped
- ½ small turnip, peeled and finely chopped
- 5 fl. oz. [⅝ cup] chicken stock
- 8 oz. [2 cups] **Hot Water Crust Pastry dough**
- ½ teaspoon black pepper
- 1 tablespoon chopped fresh parsley
- 1 egg, lightly beaten

Place the mutton in a large saucepan. Pour in enough water just to cover and add 1 teaspoon of salt, the bouquet garni and the two whole onions. Place the pan over moderately high heat and bring the water to the boil, skimming off any scum that rises to the surface. Reduce the heat to low, cover the pan and simmer the mutton for 1 to 1¼ hours or until it is tender when pierced with the point of a sharp knife.

Remove the pan from the heat and allow the mutton to cool in the cooking liquid. When the mutton has cooled, skim off any fat that has formed on the surface of the liquid. Using two large spoons, lift the meat out of the pan and place it on a chopping board. Discard the cooking liquid and vegetables.

With a sharp knife, cut the mutton into very small pieces. Place them in a large mixing bowl.

Preheat the oven to hot 425°F (Gas Mark 7, 220°C). With the tablespoon of butter, lightly grease 15 patty tins and set them aside.

Place the chopped onion, carrot and turnip in a small saucepan and pour over the chicken stock. Place the pan over moderate heat and cook the vegetables for 10 minutes or until they are tender.

Meanwhile, divide the dough in half and set one half aside. On a lightly floured surface, roll out the other half to a circle about ¼-inch thick. With a 3-inch pastry cutter, cut the dough into 15 circles. Line the prepared patty tins with the circles.

Roll out the remaining dough to a circle about ¼-inch thick and, using a 2-inch pastry cutter, cut the dough into 15 circles. Set the circles aside.

Remove the pan containing the vegetables from the heat and drain the vegetables, reserving the cooking liquid. Add the vegetables to the meat, then add the remaining salt, the pepper, parsley and enough of the reserved liquid to moisten the mixture. Stir well to blend.

Spoon the mixture into the prepared patty tins and cover with the reserved dough circles, crimping the dough together at the edges to seal. With a sharp knife, cut a small slit in the tops. With a pastry brush, brush the tops of the pies with the beaten egg.

Place the patty tins in the oven and bake the pies for 20 to 30 minutes or until the pastry is golden brown. Remove the pies from the oven and let them cool slightly in the patty tins. Carefully remove the pies from the tins and place them on a wire rack to cool completely before serving.

Myrtle

Myrtle is an evergreen shrub which grows prolifically all over Europe.

In early history the berries of the myrtle tree were used in place of pepper.

Naan

Naan (nahn) is Indian flat leavened bread, oval or leaf-shaped, which is generally eaten hot with KEBABS. Naan is traditionally cooked in a tandoor, a special clay oven, and it is often sprinkled with poppy or sesame seeds before baking.

Naartje

Naartje is a thin-skinned tangerine fruit of the *citrus reticulata* family, native to South Africa. Naartje is mainly eaten raw as a dessert fruit, or in fruit salads, although it may also be made into jams and jellies, and crystallized [candied].

Nabobeep Salad

   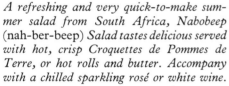

A refreshing and very quick-to-make summer salad from South Africa, Nabobeep (nah-ber-beep) Salad tastes delicious served with hot, crisp Croquettes de Pommes de Terre, or hot rolls and butter. Accompany with a chilled sparkling rosé or white wine.

4 SERVINGS

5 fl. oz. [⅝ cup] mayonnaise
3 tablespoons double [heavy] cream, whipped until thick but not stiff
2 teaspoons lemon juice
¾ teaspoon salt
½ teaspoon black pepper
1½ teaspoons mild curry powder
1 x 2½ lb. cooked chicken, boned and cut into ½-inch cubes
6 oz. small button mushrooms, stalks removed, wiped clean and sliced
2 medium-sized red eating apples, cored and diced
2 oz. [¼ cup] walnuts, chopped
6 large, flat lettuce leaves, washed and shaken dry

In a medium-sized mixing bowl, beat the mayonnaise, cream, lemon juice, salt, pepper and curry powder together with a wooden spoon until the mixture is well blended. Add the chicken cubes, mush-rooms, apples and walnuts. Toss the mixture well with two large spoons. Place the bowl in the refrigerator and chill for 1 hour.

Meanwhile, lay the lettuce leaves on the bottom of a medium-sized chilled serving dish. Set aside.

Remove the salad from the refrigerator and toss it well. Pile the salad on the lettuce leaves and serve immediately.

Nabob's Delight

    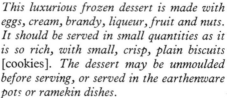

This luxurious frozen dessert is made with eggs, cream, brandy, liqueur, fruit and nuts. It should be served in small quantities as it is so rich, with small, crisp, plain biscuits [cookies]. The dessert may be unmoulded before serving, or served in the earthenware pots or ramekin dishes.

6 SERVINGS

6 glacé cherries, chopped
1-inch piece candied angelica, finely chopped
2 tablespoons raisins
2 tablespoons finely chopped candied orange peel
2 oz. [½ cup] flaked blanched almonds
10 blanched hazelnuts, finely chopped
2 fl. oz. [¼ cup] brandy
2 tablespoons orange-flavoured liqueur
2 teaspoons vegetable oil
10 fl. oz. single cream [1¼ cups light cream]
1 vanilla pod
4 egg yolks
2 tablespoons sugar
2 teaspoons arrowroot
5 fl. oz. double cream [⅝ cup heavy cream], whipped until thick but not stiff

Place the cherries, angelica, raisins, orange peel and nuts in a small mixing bowl. Stir in the brandy and orange-flavoured liqueur. Cover the bowl with aluminium foil and set the mixture aside to marinate for 1 hour, stirring occasionally.

Set the thermostat of the refrigerator to its coldest setting.

With the 2 teaspoons of oil, grease 6 small earthenware pots or ramekin dishes. Place the pots or dishes, upside-down, on kitchen paper towels and set them aside to drain for 30 minutes. Place the pots or dishes in the refrigerator to chill while you finish the dessert.

In a small saucepan, scald (bring to just under boiling point) the single [light] cream with the vanilla pod over moderate heat. Remove the pan from the heat and

set the mixture aside to infuse for 15 minutes.

Meanwhile, in a medium-sized heat-proof mixing bowl, beat the egg yolks, sugar and arrowroot together with a wire whisk or rotary beater until the mixture is pale and frothy.

Remove and discard the vanilla pod from the cream. Pour the cream in a thin stream on to the egg yolk and sugar mixture, whisking constantly.

Place the bowl in a pan half filled with hot water. Set the pan over low heat. Cook the custard, stirring constantly with a wooden spoon, for 10 to 12 minutes, or until it coats the back of the spoon. Do not allow the custard to boil or the eggs will scramble.

Remove the pan from the heat. Lift the bowl out of the pan and set the custard aside to cool completely.

Drain the fruit and nuts and reserve 2 tablespoons of the marinade. Fold the fruit and nuts, with the reserved marinade, into the cold custard. Beat in the double [heavy] cream and combine the mixture thoroughly.

Place the bowl in the frozen food

Stir in the cream and soy sauce. Cook the cabbage mixture, stirring constantly, for 4 minutes or until the sauce comes to the boil.

Remove the pan from the heat. Turn the mixture into a warmed serving dish and serve immediately.

Najafabad Biscuits [Cookies]

Simple, easy-to-make biscuits [cookies] Najafabad Biscuits [Cookies] are subtly flavoured with essences and cloves. The low baking temperature gives the biscuits [cookies] a light, almost sponge-like texture.

ABOUT 16 BISCUITS [COOKIES]

6 oz. [¾ cup] plus 1 teaspoon butter, softened
8 oz. [2 cups] flour
¼ teaspoon salt
1 teaspoon baking powder
¼ teaspoon ground cloves
6 oz. [¾ cup] castor sugar
2 egg yolks
1 teaspoon almond essence
1 teaspoon vanilla essence
grated rind of 1 lemon
8 to 10 whole blanched almonds, halved

Preheat the oven to cool 300°F (Gas Mark 2, 150°C). Lightly grease a large baking sheet with the teaspoon of butter. Set aside.

Sift the flour, salt, baking powder and cloves into a medium-sized mixing bowl. Set aside.

In a large mixing bowl, cream the remaining butter and the sugar together with a wooden spoon until the mixture is light and fluffy. Using a wooden spoon, beat in the egg yolks. Add the almond and vanilla essences and lemon rind. Using a metal spoon, fold in the flour mixture and stir until the mixture forms a soft dough.

Knead the dough lightly. Break off small pieces of the dough and roll them into balls. Place the balls on the prepared baking sheet, fairly close together, and, using your fingertips, flatten them slightly. Press an almond half into each ball of dough.

Place the baking sheet in the oven and bake for 15 minutes. Increase the oven temperature to moderate 350°F (Gas Mark 4, 180°C) and bake for a further 15 to 20 minutes, or until the biscuits [cookies] are a pale golden brown and have spread into one another.

Remove the baking sheet from the oven. Using a palette knife or spatula, carefully transfer the biscuits [cookies] to a wire rack to cool completely before serving.

A superb frozen dessert, Nabob's Delight is rich with fruit, nuts, cream, brandy and orange liqueur.

storage compartment of the refrigerator and freeze for 1 hour, beating the mixture vigorously with a wooden spoon every 5 minutes.

When the mixture is just beginning to freeze and is very thick but still smooth, remove the bowl from the storage compartment. Remove the oiled pots or dishes from the refrigerator.

Spoon the mixture into the chilled pots or dishes and place them in the frozen food storage compartment. Freeze for 1½ to 2 hours, or until the dessert is completely frozen and firm to the touch.

Remove the dessert from the refrigerator and serve.

Nai-yu-ts'ai-hsin

CHINESE CABBAGE IN CREAM SAUCE

Nai-yu-ts'ai-hsin (nye-yoo-sye-shun) *is a*

Chinese dish of cabbage stir-fried and coated in a cream sauce. Serve it as a vegetable accompaniment to Chinese meat or fish dishes.

4-6 SERVINGS

1 tablespoon butter
1 tablespoon sesame oil
3 small spring onions [scallions], thinly sliced
2 small Chinese cabbages, coarse outer leaves removed, washed and coarsely shredded
½ teaspoon salt
½ teaspoon black pepper
1 tablespoon white wine vinegar
4 fl. oz. single cream [½ cup light cream]
2 teaspoons soy sauce

In a large frying-pan, melt the butter with the oil over moderate heat. When the foam subsides, add the spring onions [scallions] and cabbage and stir-fry for 3 minutes. Sprinkle over the salt, pepper and vinegar. Combine the mixture well and stir-fry for a further 2 to 3 minutes, or until the cabbage is cooked but still crisp.

Nakompatoa Forowee

SALTED FISH FRIED WITH VEGETABLES

A typical West African dish of salted fish fried with yam, tomatoes, pimientos and flavoured with garlic and coconut, Nakompatoa Forowee (nah-kohm-pah-toh-ah foh-oh-ee) makes a light lunch or supper without any accompaniment.

4 SERVINGS

1½ lb. dried salted nakompatoa fish, or any dried salted white fish, soaked in cold water for 24 hours and drained
1 bay leaf
3 to 4 tablespoons peanut oil
2 lb. yam, cooked until just tender, peeled, drained and sliced
1 large garlic clove, crushed
4 tablespoons chopped pimientos
4 medium-sized tomatoes, blanched, peeled and chopped
1 tablespoon finely chopped fresh thyme, or 1½ teaspoons dried thyme
½ teaspoon black pepper
4 fl. oz. [½ cup] coconut milk, made with 2 oz. [¼ cup] creamed coconut dissolved in 4 fl. oz. [½ cup] water
3 hard-boiled eggs, coarsely chopped

Place the fish and bay leaf in a medium-sized saucepan. Pour over enough cold water to cover the fish.

Set the pan over moderately high heat and bring the water to the boil. Cover the pan, reduce the heat to moderately low and simmer for 8 to 10 minutes, or until the fish flakes easily when tested with a fork.

Remove the pan from the heat. With a slotted spoon, remove the fish from the pan and place it in a colander. Discard the cooking liquid. Rinse the fish under warm running water to remove excess saltiness. Pat the fish dry with kitchen paper towels.

Place the fish on a chopping board. With a sharp-pointed knife, skin and bone the fish and cut it into large chunks. Set aside.

In a large frying-pan, heat 3 tablespoons of the oil over moderate heat. When the oil is hot, add the yam slices and fry them for 3 to 4 minutes on each side, or until they are golden brown and crisp.

With a slotted spoon, remove the yam slices from the pan and place them in a medium-sized warmed serving dish. Keep hot.

Add the fish pieces to the pan, adding more oil if necessary, and fry, stirring and turning occasionally with the slotted spoon, for 4 to 5 minutes, or until the fish pieces are golden brown. Remove the pan from the heat.

With a slotted spoon, remove the fish

Nakompatoa Forowee, from West Africa, is an unusual mixture of fried yam, salted fish, vegetables and coconut.

from the pan and place it over the yam slices in the dish. Keep hot.

Pour off all but 1 tablespoon of the oil in the frying-pan.

Return the pan to the heat and add the garlic, pimientos, tomatoes, thyme and pepper. Fry the mixture, stirring constantly, for 3 minutes.

Stir in the coconut milk and increase the heat to moderately high. Boil the mixture, stirring constantly, for 3 to 4 minutes, or until it has thickened slightly.

Remove the pan from the heat. Spoon the coconut mixture over the fish and yam. Sprinkle over the chopped hard-boiled eggs and serve immediately.

Nalesniki

CREPES STUFFED WITH CHEESE

A savoury dish with a Russian flavour, Nalesniki (ny-ah-lehss-nee-kee) are crêpes filled with a tasty cheese mixture. Serve them for a filling breakfast, or as a light supper dish.

4-6 SERVINGS

8 fl. oz. [1 cup] savoury Crêpe Batter

1 lb. [2 cups] cottage cheese
3 oz. [⅜ cup] butter, softened
2 eggs, separated
    grated rind and juice of 1 orange
2 oz. [¼ cup] castor sugar
½ teaspoon vanilla essence
4 fl. oz. [½ cup] sour cream
2 tablespoons chopped stoned dates

Fry the crêpes according to the instructions in the basic recipe and keep them warm.

Place the cottage cheese in a fine nylon strainer set over a medium-sized bowl. Using the back of a wooden spoon, rub the cheese through the strainer. Set the cheese aside.

In a large mixing bowl, cream 1 ounce [2 tablespoons] of the butter and the egg yolks together with a wooden spoon until the mixture is light and fluffy. Beat in the cheese. Add the orange rind, sugar, vanilla essence and sour cream and beat well until all the ingredients are thoroughly combined. Stir in the chopped dates.

In a medium-sized mixing bowl, beat the egg whites with a wire whisk or rotary beater until they form stiff peaks. Using a metal spoon, carefully fold the egg whites into the cheese mixture.

Lay the crêpes out flat. Place a little of the cheese filling near the edge of each crêpe. Turn the sides in, then roll the crêpe up. Repeat the process until all the crêpes have been filled.

In a large frying-pan, melt the remaining butter over moderate heat. When the foam subsides, place a few of the crêpe rolls, seam sides down, in the pan and fry for 3 to 4 minutes on each side or until they are golden brown. With a slotted spoon, transfer the crêpes to a serving dish and keep warm while you cook the remaining crêpes in the same way.

When all the crêpes have been cooked, sprinkle over the orange juice and serve at once.

Namasu Maguro
TUNA AND VEGETABLE SALAD

   ⧖⧖

An adaptation of a traditional Japanese dish, Namasu Maguro (nah-mah-soo mah-goor-oh) should ideally be made with daikon, a Japanese white radish, but turnip may be substituted. Serve Namasu Maguro as an hors d'oeuvre or as part of a formal Japanese meal.

4 SERVINGS

1 large white turnip, peeled and
    cut into julienne strips
1 large carrot, scraped and cut into
    julienne strips
1 small red pepper, white pith
    removed, seeded and cut into
    julienne strips
4 fl. oz. [½ cup] sake
7 oz. canned tuna fish,
    drained and finely flaked
1 tablespoon sugar
4 fl. oz. [½ cup] white wine vinegar

Low Cal

Place the turnip, carrot and red pepper in a large bowl. Pour over the sake and toss well to mix. Set aside to marinate at room temperature for 1 hour, basting the vegetables from time to time.

Drain the vegetables and place them in a medium-sized salad bowl. Discard the marinating liquid. Stir in the tuna fish, then the sugar and vinegar. With two large spoons, toss the mixture to coat thoroughly. Serve at once.

Russian Nalesniki are crêpes stuffed with cottage cheese, flavoured with orange, dates and sour cream.

Delectable little Nantes Cakes, with orange and almonds, are coated with apricot jam, kirsch-flavoured fondant and maraschino cherries.

Nanban Zuke

FRIED FISH WITH VINEGAR DRESSING

An adaptation of a Middle Eastern dish, Nanban Zuke (nahn-bahn zook) is lightly cooked fish soaked in a vinegar dressing. We have used turbot, but any firm white fish fillets may be used instead.

4 SERVINGS

2 oz. [½ cup] seasoned flour made
   with 2 oz. [½ cup] flour, ½ teaspoon
   salt, ¼ teaspoon black pepper
   and ⅛ teaspoon ground ginger
2 lb. turbot fillets
2 oz. [¼ cup] butter
4 fl. oz. [½ cup] chicken stock
2 tablespoons white wine vinegar
1 tablespoon soy sauce
1 teaspoon sugar
⅛ teaspoon salt

Low Cal

Place the seasoned flour on a plate and dip the fillets, one by one, in it, shaking off any excess.

In a large frying-pan, melt the butter over moderate heat. When the foam subsides, place the fillets in the pan and fry for 7 to 8 minutes on each side or until the flesh flakes easily when tested with a fork. Remove the pan from the heat and, using tongs or a slotted spoon, transfer the fish to a warmed serving dish. Keep warm while you make the dressing.

Place the stock, vinegar, soy sauce, sugar and salt in a medium-sized saucepan. Set the pan over moderate heat, and cook, stirring occasionally, for 3 to 4 minutes or until the dressing is hot. Remove the pan from the heat. Pour the dressing over the fish and leave for 5 minutes before serving.

Nantais Biscuits [Cookies]

Sweet biscuits [cookies] made crunchy with a sugar and nut topping, Nantais Biscuits [Cookies] are delicious served with tea or coffee. They will keep well if stored in an airtight tin.

ABOUT 24 BISCUITS [COOKIES]

4 oz. [½ cup] plus 1 teaspoon butter,
   softened
1 lb. [4 cups] flour
½ teaspoon salt
6 oz. [1 cup] ground almonds
14 oz. [1¾ cups] plus 4 tablespoons
   castor sugar
3 eggs
2 fl. oz. [¼ cup] kirsch
2 oz. [⅓ cup] blanched almonds,
   finely chopped
1 egg, lightly beaten

With the teaspoon of butter, lightly grease a large baking sheet. Set aside.

Sift the flour and salt together into a medium-sized mixing bowl. Stir in the ground almonds. Set aside.

In a large mixing bowl, cream the remaining butter and the 14 ounces [1¾ cups] of sugar together with a wooden spoon until the mixture is light and fluffy. Beat in the eggs, one at a time, beating well between each addition. Add the kirsch.

Continue beating the mixture until it is smooth. Using a metal spoon, fold in the flour mixture and stir the mixture until it forms a soft dough. Knead the dough lightly and wrap it in greaseproof or waxed paper. Place the dough in the refrigerator to chill for 30 minutes.

Preheat the oven to fairly hot 375°F (Gas Mark 5, 190°C).

Remove the dough from the refrigerator. Turn it out on to a lightly floured working surface and roll it out to a circle approximately ¼-inch thick. Using a 3-inch pastry cutter, cut out circles of dough and place them on the prepared baking sheet.

In a small bowl, mix the 4 tablespoons of sugar and the chopped almonds together. Using a pastry brush, brush the dough circles with the beaten egg and sprinkle over the sugar and nut mixture.

Place the baking sheet in the centre of the oven and bake for 15 to 20 minutes or until the biscuits [cookies] are golden brown.

Remove the baking sheet from the oven and let the biscuits [cookies] cool slightly on the baking sheet. Carefully transfer the biscuits [cookies] to a wire rack to cool completely before serving.

Nantes Cakes

These delicious little cakes, covered with kirsch-flavoured fondant icing, make an attractive addition to any tea table.

15 CAKES

4 oz. [½ cup] plus 1 tablespoon
   butter, softened
2 oz. [½ cup] slivered almonds, cut
   into strips
¼ teaspoon salt
½ teaspoon baking powder
4 oz. [½ cup] castor sugar
   grated rind of 1 orange
2 eggs
4 oz. [1 cup] flour, sifted
2 tablespoons apricot jam, melted
8 maraschino cherries, halved

Veal cooked with colourful vegetables and an aromatic blend of garlic, lemon, coconut and spices, Nantwinam Kyewee is an exciting African dish.

FONDANT ICING
4 oz. [½ cup] Fondant
1 tablespoon sugar dissolved in
   1 tablespoon water
1 teaspoon kirsch

Preheat the oven to moderate 350°F (Gas Mark 4, 180°C). With the tablespoon of butter, grease 15 patty tins. Sprinkle a few almond strips into the bottom of each tin and set aside.

In a large mixing bowl, cream the remaining butter with a wooden spoon until it is soft. Add the salt, baking powder, sugar and orange rind and continue beating until the mixture is light and fluffy. Using a wire whisk or rotary beater, beat in the eggs, one at a time, adding a little of the flour with each egg. Beat the mixture well. Using a metal spoon, fold in the remaining flour and mix until all the ingredients are well combined.

Spoon the mixture into the prepared patty tins. Place the tins in the centre of the oven and bake for 25 to 30 minutes or until the cakes spring back when lightly pressed with a fingertip.

Remove the tins from the oven and turn the cakes out on to a wire rack to cool completely.

Meanwhile, in a small bowl placed over a pan of hot water, soften the fondant over low heat. Using a wooden spoon, beat in the sugar mixture and the kirsch Remove the pan from the heat.

When the cakes are cold, using a pastry brush, brush the tops with the melted jam. With a palette knife, spread the fondant icing over the jam. Place a cherry half on each cake. When the icing has set, the cakes are ready to serve.

Nantua, à la

A la Nantua (ah lah nahn-too-ah) is a French culinary term applied to dishes which are either garnished with crayfish tails or masked with a CRAYFISH purée mixture. The name is also occasionally applied to sauces which have crayfish as their main ingredient.

Nantwinam Kyewee

VEAL CHOPS MARINATED IN COCONUT MILK

An unusual blend of veal, lemon, coconut, ginger, chilli, garlic and tomatoes, Nantwinam Kyewee (nant-wee-nam kye-wee) tastes excellent served on a bed of rice or accompanied by fried yams or sweet potatoes and a crisp green salad.

4 SERVINGS
1 garlic clove, crushed
2 fl. oz. [¼ cup] fresh lemon juice
4 fl. oz. [½ cup] coconut milk, made with 2 oz. [¼ cup] creamed coconut dissolved in 4 fl. oz. [½ cup] water
1-inch piece fresh root ginger, peeled and thinly sliced
4 veal chops, 1-inch thick
1 teaspoon salt
½ teaspoon black pepper
⅛ teaspoon turmeric (optional)
2 oz. [¼ cup] butter
2 medium-sized shallots, finely chopped
1 large red pepper, white pith removed, seeded and coarsely chopped
1 large green pepper, white pith removed, seeded and coarsely chopped
1 small green chilli, seeds removed and finely diced
1 tablespoon finely chopped fresh thyme, or ¾ teaspoon dried thyme
14 oz. canned peeled tomatoes, coarsely chopped

In a medium-sized shallow dish, combine the garlic, lemon juice, coconut milk and ginger. Place the chops in the dish and set aside in a cool place to marinate for 2 hours, basting and turning the chops over every 30 minutes.

Remove the chops from the marinade. Discard all but 1 tablespoon of the marinade. Dry the chops with kitchen paper towels and rub them all over with the salt, pepper and the turmeric, if you are using it. Set aside.

In a large frying-pan, melt the butter over moderate heat. When the foam subsides, add the shallots, peppers and chilli. Fry the vegetables, stirring occasionally, for 5 minutes, or until the shallots are soft and translucent but not brown. With a slotted spoon, remove the vegetables from the pan and set them aside to drain on kitchen paper towels.

Add the chops to the pan and fry them for 5 minutes on each side.

Reduce the heat to moderately low. Return the shallots, peppers and chilli to the pan. Sprinkle over the thyme and stir in the chopped tomatoes with the can juice, and the reserved marinade.

Stir well and cover the pan. Simmer for 20 to 30 minutes, stirring and turning the chops over occasionally, or until the chops are cooked and tender when pierced with the point of a sharp knife.

Remove the pan from the heat. With a slotted spoon, remove the chops from the pan and transfer them to a heated serving dish. If the sauce looks too liquid, place the pan over high heat and boil, stirring constantly, for 2 or 3 minutes, or until some of the liquid has evaporated and the sauce has thickened slightly.

Pour the sauce over the chops and serve immediately.

Nanymo Squares

Chocolate-covered crunchy biscuits [cookies] with a sweet coconut filling, Nanymo Squares are absolutely scrumptious with coffee and tea.

9 SQUARES

5 oz. [⅝ cup] plus 1 teaspoon butter
2 fl. oz. golden syrup [¼ cup light corn syrup]
2 oz. [⅓ cup] soft brown sugar
3 tablespoons cocoa powder
2 eggs
1 teaspoon vanilla essence
8 oz. [2 cups] crushed shortbread biscuits [cookies]
4 oz. desiccated coconut [1 cup shredded coconut]
3 oz. [½ cup] pecans, chopped
12 oz. icing sugar [3 cups confectioners' sugar], sifted
4 oz. dark [semi-sweet] cooking chocolate, melted

Lightly grease a 9-inch square baking tin with the teaspoon of butter. Set aside.

Place 2 ounces [¼ cup] of the remaining butter, the syrup, sugar, cocoa powder, 1 egg and the vanilla essence in a large saucepan. Set the pan over very low heat and, stirring constantly with a wooden spoon, cook the mixture for 2 to 3 minutes or until it is smooth and thin. Remove the pan from the heat.

Stir in the crushed biscuits [cookies], coconut and nuts beating until all the ingredients are thoroughly combined.

Press the crumb mixture into the prepared baking tin with the back of a wooden spoon.

In a large bowl, cream the remaining butter with a wooden spoon until it is soft. Beat in the remaining egg and the icing [confectioners'] sugar, a little at a time. Using a flat-bladed knife, spread the sugar mixture on to the crumb base. Place in the refrigerator to chill for 30 minutes.

Remove the tin from the refrigerator. Spread the melted chocolate over the top and return the tin to the refrigerator to chill for 1 hour or until the chocolate has set.

Cut into squares and serve.

Nap

Nap is a now almost obsolete culinary term which is used to describe the coating of foods or moulded dishes with a sauce or liquid. The liquid should be thick enough to stay in place, but not so thick that it obscures the shape of the coated food or dish.

Napoleon

Napoleon (nah-poh-lay-ohn) is the name used outside France for MILLE-FEUILLE, a puff pastry concoction filled with CREME PATISSIERE, or cream, and sprinkled with sugar. The main difference between the two cakes is that the mille-feuille is covered with icing [confectioners'] sugar, whereas the Napoleon is covered with a white frosting and decorated with lines of melted chocolate or chocolate icing.

Napoleons are traditionally sweet, but, like mille-feuille, they may be made with savoury fillings.

Napoleon au Fromage Blanc
PUFF PASTRY LAYERS WITH CREAM CHEESE FILLING

Napoleon au Fromage Blanc (nah-poh-lay-ohn oh froh-maj blahn) is a superb concoction of crisp layers of puff pastry sandwiched with a savoury cream cheese, vegetable and shrimp filling. Serve it with a salad or as a centrepiece for a cold buffet. For a more

Light-as-air pastry layers filled with cream cheese, shrimps and vegetables, Napoleon au Fromage Blanc is an impressive dish from France.

decorative effect, arrange sliced cucumber, tomatoes, hard-boiled eggs and black olives around the edge of the Napoleon.

6-8 SERVINGS

PASTRY
12 oz. [3 cups] flour
½ teaspoon salt
12 oz. [1½ cups] butter
6 fl. oz. [¾ cup] iced water
FILLING
1 lb. cream cheese
2 fl. oz. double cream [¼ cup heavy cream], whipped until thick but not stiff
2 teaspoons tarragon vinegar
1 teaspoon lemon juice
3 fl. oz. [⅜ cup] mayonnaise
2 teaspoons prepared French mustard
½ teaspoon salt
½ teaspoon black pepper
⅛ teaspoon cayenne pepper
1 tablespoon paprika
1 tablespoon finely chopped fresh chives
8 oz. potted shrimps, drained and coarsely chopped
1 small red pepper, white pith removed, seeded and finely chopped
1 small green pepper, white pith removed, seeded and finely chopped
2 small shallots, very finely diced
10 cooked shrimps, in their shells

First, make the pastry. Sift the flour and salt into a medium-sized mixing bowl. Add 3 ounces [⅜ cup] of the butter and cut it into the flour with a table knife. Using your fingertips, rub the butter into the flour until the mixture resembles fine breadcrumbs. Add the water and mix it into the dough with the knife. With your hands, lightly knead the dough until it is smooth.

Shape the dough into a ball, wrap it in greaseproof or waxed paper and place it in the refrigerator to chill for 15 minutes.

Meanwhile, put the remaining butter between two sheets of greaseproof or waxed paper. Using a rolling pin or the back of a wooden spoon, beat the butter into an oblong approximately ¾-inch thick. Set aside.

Place the dough on a lightly floured board or marble slab and, using a floured rolling pin, roll it out into an oblong approximately ¼-inch thick. Place the slab of butter in the centre of the dough.

Fold the dough in three over the butter to enclose it and to make a parcel. Place the dough in the refrigerator to chill for 10 minutes.

Place the dough on the board or slab with the folded ends facing you. Roll the dough out into an oblong and fold it in three. Roll it out again and fold it in three. Chill the dough in the refrigerator for 15 minutes. Repeat the rolling and folding twice more.

Preheat the oven to hot 425°F (Gas Mark 7, 220°C). Dampen a large baking sheet with cold water and set it aside.

Cut the dough into three equal pieces.

Roll out each piece into an oblong approximately 4-inches wide and 12-inches long. Trim the oblongs with a sharp knife to make them the same size and straighten the edges. Discard any leftover dough.

Prick the oblongs all over with a fork. Wrap two of the oblongs in greaseproof or waxed paper and place them in the refrigerator.

Place the third oblong on the prepared baking sheet. Place the baking sheet in the centre of the oven and bake for 10 to 12 minutes, or until the pastry is crisp and golden brown.

Remove the baking sheet from the oven

and allow the pastry to cool on the sheet for 10 minutes before carefully transferring it to a wire rack to cool completely.

Wetting the baking sheet with cold water each time, bake and cool the remaining oblongs in the same way.

While the pastry is cooling, make the filling. In a large mixing bowl, beat the cream cheese with a wooden spoon until it is smooth. Beat in the cream, vinegar, lemon juice, 2 tablespoons of the mayonnaise, the mustard, salt, pepper, cayenne and paprika. Blend the mixture until it is smooth. Add the chives, potted shrimps, peppers and shallots and combine the mixture thoroughly. Chill the mixture in the refrigerator for 30 minutes.

Place one of the pastry oblongs on a large serving platter. Spoon half of the filling on to the pastry. With a flat-bladed knife, spread it evenly to the edges of the pastry. Place a second pastry oblong on top and spread over the remaining filling. Cover with the last pastry layer.

Spoon or pipe the remaining mayonnaise in an even line along the centre of the top pastry layer.

Arrange the shrimps, side by side, over the line of mayonnaise, pressing them down lightly with your fingers.

Place the platter in the refrigerator and chill the napoleon for 30 minutes before serving.

Naranjas al Kirsch
FRUIT SOAKED IN KIRSCH

Naranjas al Kirsch (nah-ran-jas ahl kee-rsh), *a Spanish dish of oranges, cherries, raspberries and almonds soaked in kirsch, makes a refreshing dessert, the perfect ending to a rich meal. Serve the dessert on its own, or with whipped cream.*

4 SERVINGS

6 medium-sized oranges, peeled, white pith removed and thinly sliced
4 oz. black cherries, stoned and halved
8 oz. raspberries
2 tablespoons castor sugar
¼ teaspoon ground allspice
2 oz. [½ cup] flaked almonds
4 fl. oz. [½ cup] kirsch

Place the fruit in alternating layers in a medium-sized shallow serving dish, sprinkling a little of the sugar, allspice and flaked almonds over each layer.

Fresh, juicy fruit with almonds and allspice soaked in kirsch, Naranjas al Kirsch is a refreshing dessert.

Pour over the kirsch. Cover the dish with aluminium foil and place it in the refrigerator. Marinate the fruit for 2 hours, basting occasionally with the kirsch.

Remove the dish from the refrigerator. Remove and discard the aluminium foil. Toss the fruit well with two large spoons and serve immediately.

Narbonne Biscuits [Cookies]

Narbonne Biscuits [Cookies] are unusual wine-flavoured biscuits [cookies], deep-fried until crisp. Try cutting the dough with different shapes of pastry cutters — hearts, flowers, diamonds — for a more decorative effect. You may, if you like, sprinkle the cooked biscuits [cookies] with a little sugar just before serving.

ABOUT 36 BISCUITS [COOKIES]

2 tablespoons lemon juice
2 fl. oz. [¼ cup] dry sherry
2 fl. oz. [¼ cup] Marsala
4 fl. oz. [½ cup] rosé wine
3 oz. [½ cup] soft brown sugar
12 oz. [3 cups] flour
⅛ teaspoon salt
½ teaspoon ground allspice

2 eggs, well beaten with 2 tablespoons milk
sufficient vegetable oil for deep-frying

In a medium-sized heavy saucepan, combine the lemon juice, sherry, Marsala, wine and sugar.

Set the pan over moderate heat and cook the mixture, stirring constantly, for 3 minutes, or until the sugar has dissolved. Increase the heat to high and bring the mixture to the boil.

Remove the pan from the heat and sift in the flour, salt and ground allspice. Beat the mixture with a wooden spoon until it is smooth and comes away from the sides of the pan. Allow the mixture to cool to lukewarm. When it is cool, beat in the egg and milk mixture. Set the dough aside to cool completely.

Turn the cooled dough out on to a lightly floured board or marble slab and knead it for 5 minutes, or until it is smooth and elastic. Shape the dough into a ball.

Using a lightly floured rolling pin, roll out the dough into a circle approximately ⅛-inch thick. With a 2-inch round pastry cutter, cut the dough into circles and set aside.

Narbonne Biscuits [Cookies] are made with sherry, Marsala and wine and deep-fried until they are crisp.

Gather up the leftover dough pieces and knead them together. Roll out the dough into a circle approximately ⅛-inch thick and cut it into circles. Set the circles aside.

Fill a deep-frying pan one third full of vegetable oil. Place the pan over moderate heat and heat the oil until it reaches 375°F on a deep-fat thermometer, or until a small cube of stale bread dropped into the oil turns golden brown in 40 seconds.

With a slotted spoon, lower four or five of the dough circles into the hot oil. Fry them for 1½ minutes, or until they are crisp and golden and have risen to the surface of the oil.

With the slotted spoon, remove the biscuits [cookies] from the oil and drain them on kitchen paper towels. Place the drained biscuits [cookies] on a plate and keep them warm while you fry and drain the remaining biscuits [cookies] in the same way.

Serve the biscuits [cookies] immediately, or allow them to cool completely before serving.

Nargisi Koftas

MEATBALLS STUFFED WITH HARD-BOILED
EGGS

*Hard-boiled eggs covered with a layer of
spiced minced [ground] meat and deep-fried,
Nargisi Koftas (nahr-gee-see kohf-tahs)
may be described as Scotch eggs Indian-style.
Garnish the koftas with thinly sliced onion
rings and serve with a chutney. Nargisi
Koftas are sometimes added to a curry sauce
and served with rice.*

4 SERVINGS

1¼ lb. minced [ground] lamb or beef
1-inch piece fresh root ginger,
   peeled and finely chopped
½ teaspoon hot chilli powder
1 teaspoon ground cumin
1 tablespoon ground coriander
1 onion, finely chopped
2 garlic cloves, crushed
1½ oz. [3 tablespoons] gram or
   chick-pea flour
1 teaspoon salt
½ teaspoon black pepper
1 egg
8 hard-boiled eggs
   sufficient vegetable oil for
   deep-frying

In a large mixing bowl, combine the
minced [ground] meat, ginger, chilli
powder, cumin, coriander, onion, garlic,
gram or chick-pea flour, salt, pepper and
the egg. Using your hands, mix and knead
the ingredients together well.

If you have an electric blender, blend
the ginger, garlic and onion together to
make a fine purée before mixing them
with the other ingredients.

Divide the meat mixture into 8
equal portions. Using wetted hands, roll
each portion into a ball. Flatten a meat-
ball in the palm of your hand and place a
hard-boiled egg in the centre. Work the
meat mixture up and around the egg until
the egg is completely enclosed.

Place the koftas in a greased dish and
put them in the refrigerator to chill for 30
minutes.

Fill a deep-frying pan one-third full of
vegetable oil. Place the pan over moderate
heat and heat the oil until it reaches
375°F on a deep-fat thermometer or until
a cube of stale bread dropped into the oil
turns golden brown in 40 seconds.

Add the koftas, three or four at a time,
and fry them for 2 to 3 minutes or until
they are a rich brown colour.

Using a slotted spoon, transfer the

koftas to a plate lined with kitchen paper
towels. Keep them hot while you fry the
remaining koftas.

Arrange the koftas on a heated serving
dish and serve immediately.

Nariel Chatni

COCONUT CHUTNEY

*A fresh-tasting chutney which is a perfect
accompaniment to curry, Nariel Chatni
(nahr-yale chat-nee) must be served fresh.
At the most it will keep for 2 to 3 days if
covered and stored in the refrigerator.*

ABOUT 4 OUNCES

2 oz. desiccated coconut [½ cup
   shredded coconut] soaked in
5 fl. oz. [⅝ cup] yogurt for 1 hour
   juice and grated rind of 1 lemon
1-inch piece fresh root ginger,
   peeled and sliced
1 green chilli, chopped
1 garlic clove, sliced
1 medium-sized onion, roughly
   chopped

Place the coconut mixture and lemon
juice in an electric blender. Blend for 1 to

Nariel Samosas, coconut, raisin and puff pastry turnovers, and Nargisi Koftas, hard-boiled eggs coated with meat and spices, are both from India.

2 minutes or until the mixture has become a purée. Add the lemon rind, ginger, chilli, garlic and onion and blend for 1 minute more.

If you do not have a blender, finely chop or mince all the ingredients and mix them together in a mixing bowl.

Serve immediately or cover and store in the refrigerator until needed.

Nariel Samosas

COCONUT TURNOVERS

Nariel Samosas (nahr-yale sahm-oh-sahs) *are little puff pastry turnovers served as a snack in Indian homes. They are light and delicate and particularly good with tea.*

24 PASTRIES

2 oz. desiccated coconut [$\frac{1}{2}$ cup shredded coconut] soaked in 3 fl. oz. [$\frac{3}{8}$ cup] milk
$\frac{1}{2}$ teaspoon cardamom seeds, crushed
2 oz. [$\frac{1}{3}$ cup] seedless raisins
2 oz. [$\frac{1}{3}$ cup] soft brown sugar
1 egg white, lightly beaten

PASTRY
12 oz. [3 cups] flour
$\frac{1}{2}$ teaspoon salt
12 oz. [$1\frac{1}{2}$ cups] unsalted butter
6 fl. oz. [$\frac{3}{4}$ cup] iced water

First, make the pastry. Sift the flour and salt into a medium-sized mixing bowl. With a table knife, cut 3 ounces [$\frac{3}{8}$ cup] of the butter into the flour. With your fingertips, rub the butter into the flour until the mixture resembles coarse breadcrumbs. Add the water and mix to a firm dough. Knead the dough to make it pliable and form it into a ball. Cover with greaseproof or waxed paper and place the dough in the refrigerator to chill for 15 minutes.

Put the remaining butter between two pieces of greaseproof or waxed paper and beat it with the back of a wooden spoon or a wooden mallet into a flat oblong slab about $\frac{3}{4}$-inch thick.

On a floured board, roll out the dough into a rectangular shape about $\frac{1}{4}$-inch thick. Place the slab of butter in the centre of the dough and fold the dough over it to make a parcel. Chill the dough in the refrigerator for 10 minutes.

Place the dough, with the folds downwards, on the board and roll it out away from you into a rectangle. Fold the rectangle in three. Turn so that the open end is facing you and roll out again. Chill in the refrigerator for 15 minutes. Repeat this twice more.

Preheat the oven to hot 425°F (Gas Mark 7, 220°C).

In a small mixing bowl, combine the coconut mixture, cardamom, raisins and sugar.

On a lightly floured board roll out the dough very thinly. Using a 3-inch pastry cutter, cut the dough into 24 circles.

Place a spoonful of the coconut mixture in the centre of each circle. Dampen the edges with water, fold the dough in half and pinch the edges together to seal.

Place the turnovers on a baking sheet. Brush them with the egg white and put them in the oven. Bake for 15 to 20 minutes, or until the turnovers are crisp and golden.

Remove the baking sheet from the oven. Using a spatula, transfer the turnovers to a wire rack. Serve when cool.

Nasi Goreng

INDONESIAN RICE

Nasi Goreng (naah-zi gaw-reng) *is almost the Indonesian national dish, a delicious rice, meat and vegetable mixture. Serve it with sliced tomatoes, cucumber and chutney and accompany with lots of cold lager.*

4-6 SERVINGS

12 oz. [2 cups] long-grain rice, washed, soaked in cold water for 30 minutes and drained
$1\frac{1}{4}$ pints [$3\frac{1}{8}$ cups] cold water
1 teaspoon salt
2 tablespoons vegetable oil
3 eggs, lightly beaten
1 medium-sized onion, very finely chopped
2 green chillis, very finely chopped
1 garlic clove, crushed
1 lb. cooked chicken meat, cut into thin slices
8 oz. prawns or shrimps, shelled and chopped
2 celery stalks, trimmed and finely chopped
2 tablespoons soy sauce

Low Cal

Put the rice in a large saucepan. Pour over the water and add the salt. Bring the water to the boil over high heat. Cover the pan, reduce the heat to very low and simmer for 15 minutes or until the rice is tender and has absorbed all the liquid.

Remove the pan from the heat and set aside.

In a small frying-pan, heat half of the oil over moderate heat. When the oil is hot, add the eggs and fry for 3 minutes on each side or until they are set in a thin omelet. Remove the pan from the heat. Slide the omelet on to a plate. Cut it into thin strips about 2-inches long and $\frac{1}{2}$-inch wide. Set aside.

In a large frying-pan, heat the remaining oil over moderate heat. When the oil is hot, add the onion, chillis and garlic to the pan and fry, stirring occasionally, for 5 to 7 minutes, or until the onion is soft and translucent but not brown. Add the chicken, prawns or shrimps, and celery and cook, stirring occasionally, until they are well mixed.

Add the cooked rice, soy sauce and omelet strips and cook, stirring occasionally, for 3 minutes or until all the ingredients are warmed through.

Remove the pan from the heat and transfer the mixture to a warmed serving dish. Serve immediately.

Nasturtium

A common flowering plant, nasturtium is grown both for decoration and for food, since its leaves, petals and buds are all edible. The leaves and petals of the nasturtium are similar to watercress and are used in the same way — usually chopped, raw in salads. The buds and seeds, when young, are often pickled in vinegar and used to flavour sauces and as garnishes.

Nasturtium Buds, Pickled

Pickled nasturtium buds have a slightly bitter, peppery taste and are sometimes used in savoury dishes in place of capers.

ABOUT 10 FLUID OUNCES

12 oz. [4 cups] nasturtium buds
10 fl. oz. [$1\frac{1}{4}$ cups] malt vinegar
5 black peppercorns
5 white peppercorns
1 teaspoon mustard seeds
1 teaspoon coriander seeds
1 mace blade

Low Cal

Gather the nasturtium buds on a dry day and leave them at room temperature in an airy place for 3 days.

Pour the vinegar into a small saucepan and add the peppercorns, mustard seeds, coriander seeds and mace. Place the pan over high heat and bring the mixture to the boil. Boil for 4 minutes, then remove the pan from the heat. Set aside for 30 minutes.

Place the nasturtium buds in a large, warmed preserving jar and strain the spiced vinegar over them. Leave to cool and then seal the jar. Leave the jar for 2 to 3 months before using.

Nasturtium Spread

A tasty spread made from cream cheese and nasturtium leaves, Nasturtium Spread may be used on toast or crispbread for a quick snack or as a savoury dip. It should be eaten as soon as it is made, however, as it will discolour if set aside.

4 OUNCES

- 4 oz. cream cheese
- 2 teaspoons finely chopped nasturtium leaves
- ½ teaspoon paprika
- 3 nasturtium flowers

In a small mixing bowl, combine all the ingredients, except the nasturtium flowers, beating with a wooden spoon until they are well blended.

Transfer the mixture to a serving bowl and garnish with the nasturtium flowers. Serve at once.

Nasu Karashi Sumiso-ae

AUBERGINES [EGGPLANT] WITH MUSTARD DRESSING

A spicy and easy to make dish, Nasu Karashi Sumiso-ae (na-soo kah-rah-shee soo-mee-soh-eye) is served as a pickle with rice as part of a Japanese meal. Small young aubergines [eggplant] are most suitable for this dish; however, if you use the larger variety, the skins should be partly peeled, as they tend to be a little tough.

4 SERVINGS

- 2 pints [5 cups] water
- 1 teaspoon salt
- 4 small aubergines [eggplant], cut lengthways
- 3 tablespoons miso paste
- 2 tablespoons white wine vinegar
- 4 tablespoons sugar
- 2 teaspoons dry mustard dissolved in 2 teaspoons lukewarm water

In a medium-sized saucepan, bring the water to the boil over high heat. Add the salt and the aubergine [eggplant] slices. When the water comes to the boil again, reduce the heat to moderate and cook for 8 to 10 minutes, or until the slices are tender. Remove the pan from the heat and drain the aubergine [eggplant] slices in a colander. Set aside to cool.

When the aubergine [eggplant] slices are cool, transfer them to a plate and place it in the refrigerator to chill for 30 minutes.

In a medium-sized mixing bowl, combine the miso paste, wine vinegar and sugar. Add the dissolved mustard and mix well. Remove the aubergine [egg-plant] slices from the refrigerator and add them to the mustard dressing.

Toss the aubergine [eggplant] slices in the dressing and mix well, ensuring that all the slices are well coated with the dressing.

Arrange the aubergine [eggplant] slices on a serving dish and serve immediately.

Natalie's Dream Dessert

A beautiful chocolate dessert, Natalie's Dream Dessert should be served in small quantities as it is so rich. You may, if you like, serve the dessert with small plain biscuits [cookies].

6 SERVINGS

- 6 oz. dark [semi-sweet] chocolate, broken into small pieces
- 2 tablespoons water
- 1 tablespoon rum
- 6 oz. [¾ cup] castor sugar
- 6 oz. [¾ cup] unsalted butter, cut into small pieces
- 3 large eggs, separated
- 8 fl. oz. double cream [1 cup heavy cream]

In a medium-sized saucepan, melt the chocolate with the water and rum over low heat, stirring occasionally with a wooden spoon. When the chocolate has melted and the mixture is smooth, add the sugar and cook, stirring constantly, until the sugar has dissolved.

Remove the pan from the heat. Beat in the unsalted butter, a few pieces at a time, beating until it is thoroughly blended into the chocolate mixture. Set the mixture aside to cool to lukewarm, stirring occasionally.

When the mixture has cooled, beat in the egg yolks and combine the mixture thoroughly. Set aside.

In a medium-sized mixing bowl, beat the egg whites with a wire whisk or rotary beater until they form stiff peaks. With a metal spoon, fold the egg whites into the chocolate mixture. Spoon the mixture into 6 serving glasses or ramekin dishes and place them in the refrigerator. Chill the dessert for 2 hours, or until it has set.

Just before the dessert is ready, pour the cream into a small mixing bowl. Using a wire whisk or rotary beater, beat the cream until it is stiff. Spoon the cream into a small forcing bag fitted with a medium-sized star-shaped nozzle.

Remove the glasses or ramekin dishes from the refrigerator. Pipe the cream over the chocolate mixture to cover it completely, bringing the cream up into decorative swirls.

Serve immediately.

Nautical Stew

This filling and tasty stew is made, with the exception of the meat and onion, from canned ingredients. It is an ideal dish to make in a pressure cooker and, as the name suggests, in the galley of a yacht!

4-6 SERVINGS

- 3 tablespoons vegetable oil
- 2 lb. stewing steak, cut into 1-inch cubes
- 1 large onion, sliced
- 1¼ teaspoons salt
- 1 tablespoon paprika
- 1 tablespoon flour
- 14 oz. canned peeled tomatoes
- 28 oz. canned baked beans
- 14 oz. canned red or green peppers, drained and sliced
- 2 fl. oz. [¼ cup] brandy

In a large flameproof casserole, heat the oil over moderate heat. Add the meat cubes, a few at a time, and fry, turning them frequently, for 5 to 6 minutes or until they are brown. Using a slotted spoon, transfer the meat cubes to a warmed plate. Keep warm while you brown the remaining meat cubes in the same way.

Add the onion to the casserole and fry, stirring occasionally, for 8 to 10 minutes or until it is golden brown. Stir in the salt, paprika and flour and cook, stirring constantly, for 1 minute. Add the tomatoes with the can juice, and stir well. Return the meat to the casserole. When the mixture begins to bubble, cover the casserole, reduce the heat to low and simmer for 1½ hours.

Uncover the casserole and stir in the baked beans and peppers. Increase the heat to moderate. When the stew comes to the boil again, cover the casserole, reduce the heat to low and continue cooking for a further 30 minutes. If the stew is too liquid continue this final cooking with the casserole uncovered.

Stir in the brandy and taste the stew. Add more salt if necessary. Remove the casserole from the heat and serve immediately, from the casserole.

Navarin

Navarin (nah-vah-ran) is the French term for a stew of mutton, to which potatoes and onions are added. When a variety of spring vegetables, such as carrots, turnips and peas is added, the dish is called NAVARIN PRINTANIER.

Easy to prepare Nautical Stew is made from meat and canned vegetables.

Navarin de Mouton

MUTTON STEW

A classic French dish, Navarin de Mouton (nah-vah-ran d'moo-ton) is nourishing and relatively inexpensive. Great care should be taken to remove as much grease as possible from the cooking liquid. Serve this dish with a green vegetable and a full-blooded red wine such as a Nuits St. Georges.

6 SERVINGS

2 oz. [¼ cup] butter
3 tablespoons olive oil
2 garlic cloves, crushed
1½ lb. boned breast of mutton, trimmed of excess fat and cut into 1-inch cubes
1½ lb. boned leg of mutton, cut into 1-inch cubes
1 tablespoon flour
1 teaspoon salt
½ teaspoon black pepper
2 tablespoons tomato purée

1 pint [2½ cups] brown stock
bouquet garni, consisting of 4 parsley sprigs, 1 thyme spray and 1 bay leaf tied together
6 small onions, peeled
12 small potatoes, peeled

In a large saucepan, melt half of the butter with 2 tablespoons of the oil over moderate heat. When the foam subsides, add the garlic cloves and the meat cubes, a few at a time. Fry, stirring occasionally,

for 6 to 8 minutes, or until the cubes are evenly browned.

With a slotted spoon, transfer the meat cubes to a warmed plate. Keep warm while you brown the remaining cubes in the same way.

Remove the pan from the heat and pour off half of the fat. Return the meat to the pan and sprinkle over the flour, salt and pepper. Place the pan over moderate heat and cook, stirring constantly, for 3 minutes.

Stir in the tomato purée and the stock. Increase the heat to high and bring the stock to the boil. Reduce the heat to low and add the bouquet garni. Cover the pan and simmer for 1 hour.

Meanwhile, in a large frying-pan, melt the remaining butter with the remaining oil over moderate heat. When the foam subsides, add the onions and potatoes. Fry, stirring frequently, for 6 to 8 minutes or until the vegetables are lightly browned all over.

Remove the pan from the heat. With a slotted spoon, transfer the vegetables to a dish.
Set aside.

With a large spoon, skim any grease off the surface of the cooking liquid in the saucepan. Add the onions and potatoes. Simmer, covered, for a further 20 to 25 minutes or until the meat and vegetables are tender when pierced with the point of a sharp knife.

Remove the pan from the heat. With a large spoon, skim any grease off the surface of the cooking liquid. Remove and discard the bouquet garni. Turn the stew into a warmed serving dish and serve immediately.

Navarin Printanier

MUTTON STEW WITH FRESH SPRING
VEGETABLES

   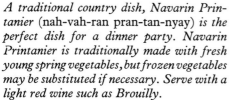

A traditional country dish, Navarin Printanier (nah-vah-ran pran-tan-nyay) is the perfect dish for a dinner party. Navarin Printanier is traditionally made with fresh young spring vegetables, but frozen vegetables may be substituted if necessary. Serve with a light red wine such as Brouilly.

6 SERVINGS

4 oz. salt pork, diced
1½ lb. boned breast of mutton, trimmed of excess fat and cut into 2-inch cubes
1½ lb. boned shoulder of mutton, trimmed of excess fat and cut into 2-inch cubes
2 tablespoons soft brown sugar
1 teaspoon salt
½ teaspoon black pepper
½ tablespoon flour
6 medium-sized tomatoes, blanched, peeled, seeded and chopped
2 pints [5 cups] chicken stock
bouquet garni, consisting of 4 parsley sprigs, 1 thyme spray and 1 bay leaf tied together
2 oz. [¼ cup] butter
12 small potatoes, peeled
6 small turnips, peeled
6 small carrots, scraped
12 small onions, peeled
½ tablespoon sugar

In a large, heavy-bottomed saucepan, fry the salt pork over moderate heat for 8 to 10 minutes, or until it resembles small croûtons and has rendered most of its fat. Stir occasionally to prevent it from sticking to the bottom of the pan. With a slotted spoon, transfer the salt pork to a large plate.

Add the meat cubes, a few at a time, to the pan and fry, stirring and turning occasionally, for 6 to 8 minutes, or until the meat is lightly and evenly browned.

With a slotted spoon, transfer the meat to the plate with the salt pork. Keep warm while you brown the remaining meat cubes in the same way.

Remove the pan from the heat and pour off half of the fat. Return the meat cubes and salt pork to the pan and sprinkle over the sugar, salt and pepper. Place the pan over moderate heat and cook, stirring constantly, for 3 minutes, or until the sugar has caramelized. Add the flour to the pan and cook for a further 3 minutes, stirring constantly.

Stir in the tomatoes, stock and bouquet garni. Increase the heat to high and bring the liquid to the boil. Reduce the heat to low, cover and simmer for 1 hour.

Meanwhile prepare the vegetables. In a large frying-pan, melt the butter over

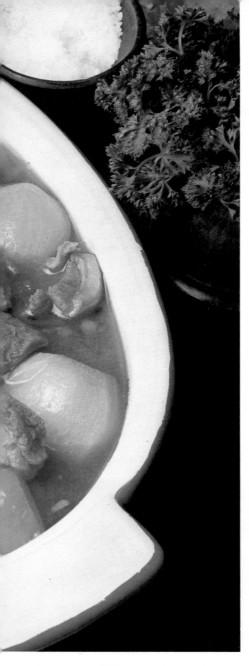

moderate heat. When the foam subsides, add the potatoes, turnips, carrots and onions and cook, stirring occasionally, for 8 to 10 minutes or until the onions are golden brown. Stir in the sugar and cook for a further 3 minutes or until the sugar has dissolved. Remove the pan from the heat. With a slotted spoon, transfer the vegetables to a dish and keep warm.

Remove the saucepan from the heat. With a metal spoon, skim off any grease from the surface of the cooking liquid. Add the browned vegetables and stir well. Return the pan to the heat and cook for 25 minutes, or until the meat and vegetables are tender when pierced with the point of a sharp knife.

Remove the pan from the heat. With a metal spoon, skim off any grease from the surface of the cooking liquid. Remove and discard the bouquet garni. Transfer the stew to a warmed, deep serving dish. Serve immediately.

Navarin Printanier is a classic mutton stew from France. Traditionally, fresh spring vegetables are used, but you may substitute frozen ones.

Navets Glacés
GLAZED TURNIPS

A traditional French dish, Navets Glacés (nah-vay glah-say) is a delicious accompaniment to roast duck or grilled [broiled] chops.

4 SERVINGS

1 oz. [2 tablespoons] butter
1 tablespoon olive oil
1½ lb. young turnips, peeled and quartered
2 tablespoons soft brown sugar
6 fl. oz. [¾ cup] chicken stock

In a medium-sized saucepan, melt the butter with the oil over moderate heat. When the foam subsides, add the turnips and cook, stirring occasionally, for 7 minutes, or until the turnips are golden brown. Add the sugar and cook, stirring occasionally, for a further 5 minutes.

Increase the heat to high, pour in the chicken stock and bring it to the boil. Cover the pan, reduce the heat to low and simmer the turnips for 30 minutes, or until they are tender but still firm and almost all of the stock has been absorbed.

Remove the pan from the heat and transfer the turnips to a warmed serving dish. Serve immediately.

Navets au Gratin
TURNIPS BAKED WITH CHEESE AND BREADCRUMBS

An inexpensive dish, Navets au Gratin (nah-vay oh gra-tan) is easy to prepare and quite delicious. Serve as a light vegetable lunch or as an accompaniment to meat or poultry.

4-6 SERVINGS

1 oz. [2 tablespoons] plus 1 teaspoon butter, cut into small pieces
2 lb. small turnips, peeled and sliced
1 large onion, thinly sliced and pushed out into rings
2 garlic cloves, crushed
1 teaspoon salt
½ teaspoon black pepper
2 tablespoons chopped fresh parsley
4 fl. oz. [½ cup] chicken stock
2 tablespoons dry white breadcrumbs
2 oz. [½ cup] Parmesan cheese, grated

Preheat the oven to fairly hot 375°F (Gas Mark 5, 190°C).

With the teaspoon of butter, lightly grease a medium-sized ovenproof dish.

Place about one-third of the turnip slices on the bottom of the dish. Cover with half of the onion rings and half of the garlic. Sprinkle over half of the salt, pepper and parsley. Cover with another third of the turnip slices and then with the remaining onion rings, garlic, salt, pepper and parsley. Put the remaining turnip slices on top. Pour over the chicken stock and dot the remaining butter over the top.

In a small bowl, combine the breadcrumbs and grated cheese, mixing with a fork until they are well blended. Sprinkle the mixture evenly over the top of the vegetables.

Place the dish in the centre of the oven and bake for 45 to 55 minutes, or until the turnips are tender but still firm.

Remove from the oven and serve immediately.

Navets au Petit Salé
TURNIPS WITH SALT PORK

When treated imaginatively, turnips make a delicious accompaniment to any meat dish. Serve Navets au Petit Salé (nah-vay oh peh-tee sah-lay) with roast chicken or roast beef for a delightful and sustaining Sunday lunch.

6 SERVINGS

4 oz. salt pork, diced
1 tablespoon butter
2 medium-sized onions, finely chopped
2 lb. small turnips, peeled and sliced
1 tablespoon soft brown sugar
1 tablespoon flour
2 tablespoons chopped fresh parsley
½ teaspoon black pepper
8 fl. oz. [1 cup] beef stock
1 tablespoon chopped fresh chives

Preheat the oven to fairly hot 375°F (Gas Mark 5, 190°C).

In a medium-sized flameproof casserole, fry the salt pork over moderate heat, stirring frequently, for 8 to 10 minutes, or until it resembles small croûtons and has rendered most of its fat. With a slotted spoon, transfer the pork to a plate and keep warm. Remove the casserole from the heat and pour off all but 1 tablespoon of the pork fat.

Return the casserole to the heat and add the butter. When the foam subsides, add the onions and cook, stirring occasionally, for 5 to 7 minutes, or until they are soft and translucent but not brown. Add the turnip slices and cook, stirring occasionally, for 7 minutes, or until they are lightly browned.

Stir in the sugar, flour, parsley and pepper and cook, stirring constantly, for a further 2 minutes. Pour over the stock, and bring to the boil.

Remove the casserole from the heat, cover and place it in the centre of the oven. Braise for 20 minutes. Uncover the casserole and continue to braise for a further 15 minutes, or until the turnips are tender when pierced with the point of a sharp knife and most of the liquid has been absorbed.

Remove the casserole from the oven and transfer the mixture to a warmed serving dish. Sprinkle over the chives and salt pork and serve immediately.

Navy Fruit Cake

A scrumptious cake, guaranteed to tempt even the strongest willed slimmer, Navy Fruit Cake combines mixed fruit with honey and rich dark rum.

ONE 10-INCH CAKE

3 lb. mixed dried fruit
4 oz. [⅔ cup] glacé cherries
8 fl. oz. [1 cup] dark rum
8 oz. [1 cup] plus 1 teaspoon butter
8 oz. [1⅓ cups] soft brown sugar
5 eggs, separated
8 oz. [2 cups] flour, sifted
5 fl. oz. [⅝ cup] clear honey

In a large mixing bowl, soak the dried fruit and glacé cherries in the rum. Set aside.

Preheat the oven to warm 325°F (Gas Mark 3, 170°C). With the teaspoon of butter, grease a round, deep, loose-bottomed 10-inch cake tin and line it with greaseproof or waxed paper. Set aside.

In a large mixing bowl, cream the remaining butter and the sugar together with a wooden spoon until the mixture is light and fluffy. Add the egg yolks, one at a time, beating well between each addition. Beat in a spoonful of flour with each egg yolk. Fold in the remaining flour.

Add the mixed fruit and glacé cherries, with the rum, to the mixture and blend well. Stir in the honey. Mix the ingredients together thoroughly.

In a medium-sized mixing bowl beat the egg whites with a wire whisk or rotary beater until they form stiff peaks. Fold into the batter.

Spoon the cake mixture into the cake tin and place it in the centre of the oven. Bake for 2 to 2½ hours. Reduce heat to 300°F (Gas Mark 2, 150°C) for a further 1 to 1½ hours. Cover with a double thickness of greaseproof paper halfway through cooking to prevent overbrowning.

Remove the cake from the oven and turn it out on to a wire rack to cool completely before serving.

Nazkhatun

AUBERGINE [EGGPLANT] HORS D'OEUVRE

Nazkhatun (nahz-hah-tun), a dish of Middle Eastern origin, makes an excellent and refreshing hors d'oeuvre. Serve it on thin triangles of black bread, garnished with lemon slices.

Honey, fruit, brown sugar and dark rum combine to make Navy Fruit Cake quite irresistible!

4 SERVINGS

2 medium-sized aubergines
  [eggplant]
2 tablespoons vegetable oil
1 medium-sized onion, finely
  chopped
2 garlic cloves, finely chopped
½ teaspoon salt
¼ teaspoon black pepper
1 tablespoon tomato purée
2 teaspoons wine vinegar
1 tablespoon lemon juice
2 tablespoons chopped fresh
  parsley

(Low Cal)

Half fill a large saucepan with water. Add the aubergine [eggplant] and set the pan over high heat. When the water comes to the boil, reduce the heat to low, cover the pan and simmer for 15 minutes.

Remove the pan from the heat and drain the aubergines [eggplant] in a colander. Place them on a chopping board and carefully peel off and discard the skins. Using a kitchen fork, mash the aubergine [eggplant] flesh. Set aside.

In a large frying-pan, heat the oil over moderate heat. When the oil is hot, add the onion and garlic and fry, stirring occasionally, for 5 to 7 minutes, or until the onion is soft and translucent but not brown.

Add the aubergine [eggplant] flesh, the salt, pepper, tomato purée and vinegar. Reduce the heat to low and, stirring constantly, simmer the mixture for 5 minutes. Stir in the lemon juice and parsley.

Remove the pan from the heat. Transfer the mixture to a serving bowl and leave to cool. Place the bowl in the refrigerator to chill for 1 hour before serving.

Neapolitan Beef Stew

A delightful and sustaining dish, Neapolitan Beef Stew is a mixture of lean beef cubes, tomatoes, oregano and Mozzarella cheese. Serve with noodles and a mixed green salad and, to drink, a light red Valpolicella wine.

4 SERVINGS

3 oz. [⅜ cup] butter
2 lb. lean stewing beef, cut into
  1-inch cubes
2 medium-sized onions, thinly
  sliced
2 garlic cloves, crushed
2 celery stalks, trimmed and
  chopped
1 large green pepper, white pith
  removed, seeded and chopped
14 oz. canned peeled tomatoes
2 tablespoons tomato purée
1 teaspoon salt
½ teaspoon black pepper

Popular Neapolitan Ice-Cream is a mixture of chocolate, vanilla and strawberry ice-cream layers.

2 teaspoons dried oregano
4 fl. oz. [½ cup] dry red wine
2 oz. Mozzarella cheese, cubed
1 oz. [¼ cup] Parmesan cheese,
  grated

In a large flameproof casserole, melt 2 ounces [¼ cup] of the butter over moderate heat. When the foam subsides, add the beef cubes, a few at a time, and cook, stirring and turning occasionally, for 6 to 8 minutes, or until they are lightly and evenly browned. With a slotted spoon, transfer the beef cubes to a plate. Keep them warm while you brown the remaining cubes in the same way.

Add the remaining butter to the casserole. When the foam subsides, add the onions and garlic and cook, stirring occasionally, for 5 to 7 minutes or until the onions are soft and translucent but not brown. Add the celery and green pepper to the casserole and cook, stirring occasionally, for 5 minutes.

Add the tomatoes with the can juice, the tomato purée, salt, pepper and oregano and stir well to mix. Return the beef cubes to the casserole and pour over the wine. Bring the liquid to the boil, stirring occasionally. Reduce the heat to low, cover the casserole and simmer the stew for 2 to 2½ hours or until the meat is very

tender when pierced with the point of a sharp knife.

Stir in the Mozzarella cubes and, stirring frequently, cook the stew for 5 to 8 minutes or until the cheese has melted. Remove the casserole from the heat and serve at once, with the grated cheese.

Neapolitan Ice-Cream

Neapolitan Ice-Cream is a mixture of differently coloured and flavoured layers of ice-cream frozen together in a brick mould. Commercially, the flavours are generally strawberry, vanilla and pistachio or chocolate ice-cream.

To make Neapolitan Ice-Cream, use the recipe for Ice-Cream made with a Mousse Base. Make 6 fluid ounces [¾ cup] each of vanilla, strawberry and pistachio or chocolate ice-cream.

To make this amount of pistachio ice-cream, pound to a paste 2½ ounces [½ cup] pistachio nuts together with 1 tablespoon of blanched almonds. Stir this paste into the scalded cream. When the cream is cool, add a few drops of green food colouring and then continue with the recipe.

Freeze the three different ice-creams separately. When they are half frozen, fill a 1-pint [1½-pint] brick mould first with the strawberry, then with the vanilla and lastly with the pistachio or chocolate ice-cream. Cover the mould with aluminium foil and place it in the frozen food storage compartment of the refrigerator to freeze

Traditional Neapolitan Pizzas, made with tomatoes, anchovies, Mozzarella cheese and oregano should be served sizzling hot, with an Italian wine.

---

for 1 hour, or until the ice-cream is completely frozen and firm to the touch.

To serve, remove the mould from the compartment. Remove the aluminium foil and dip the bottom of the mould in cold water. Invert a chilled serving dish over the mould and reverse the two, giving the mould a good shake. The ice-cream should slide out easily. The ice-cream is now ready to slice and serve.

Neapolitan Pizzas

A traditional Italian dish from Naples, Neapolitan Pizzas make a delicious meal, which is both inexpensive and filling. Serve Neapolitan Pizzas with a crisp green salad and a bottle of dry white Italian wine, such as Orvieto Secco.

2 SERVINGS

½ oz. fresh yeast
¼ teaspoon sugar
4 fl. oz. [½ cup] plus 1 tablespoon lukewarm water
8 oz. [2 cups] flour

1 teaspoon salt
2 teaspoons olive oil
FILLING
2 tablespoons tomato purée
4 medium-sized tomatoes, blanched, peeled, seeded and coarsely chopped
8 oz. Mozzarella cheese, sliced
8 anchovy fillets, cut in half
¼ teaspoon black pepper
2 teaspoons chopped fresh oregano or 1 teaspoon dried oregano

Crumble the yeast into a small bowl. Add the sugar and 1 tablespoon of the water and cream the water and yeast together. Set the bowl aside in a warm, draught-free place for 15 to 20 minutes, or until the yeast mixture is puffed up and frothy.

Sift the flour and salt into a warmed, large mixing bowl. Make a well in the centre and pour in the yeast mixture and the remaining water.

Using your fingers or a spatula, gradually draw the flour into the liquids. Continue mixing until all the flour is incorporated and the dough comes away from the sides of the bowl.

Turn the dough out on to a lightly floured board or marble slab and knead it for about 10 minutes, reflouring the surface if the dough becomes sticky. The dough should be elastic and smooth.

Rinse, thoroughly dry and lightly grease the large mixing bowl. Shape the dough into a ball and return it to the bowl. Dust the top of the dough with a little flour and cover the bowl with a clean, damp cloth. Set the bowl in a warm, draught-free place and leave it for 45 minutes to 1 hour, or until the dough has risen and has almost doubled in bulk.

Preheat the oven to very hot 450°F (Gas Mark 8, 230°C). With 1 teaspoon of the olive oil, lightly grease a large baking sheet and set aside.

Turn the risen dough out of the bowl on to a floured surface and knead it for 3 minutes. Cut the dough in half. With a lightly floured rolling pin, roll out each dough half to a circle about ¼-inch thick. Carefully arrange the dough circles, well apart, on the prepared baking sheet.

Spoon a tablespoon of tomato purée on to each circle and spread it out with a table knife. Decorate each circle with half of the tomatoes, cheese and anchovy fillets and sprinkle over the black pepper and oregano. Moisten each pizza with the remaining olive oil.

Place the pizzas in the centre of the oven and bake for 15 to 20 minutes, or until the dough is cooked and the cheese has melted. Remove from the oven and transfer the pizzas to a warmed serving dish. Serve immediately.

Neapolitan Stuffed Peppers

Inexpensive and easy-to-make, Neapolitan Stuffed Peppers make a filling main course. Serve with pasta, a mixed salad and lots of Chianti wine.

4 SERVINGS

2 fl. oz. [¼ cup] plus 1 teaspoon olive oil
4 large green peppers
1 oz. [2 tablespoons] butter
1 large onion, finely chopped
2 garlic cloves, crushed
4 medium-sized tomatoes, blanched, peeled, seeded and finely chopped
8 large black olives, stoned and finely chopped
4 anchovy fillets, chopped
4 oz. mushrooms, wiped clean and chopped
1 teaspoon salt
½ teaspoon black pepper
1 tablespoon chopped fresh basil, or 1½ teaspoons dried basil
2 oz. [1 cup] fresh breadcrumbs
2 oz. [½ cup] Parmesan cheese, grated

Preheat the oven to fairly hot 375°F (Gas Mark 5, 190°C).

With the teaspoon of olive oil, lightly grease a medium-sized baking dish and set it aside.

With a sharp knife, slice off and reserve 1-inch from the wider end of each pepper. Carefully remove and discard the white pith and seeds from the inside of each pepper. Set the peppers aside.

In a medium-sized saucepan, melt the butter with the remaining oil over moderate heat. When the foam subsides, add the onion and garlic and cook, stirring occasionally, for 5 to 7 minutes, or until the onion is soft and translucent but not brown. Add the tomatoes, olives, anchovies, mushrooms, salt, pepper and basil and cook for a further 5 minutes, stirring occasionally.

Remove the saucepan from the heat and stir in the breadcrumbs.

Spoon equal amounts of the stuffing mixture into each pepper and replace the reserved tops. Stand the peppers upright in the baking dish and place the dish in the centre of the oven. Bake for 45 minutes.

Remove the dish from the oven. Remove the tops and keep warm. Sprinkle each pepper with equal amounts of the grated cheese and return them to the oven. Continue to bake for a further 5 to 10 minutes, or until the topping is golden brown and the peppers are cooked.

Remove the peppers from the oven and replace the tops. Transfer to a warmed serving dish and serve immediately.

Neapolitan Veal Chops, with its sauce of wine, cream, garlic and sage, is a rich dinner party dish.

Neapolitan Veal Chops

A delicate dish of veal chops with mushrooms and a creamy tomato sauce flavoured with a hint of sage, Neapolitan Veal Chops should be served with creamed potatoes and a green vegetable or salad.

4 SERVINGS

4 veal chops
1 teaspoon salt
¼ teaspoon black pepper
2 garlic cloves, crushed
1 oz. [2 tablespoons] butter
2 tablespoons olive oil
6 medium-sized tomatoes, blanched, peeled, seeded and coarsely chopped
8 oz. button mushrooms, wiped clean and thinly sliced
1 tablespoon chopped fresh sage or ¼ teaspoon dried sage
2 fl. oz. [¼ cup] chicken stock
2 fl. oz. [¼ cup] white wine
2 fl. oz. double cream [¼ cup heavy cream]

Preheat the oven to moderate 350°F (Gas Mark 4, 180°C).

Place the veal chops on a flat working surface and rub the salt, pepper and crushed garlic all over them.

In a large flameproof casserole, melt the butter with the oil over moderate heat.

When the foam subsides add the veal chops, two at a time, and fry them for 6 to 8 minutes, turning once, or until they are golden brown all over. With a slotted spoon transfer the chops to a warmed dish and keep warm while you brown the remaining chops in the same way.

Add the tomatoes to the casserole. Cook, stirring frequently, for 5 minutes. Add the mushrooms and sage and continue to cook, stirring frequently, for a further 3 minutes.

Replace the veal chops in the casserole. Pour over the chicken stock and white wine. Cover the casserole and place it in the centre of the oven. Braise for 30 minutes. Uncover the casserole and continue braising for a further 15 minutes, or until the meat is tender when pierced with the point of a sharp knife.

Remove the casserole from the oven. With a slotted spoon transfer the veal chops and mushrooms to a warmed serving dish. Keep warm.

Place the casserole over high heat and bring the cooking liquid to the boil. Boil, stirring occasionally, for 5 to 8 minutes or until the liquid has reduced to half the original quantity. Remove the casserole from the heat.

With a wooden spoon stir in the cream. Pour the cream sauce over the chops and serve immediately.

Near Eastern Pork with Peanuts and Grapes

Tender pork fillet, gently cooked with juicy grapes and sprinkled with toasted peanuts, Near Eastern Pork with Peanuts and Grapes is an exotic dish to serve at a special dinner party. If peanuts are not available, use any type of nut — although the flavour will, naturally, be slightly different.

6-8 SERVINGS

2 tablespoons peanut oil
2 lb. pork fillet, cut into 1-inch cubes
1 teaspoon salt
½ teaspoon black pepper
2½ oz. [½ cup] unsalted peanuts, ground
2 tablespoons soy sauce
¼ teaspoon mild chilli powder
1 lb. seedless white grapes, halved
2½ oz. [½ cup] unsalted peanuts, finely chopped and toasted

In a large frying-pan, heat the oil over moderate heat. When the oil is hot add the pork cubes. Cook the pork, stirring and turning occasionally, for 5 to 10 minutes or until the cubes are lightly and evenly browned.

Add the salt, pepper, ground peanuts, soy sauce and chilli powder and mix well.

Reduce the heat to low. Add the grapes and simmer the mixture for 15 to 20 minutes, or until the pork is very tender when pierced with the point of a sharp knife.

Remove the pan from the heat and transfer the mixture to a warmed serving dish. Sprinkle with the chopped peanuts and serve at once.

Neck of Lamb with Marjoram and Orange

Neck of lamb braised in wine and orange juice gives the meat a luscious, juicy texture. Served with a mildly sweet sauce, this dish is sure to be a success.

4-6 SERVINGS

1 x 5 lb. best end of neck of lamb, chined
1 teaspoon salt
½ teaspoon black pepper
1 oz. [2 tablespoons] butter
2 large onions, thinly sliced
3 tablespoons chopped fresh marjoram or 1 tablespoon dried marjoram
thinly pared rind of 1 orange
14 fl. oz. [1¾ cups] sweet white wine
4 fl. oz. [½ cup] fresh orange juice
1 tablespoon orange marmalade

Inexpensive yet exotic, Near Eastern Pork with Peanuts and Grapes makes an exciting, different supper dish for friends or family.

Preheat the oven to warm 325°F (Gas Mark 3, 170°C).

Trim off any excess fat from the lamb and rub the meat all over with the salt and pepper. Set aside.

In a medium-sized frying-pan, melt the butter over moderate heat. When the foam subsides, add the onions to the pan and fry, stirring occasionally, for 5 to 7 minutes or until they are soft and translucent but not brown. Using a slotted spoon, transfer the onions to a large oven-proof casserole. Sprinkle over the marjoram and orange rind and lay the meat on top. Pour over the wine and the orange juice.

Cover the casserole and place it in the oven. Braise, basting occasionally and adding more wine if necessary, for 2 to 2½ hours or until the meat is very tender when pierced with the point of a sharp knife.

Remove the casserole from the oven. With tongs or two large spoons, remove the meat from the casserole and place it on a warmed serving dish.

Skim off any fat from the cooking

liquid and strain it into a medium-sized mixing bowl. Stir the marmalade into the cooking liquid.

Using a sharp-bladed knife, cut the meat between the bones into chops. Pour over the sauce and serve at once.

Neck of Veal, Braised

A very simple dish to make, Neck of Veal, Braised makes a delicious Sunday lunch, served with a green vegetable and boiled new potatoes. Ask your butcher to chine the veal as this makes it easier to carve.

4 SERVINGS

1 x 4 lb. best end of neck of veal, chine bone removed
1 teaspoon salt
½ teaspoon black pepper
¼ teaspoon ground cloves
¼ teaspoon ground mace
4 streaky bacon slices, rinds removed
1 medium-sized onion, finely chopped
1 large carrot, scraped and sliced
2 celery stalks, trimmed and cut into 2-inch pieces

A deliciously simple, sturdy dish, Neck of Veal, Braised is the perfect economical Sunday lunch.

bouquet garni, consisting of 4 parsley sprigs, 1 thyme spray and 1 bay leaf tied together
6 black peppercorns
1 bay leaf
12 fl. oz. [1½ cups] chicken stock
1 tablespoon lemon juice

Using a sharp knife, cut off the short pieces of rib bone from the flap on the veal. Rub the meat all over with the salt, pepper, cloves and mace and set aside.

In a large flameproof casserole, fry the bacon over moderate heat, stirring occasionally, for 5 to 6 minutes or until it is crisp and has rendered most of its fat. Using a slotted spoon, remove and discard the bacon.

Add the onion to the casserole and fry, stirring occasionally, for 5 to 7 minutes, or until it is soft and translucent but not brown. Add the carrot and celery and, stirring occasionally, cook the vegetables for 2 minutes. Stir in the bouquet garni, peppercorns and bay leaf and pour the stock on to the vegetables. Increase the heat to moderately high and bring the stock to the boil. Put the veal into the casserole, cover and reduce the heat to low. Simmer the veal for 2 hours, basting occasionally, or until it is very tender when pierced with the point of a sharp knife.

Preheat the oven to moderate 350°F (Gas Mark 4, 180°C).

Remove the casserole from the heat. Remove the lid and place the casserole in the oven. Braise, uncovered, for 20 minutes.

Remove the casserole from the oven and, with tongs or two large spoons, transfer the veal to a warmed serving dish. Skim off any fat from the cooking liquid. Strain the cooking liquid into a warmed sauceboat. Discard the contents of the strainer.

Using a sharp-bladed knife, cut between the rib bones of the veal. Sprinkle with the lemon juice and serve at once, with the cooking liquid.

Nectar

Nectar was the legendary drink of both the Greek and the Roman gods. It was then defined as a special type of dew, but the word is now used loosely to describe any delicious drink.

Nectarine

The nectarine is a variety of smooth-skinned PEACH with a firm texture and a delicate flavour. It is usually eaten raw, as a dessert fruit, but is also delicious when made into pie fillings and preserves. All peach recipes are suitable for nectarines.

To peel nectarines, first blanch them. The skins will then slip off easily.

Serve this rich and delectable Nectarine Cream Mould with whipped cream and Brandy Snaps as the perfect ending to that special dinner party.

4 SERVINGS

2 teaspoons vegetable oil
6 medium-sized nectarines,
  peeled, stoned and finely chopped
⅛ teaspoon ground allspice
3 oz. icing sugar [¾ cup confectioners'
  sugar]
2 tablespoons brandy
½ oz. gelatine dissolved in 4
  tablespoons hot water
10 fl. oz. double cream [1¼ cups
  heavy cream]

Using a pastry brush, grease a 2-pint [1½-quart] mould with the oil. Place the mould, upside-down, on kitchen paper towels and set aside to drain.

In a medium-sized mixing bowl, combine the nectarines, allspice, sugar, brandy and the dissolved gelatine. Set aside.

In a small mixing bowl, beat the cream with a wire whisk or rotary beater until it forms stiff peaks. Fold the cream into the fruit mixture. Spoon the mixture into the prepared mould.

Place the mould in the refrigerator to chill for at least 2 hours or until the mould has set and is firm to the touch.

To unmould the dessert, run a knife carefully around the edge of the mould to loosen the sides. Place a serving plate, inverted, over the mould and reverse the two, giving a sharp shake. The nectarine cream should slide out easily.

Nectarine Pie

A lovely fruity pie, dredged with brown sugar and sprinkled with lemon juice and brandy, Nectarine Pie makes a really filling dessert. Serve hot with Crème à la Vanille, or cold with freshly whipped cream.

4-6 SERVINGS

5 large nectarines, peeled, stoned
  and sliced
  grated rind of 1 lemon
1 tablespoon lemon juice
½ teaspoon grated nutmeg
4 tablespoons soft brown sugar
1 tablespoon brandy
1 tablespoon butter, melted
1 egg yolk, well beaten with 2
  tablespoons milk
2 tablespoons castor sugar

PASTRY
10 oz. [2½ cups] flour
⅛ teaspoon salt
3 oz. [⅜ cup] butter

Nectarine Chutney

Chutney can be made with a number of fruit including blackberries, gooseberries, dates and plums. Here we have used nectarines and a mixture of spices, fruit and nuts to make a delicious chutney which will give added flavour to many plain dishes. Chutney improves in flavour with keeping and can be stored for months if kept in airtight jars.

ABOUT 4 POUNDS

10 large nectarines, peeled, stoned
  and quartered
2 large crisp apples, peeled, cored
  and chopped
  grated rind and juice of 3 lemons
6 oz. [1 cup] soft brown sugar
6 oz. [1 cup] walnuts, chopped
9 oz. [1½ cups] sultanas or seedless
  raisins
2-inch piece fresh root ginger,
  bruised
2 garlic cloves, crushed
6 black peppercorns
¼ teaspoon cayenne pepper
1 teaspoon ground cinnamon
6 fl. oz. [¾ cup] white wine vinegar

Place the nectarines and apples in a large saucepan. Add the lemon rind, lemon juice, sugar, walnuts, sultanas or raisins, ginger, garlic, peppercorns, cayenne and cinnamon. Pour on half of the vinegar and stir the mixture well with a wooden spoon. Place the pan over high heat and bring the mixture to the boil.

Reduce the heat to low and simmer for 30 minutes, stirring occasionally. Pour on the remaining vinegar and simmer, stirring occasionally, for a further 1½ hours, or until the chutney is thick and smooth.

Remove the pan from the heat and pour the chutney into clean, warm jars.

Place a disc of vinegar-resistant paper inside the lid to each jar and screw the lid on tightly. Alternatively use vacuum-sealed jars.

Nectarine Cream Mould

A delicately flavoured cream, nectarine and brandy mixture, Nectarine Cream Mould makes a refreshing dessert. Serve it with whipped cream and Brandy Snaps.

2 oz. [¼ cup] vegetable fat
1 tablespoon sugar
1 egg yolk, lightly beaten
1 to 2 tablespoons water

First make the pastry. Sift the flour and salt into a large mixing bowl. Add the butter and vegetable fat and cut them into small pieces with a table knife. With your fingertips rub the fats into the flour until the mixture resembles coarse bread-crumbs. Stir in the sugar.

Add the egg yolk and 1 tablespoon of the water and mix them in with the knife. Knead the dough lightly, adding the remaining water if the dough is too dry. Form the dough into a ball and place it in the refrigerator to chill for 30 minutes.

Preheat the oven to fairly hot 375°F (Gas Mark 5, 190°C).

Break off two-thirds of the dough and place it on a lightly floured board or marble slab. Using a floured rolling pin roll out the dough into a circle ¼-inch thick and large enough to line a 9-inch pie dish. Lift the dough on the rolling pin and place it over the pie dish. With your fingers, gently ease the dough into

A marvellous combination of fruit, brown sugar, brandy and crisp pastry, Nectarine Pie is delicious hot or cold.

the dish. Trim off any excess dough with a sharp knife.

Layer the nectarine slices in the dough case, sprinkling the lemon rind, lemon juice, nutmeg and brown sugar between the layers. Pour over the brandy and melted butter.

Roll out the remaining dough into a circle large enough to cover the pie. Lift the dough on the rolling pin and place it over the pie. Using your fingers, crimp the edges together to seal the pie. Using a sharp knife, cut a small cross in the middle of the dough.

Using a pastry brush, brush the dough with the egg yolk and milk mixture and sprinkle over the castor sugar.

Place the pie in the centre of the oven and bake for 30 to 40 minutes, or until the pastry is crisp and golden brown.

Remove the pie from the oven and serve it at once or allow to cool completely before serving.

Nectarine Tartlets

A mouth-watering combination of fresh nectarines and lemon-flavoured ice-cream set in crisp rich shortcrust pastry, Nectarine Tartlets make an unusual dessert.

6 TARTLETS

8 fl. oz. double cream [1 cup heavy cream]
2 tablespoons castor sugar
10 fl. oz. [1¼ cups] lemon-flavoured ice-cream
3 large nectarines, peeled, stoned and halved
3 tablespoons Apricot Glaze
2 oz. [½ cup] slivered almonds
PASTRY
12 oz. [3 cups] flour
⅛ teaspoon salt
3 oz. [⅜ cup] vegetable fat
3 oz. [⅜ cup] butter
1 tablespoon sugar
1 egg yolk, lightly beaten
1 to 2 tablespoons water

Preheat the oven to fairly hot 400°F (Gas Mark 6, 200°C).

First make the pastry. Sift the flour and salt into a large mixing bowl. Add the vegetable fat and butter and cut them into small pieces with a table knife. With your fingertips rub the fats into the flour until the mixture resembles coarse breadcrumbs. Stir in the sugar.

Add the egg yolk and 1 tablespoon of the water and mix them in with the knife. Knead the dough lightly, adding the remaining water if the dough is too dry. Form the dough into a ball and place it in the refrigerator to chill for 30 minutes.

On a lightly floured surface, roll out the dough to a circle about ¼-inch thick. With a 6-inch pastry cutter, cut the dough into six circles. Line six 4-inch tartlet tins with the dough circles.

Place the tartlet tins on two baking sheets. Line each tin with greaseproof or waxed paper and weigh the paper down with a spoonful of dried beans or rice.

Place the baking sheets in the oven and bake the tartlet cases for 10 minutes. Remove the paper and beans or rice and continue baking for 5 minutes, or until the pastry is golden brown.

Remove the tartlet cases from the oven and set them aside to cool on a wire rack. When they are cool, remove the pastry cases from the tartlet tins. Set them aside.

In a medium-sized mixing bowl beat the cream with a wire whisk or rotary beater until it forms soft peaks. Stir in the sugar and beat for a further 30 seconds or until the cream will hold a stiff peak. Spoon the cream into a forcing bag fitted with a plain nozzle and set aside.

Put equal amounts of the ice-cream into each pastry case and top with a nectarine half, cut side down. Using a teaspoon, dribble the apricot glaze evenly over each nectarine.

Pipe the cream in decorative swirls around the edge of each tartlet. Sprinkle with the almonds and serve immediately.

Negroni

A potent cocktail from Italy, Negroni is traditionally served in tall glasses with ice cubes.

4 COCKTAILS

8 fl. oz. [1 cup] Italian vermouth
4 fl. oz. [½ cup] Campari
4 fl. oz. [½ cup] gin or vodka
8 ice cubes
6 fl. oz. [¾ cup] soda water
4 orange or lemon slices

Chill 4 tall glasses in the refrigerator for 30 minutes.

Pour the vermouth, Campari and gin or vodka into a chilled cocktail shaker. Screw on the lid and shake vigorously for 30 seconds.

Remove the glasses from the refrigerator. Place two of the ice cubes in each glass. Pour in the cocktail. Add equal amounts of the soda water, top with the orange or lemon slices and serve.

Negus

Negus is the name applied to a sweet punch of which there are several varieties. Basically, it consists of port wine, spices and sugar, and it is traditionally warmed in a large pan. The punch was invented by Colonel Francis Negus during the reign of Queen Anne.

Neige de Pêches au Champagne

PEACH AND CHAMPAGNE DESSERT

Neige de Pêches au Champagne (nayj d' pesh oh shahm-pahn-yeh) *is a luxurious frozen dessert made with peach juice and Champagne and flavoured with oranges.*

A sparkling frozen peach and champagne dessert, Neige de Pêches au Champagne is refreshing after a rich main course.

$\frac{1}{8}$ teaspoon ground allspice
$\frac{1}{2}$ oz. gelatine, dissolved in 3 tablespoons hot peach juice
1 egg white
2 very large oranges

Set the thermostat of the refrigerator to its coldest setting.

In a medium-sized saucepan, combine the peach juice, Champagne, sugar, orange rind and juice and allspice. Set the pan over moderately high heat and bring the mixture to the boil, stirring constantly. Boil for 4 minutes, stirring occasionally.

Remove the pan from the heat. Stir in the dissolved gelatine and strain the mixture into a 1½-pint [1-quart] freezer tray. Set aside to cool to lukewarm and then place the tray in the frozen food storage compartment of the refrigerator to freeze for 30 minutes.

Meanwhile, in a medium-sized mixing bowl, beat the egg white with a wire whisk or rotary beater until it forms stiff peaks.

Remove the freezer tray from the refrigerator. Whisk the chilled peach mixture into the egg white, blending it in thoroughly. Spoon the mixture back into the freezer tray and return it to the frozen food storage compartment of the refrigerator. Freeze for 1 hour.

Remove the mixture from the refrigerator and turn it out into a medium-sized mixing bowl. Whisk the mixture with a wire whisk or rotary beater for 1 minute, and then spoon it back into the freezer tray. Return the tray to the frozen food storage compartment and freeze the mixture for 4 hours, whisking every hour.

Meanwhile, wash the oranges under cold running water and pat them dry with kitchen paper towels. With a sharp knife, cut the oranges across in half. With a sharp-edged metal spoon, scoop out and discard the flesh and most of the pith, taking care to keep the shells intact.

Remove the peach mixture from the refrigerator. Turn it out into a medium-sized mixing bowl and whisk it with a wire whisk or rotary beater for 2 minutes. Spoon the mixture into the prepared orange shells.

Return the dessert to the frozen food storage compartment of the refrigerator and freeze it overnight.

Remove the oranges from the refrigerator. Place them in shallow glass bowls large enough to hold the oranges comfortably. If the Champagne mixture is very hard leave the dessert for 10 to 15 minutes at room temperature before serving.

Nelusko

Nelusko (nel-eus-koh) are small petits fours made with cherries. Brandy-soaked cherries are drained, halved, stoned and filled with cooked redcurrants or redcurrant jam. The stuffed cherries are then coated with very thick, brandy-flavoured FONDANT icing. When the fondant has set and hardened, the nelusko are put into paper cases.

Neptune's Delight

A subtle dinner dish, Neptune's Delight is a combination of halibut, prawns or shrimps, wine and cream. Serve with creamed potatoes, fresh peas and, to drink, a well-chilled Muscadet white wine.

4 SERVINGS

4 large halibut steaks
1 teaspoon salt
$\frac{1}{2}$ teaspoon black pepper
10 fl. oz. [1¼ cups] fish stock
4 fl. oz. [½ cup] dry white wine
1 oz. [2 tablespoons] butter
3 tablespoons flour
10 fl. oz. single cream [1¼ cups light cream]
12 oz. prawns or shrimps, shelled and coarsely chopped

Rub the halibut steaks all over with the salt and pepper. Arrange them in a large fish kettle or saucepan. Pour over the stock and 2 fluid ounces [¼ cup] of the wine. Place the kettle or saucepan over moderately high heat and bring the liquid to the boil. Reduce the heat to low and simmer the fish gently for 15 to 20 minutes, or until the flesh flakes easily when tested with a fork.

Meanwhile, prepare the sauce. In a medium-sized saucepan, melt the butter over moderate heat. Remove the pan from the heat and, with a wooden spoon, stir in the flour to make a smooth paste. Gradually add the cream and remaining wine, stirring constantly. Return the pan to the heat. Cook, stirring constantly, for 2 to 3 minutes or until the sauce is thick and smooth.

Reduce the heat to low and stir in the prawns or shrimps. Simmer the mixture for a further 3 minutes. Remove the pan from the heat and set aside. Keep warm.

Remove the fish kettle or saucepan from the heat. With a slotted spoon, transfer the halibut steaks to a warmed serving dish. Pour the sauce over the halibut and serve immediately.

Serve it as a refreshing ending to a rich meal. The dessert must be made the day before you serve it, as it has to freeze overnight. If you think the use of Champagne is too extravagant, substitute a sparkling white wine.

4 SERVINGS

8 fl. oz. [1 cup] fresh or bottled peach juice
8 fl. oz. [1 cup] dry Champagne
2 oz. [¼ cup] castor sugar juice and grated rind of 1 small orange

A classic iced pudding, Nesselrode Pudding is made of ice-cream flavoured with chestnuts, glacé fruit and maraschino liqueur.

Nesselrode Pudding

This classic iced pudding was invented in honour of a famous Russian Count named Nesselrode. Nesselrode Pudding is traditionally made with an ice-cream base, flavoured with maraschino, chestnut purée and glacé fruits. There are many variations of this popular recipe using different liqueurs and fruits and often lining the charlotte mould with sponge finger biscuits [cookies] as in Charlotte Russe.

8 SERVINGS

1 teaspoon vegetable oil
2 oz. [⅓ cup] raisins
3 oz. [½ cup] glacé cherries, chopped
2 oz. [⅓ cup] chopped mixed peel
4 fl. oz. [½ cup] sherry
6 oz. canned unsweetened chestnut purée
1 pint [2½ cups] Crème à la Vanille
1 pint double cream [2½ cups heavy cream], whipped until thick but not stiff
2 fl. oz. [¼ cup] Maraschino liqueur
5 marrons glacés, halved

Set the thermostat of the refrigerator to its coldest setting. With the teaspoon of vegetable oil grease a 3-pint [2-quart] charlotte mould. Set aside.

In a medium-sized mixing bowl, combine the raisins, glacé cherries and mixed peel. Pour over the sherry and set aside to soak for 30 minutes.

In a large mixing bowl, mix together the chestnut purée and crème à la vanille.

Drain the raisins, cherries and mixed peel and discard any leftover sherry. Add the fruits to the custard mixture and mix well.

In a medium-sized mixing bowl beat the whipped cream and the Maraschino together with a wire whisk or rotary beater until the mixture will hold a stiff peak. With a metal spoon fold the cream into the custard mixture.

Spoon the mixture into the charlotte mould and cover the top of the mould securely with aluminium foil.

Place the mould in the frozen food storage compartment of the refrigerator and freeze overnight, or until the pudding is firm.

When you are ready to serve the pudding, remove the foil from the top and run a knife around the edge of the mould. Dip the bottom of the mould quickly in hot water. Place a serving dish, inverted,

over the mould and reverse the two, giving a sharp shake. The pudding should slide out easily on to the dish. Decorate with the marrons glacés and serve at once.

Netherlands Pork

A delicious combination of pork, apples and apricots, Netherlands Pork makes an attractive dish for a dinner party. Serve this dish with Croquettes de Pommes de Terre and steamed broccoli.

6-8 SERVINGS

1 x 4 lb. loin of pork, boned and trimmed of excess fat
2 teaspoons salt
1 teaspoon black pepper
½ teaspoon prepared mustard
2 teaspoons dried sage
2 tablespoons raisins
1 large cooking apple, peeled, cored and thinly sliced
1 tablespoon soft brown sugar
2 oz. [¼ cup] butter
25 oz. canned apricots, drained and can juice reserved
1 tablespoon sugar
1½ teaspoons cornflour [cornstarch] dissolved in 1 tablespoon water

Preheat the oven to moderate 350°F (Gas Mark 4, 180°C).

Place the loin of pork on a flat working surface and rub the salt, pepper, mustard and sage on to both sides.

Lay the pork fat side down. Sprinkle half of the raisins over the meat. Cover the raisins with the apple. Sprinkle the brown sugar over the apple and cover with the remaining raisins. Roll the meat up and tie round with string at 1-inch intervals.

In a large flameproof roasting tin, melt the butter over moderate heat. When the foam subsides, place the pork in the tin and fry, turning the meat from time to time with two large forks, for 8 minutes, or until it is browned all over.

Remove the roasting tin from the heat and place it in the centre of the oven. Roast the meat, basting occasionally, for 2½ hours, or until it is tender and the juices run clear when the meat is pierced with the point of a sharp knife.

Fifteen minutes before the meat is cooked, preheat the grill [broiler] to high.

Arrange the apricots on a flameproof dish. Sprinkle the apricots with the sugar and place under the grill [broiler]. Grill [broil] for 5 to 6 minutes, or until the sugar has melted and the tops of the apricots are pale brown. Remove the dish from under the heat. Set aside and keep warm.

Remove the roasting tin from the oven and transfer the pork to a carving dish. Remove the string from the meat and arrange the apricots around the pork. Keep warm while you prepare the sauce.

Pour off most of the pork fat from the tin, leaving about 3 tablespoons. Place the tin over moderate heat and pour in the reserved apricot can juice. Stir in the cornflour [cornstarch] mixture and bring the sauce to the boil, stirring constantly.

Remove the tin from the heat and strain the sauce into a warmed sauceboat. Serve immediately, with the meat.

Nettles

Nettles, better known as stinging nettles or tie, make a pleasant and nourishing vegetable if picked in the spring while they are still young and tender. They have a slightly bitter taste, somewhat like spinach, and are cooked in a similar way. When gathering nettles it is always advisable to wear gloves as the nettles contain formic acid which causes skin irritation. Be careful where you pick your nettles, as they may be sprayed with insecticide, which can be poisonous.

Gather only the young tips of the nettles. Wash them thoroughly under cold water. Place them in a large saucepan with only the water which is clinging to the leaves. Place the pan over low heat and cook for approximately 10 minutes or until the nettles are tender.

Remove the pan from the heat and drain the nettles. Roughly chop up the leaves and add salt and pepper and a nut of butter. Serve immediately.

Nettle Soup

This unusual soup is easy to make and very nourishing. Serve it with Croûtons. An electric blender is necessary to achieve the smooth, creamy texture of this soup.

6 SERVINGS

1 oz. [2 tablespoons] butter
1 medium-sized onion, finely chopped
2 medium-sized potatoes, finely chopped
1 lb. young nettles, washed
15 fl. oz. [1⅞ cups] chicken stock
10 fl. oz. [1¼ cups] milk
1 teaspoon salt
½ teaspoon pepper
6 tablespoons double [heavy] cream

In a large saucepan melt the butter over moderate heat. When the foam subsides, add the onion and potatoes and cook them, stirring occasionally, for 5 to 7 minutes, or until the onion is soft and translucent but not brown.

Add the nettles to the pan and cook for a further 3 minutes, stirring frequently. Stir in the stock, milk, salt and pepper. Increase the heat to high and bring the mixture to the boil. Cover the pan, reduce the heat to low and simmer the soup for 15 to 20 minutes, or until the potatoes are tender when pierced with the point of a sharp knife.

Remove the pan from the heat. Ladle the soup into an electric blender a little at a time and blend until the soup is smooth and creamy.

Return the blended soup to the saucepan. Return the pan to moderate heat and, stirring occasionally, bring the soup to the boil. Taste the soup and add more salt and pepper if necessary.

Remove the pan from the heat and spoon the soup into individual serving bowls. Add a spoonful of double [heavy] cream to each bowl and serve immediately.

Neufchâtel Cheese

Neufchâtel (nurf-shah-tel) is a soft, yellow French cheese with a red skin, made in Neufchâtel, in the province of Normandy. This creamy loaf-shaped cheese is made from whole-milk and weighs between 3 and 4 ounces.

Neustadt Rouladen

BEEF AND SAUERKRAUT ROLLS

An easy to make dish, Neustadt Rouladen (noo-staht roo-lahd-ehn) is both attractive and delicious. Serve these beef and sauerkraut rolls with creamed potatoes and red cabbage. If, at the end of the cooking time, *the sauce is too thin, stir in a little beurre manié.*

4 SERVINGS

1½ oz. [3 tablespoons] butter
6 bacon slices, diced
12 spring onions [scallions], finely chopped
2 lb. top rump [bottom round], cut into 8 slices and pounded until thin
1 tablespoon strong prepared mustard
½ teaspoon dried marjoram
4 oz. sauerkraut
1 tablespoon vegetable oil
15 fl. oz. [1⅞ cups] brown sauce
½ teaspoon salt
¼ teaspoon black pepper

In a small frying-pan, melt 1 tablespoon of the butter over moderate heat. When the foam subsides, add the bacon and the

spring onions [scallions] and fry them, stirring occasionally, for 5 to 7 minutes or until the onions are soft and translucent but not brown. Remove the pan from the heat and set aside.

Trim and cut the flattened steak slices into neat rectangles about 4- by 3-inches. Spread the meat slices with the mustard and sprinkle the cooked bacon and onion mixture and the marjoram over the top. Put a spoonful of the sauerkraut on each slice. Roll up the meat slices and tie them with string.

In a large, deep frying-pan, melt the remaining butter with the oil over moderate heat. When the foam subsides, add the meat rolls and fry them, turning them frequently, for about 5 minutes, or until they are browned all over.

With a slotted spoon, transfer the meat rolls to a plate and keep warm.

Pour the brown sauce into the frying-pan and, stirring occasionally, bring it to the boil. Return the meat rolls to the pan. Add the salt and pepper. When the mixture comes to the boil again, cover the pan, reduce the heat to low and simmer the meat rolls for 1 to 1½ hours or until they are tender.

Using a slotted spoon, transfer the meat rolls to a heated serving dish. Pour the sauce over the meat and serve immediately.

Nevada Rice Cake

An unusual fatless cake made with ground rice as well as flour, Nevada Rice Cake is layered with pineapple jam and rum-flavoured chocolate. The cake is turned upside-down to decorate it, as a perfectly smooth, flat surface is necessary.
ONE 9-INCH CAKE

1 teaspoon butter
8 oz. [2 cups] ground rice
10 oz. [1¼ cups] castor sugar
6 large eggs
¼ teaspoon almond essence
2 oz. [½ cup] flour
⅛ teaspoon salt
FILLING
6 oz. dark [semi-sweet] cooking chocolate, broken into pieces
2 tablespoons dark rum
4 tablespoons warmed pineapple jam
2 oz. icing sugar [½ cup confectioners' sugar]

A sustaining and easy-to-make dinner dish, Neustadt Rouladen is beef rolls stuffed with a highly spiced sauerkraut mixture.

Preheat the oven to warm 325°F (Gas Mark 3, 170°C). With the teaspoon of butter, grease a 9-inch round cake tin. Sprinkle 1 tablespoon of the ground rice into the tin. Tip and rotate the tin to coat it evenly with the rice, knocking out any excess. Set aside.

To make the cake, place the sugar, eggs and almond essence in a large heatproof mixing bowl. Place the bowl in a large saucepan half-filled with hot water and set the pan over low heat.

Beat the mixture with a wire whisk or rotary beater until it is pale and frothy and thick enough to hold a ribbon trail on itself when the whisk is lifted.

Remove the pan from the heat. Lift the bowl out of the pan. With a metal spoon, fold in the remaining ground rice, flour and the salt.

Spoon the batter into the prepared cake tin and smooth it down with the back of the spoon.

Place the tin in the centre of the oven and bake for 1½ to 1¾ hours, or until a skewer inserted into the centre of the cake comes out clean.

Remove the cake from the oven and let it cool in the tin for 30 minutes before turning it out on to a wire rack to cool completely.

While the cake is cooling, prepare the filling. In a small saucepan, melt the chocolate with the rum over low heat, stirring occasionally. When the chocolate has melted and the mixture is smooth, remove the pan from the heat and keep the mixture warm.

When the cake is completely cold, slice off and discard the domed top. Slice the cake across into three equal layers.

Place the top layer on a serving plate. Spoon half of the jam on to the cake and spread it evenly to the edges with a flat-bladed knife. Smooth over half of the warm chocolate mixture. Place the middle cake layer on top. Smooth over the remaining jam and then the remaining chocolate. Place the bottom layer on top, brown-side up.

Place a 9-inch round lace-patterned doily over the top of the cake. Sift the icing [confectioners'] sugar over the doily. Lift the doily off the cake, taking care not to let any sugar remaining on the doily spill over the pattern left on the cake.

Serve the cake immediately.

A melt-in-the-mouth cake made from ground rice, Nevada Rice Cake has a warm chocolate filling.

New England Boiled Dinner

A traditional American dish, New England Boiled Dinner has been cooked in the United States for well over 200 years. It should be served with horseradish sauce and small beetroots [beets]. The cooking time depends on the quality of the meat used. It can be as little as 2¼ hours or as long as 4 hours.

6-8 SERVINGS

4 lb. salt silverside or brisket of
  beef
6 black peppercorns
1 onion
  bouquet garni, consisting of 4
  parsley sprigs, 1 thyme spray
  and 1 bay leaf tied together
1 tablespoon brown sugar
8 carrots, scraped
8 medium-sized potatoes, peeled
  and quartered
6 small onions, peeled
1 small head of cabbage, coarse
  outer leaves removed and cut
  into wedges

Put the beef in a large saucepan and cover it completely with cold water. Bring the water to the boil slowly over moderate heat. As the scum rises to the surface, skim it off with a slotted spoon.

When the scum stops rising, add the peppercorns, onion, bouquet garni and sugar.

Half cover the pan, reduce the heat to low and simmer for 2 hours. Using a slotted spoon, remove and discard the onion and the bouquet garni.

Add the carrots, potatoes and small onions and simmer gently for 30 minutes. Add the cabbage wedges and simmer for a further 10 to 15 minutes, or until the vegetables and meat are tender when pierced with the point of a sharp knife.

Remove the pan from the heat. Using two large forks, transfer the meat to a carving board. With a slotted spoon remove the vegetables and put them in a heated serving dish. Serve immediately.

New England Meat Loaf

New England Meat Loaf is made from a mixture of beef, veal and pork. It is equally good hot or cold and should be served with a spicy tomato sauce.

6-8 SERVINGS

1 lb. minced [ground] lean beef
8 oz. minced [ground] lean veal
8 oz. minced [ground] lean pork
2 bay leaves
½ teaspoon dried thyme
½ teaspoon black pepper

1 teaspoon salt
2 tablespoons finely chopped
  fresh parsley
2 garlic cloves, crushed
5 fl. oz. [⅝ cup] dry red wine
1 teaspoon vegetable oil
2 celery stalks, trimmed and finely
  chopped
2 oz. [1 cup] fresh breadcrumbs
1 egg, lightly beaten
6 streaky bacon slices, rinds
  removed

In a large mixing bowl, combine the beef, veal, pork, bay leaves, thyme, pepper, salt, parsley, garlic and wine, mixing well to blend. Set the mixture aside at room temperature for 2 to 4 hours, stirring occasionally.

Preheat the oven to moderate 350°F (Gas Mark 4, 180°C). Using a pastry brush, grease a 2-pound loaf tin with the vegetable oil. Set aside.

Remove and discard the bay leaves from the meat mixture. Add the celery, breadcrumbs and egg, stirring well to mix.

Spoon the mixture into the prepared tin. Put the bacon on top of the mixture in a criss-cross pattern. Place the tin in a baking tin half-filled with water and place it in the oven. Bake for 1 to 1½ hours or until the meat loaf has shrunk away from the sides of the tin and a skewer inserted into the centre of the loaf comes out clean.

Remove the loaf from the oven and let it stand for a minute or two. Run a knife around the sides of the tin and turn the meat loaf out on to a serving dish.

Serve immediately or leave to cool before serving.

New England Soda Bread

An old American recipe, New England Soda Bread is easy to make and simply delicious. Serve this brown bread still warm with lashings of butter and cheese, accompanied by a cool glass of beer.

2 LOAVES

2 teaspoons vegetable oil
4 oz. stale crustless bread, soaked
  overnight in 12 fl. oz. [1½ cups]
  cold water
4 fl. oz. [½ cup] molasses
1 teaspoon salt
5 oz. [1 cup] corn meal
5 oz. [1¼ cups] rye flour
5 oz. [1¼ cups] coarse wholewheat
  flour
2 teaspoons bicarbonate of soda
  [baking soda]
4 fl. oz. [½ cup] cold water

Using a pastry brush, lightly oil two 1½-

pint, round, plain moulds or pudding basins with the vegetable oil. Set aside.

Using the back of a wooden spoon, rub the soaked bread through a fine wire strainer into a medium-sized mixing bowl. Add the molasses to the puréed bread, mixing them well together with a wooden spoon. Set aside.

In another medium-sized mixing bowl, combine the salt, corn meal, rye flour, wholewheat flour and soda.

Make a well in the centre of the dry ingredients. Pour in the water and add the bread and molasses mixture. Using a wooden spoon, stir the mixture until all the ingredients are well combined.

Divide the mixture between the two moulds or basins. Cover them very securely with greased aluminium foil, tied tightly with string under the rim of each basin.

Place a rack in the bottom of a large, deep saucepan which is wide enough to hold both the basins. Put the basins on the rack and pour in enough boiling water to come halfway up around the basins. Cover the saucepan and place it over low heat. Steam the bread for 3 to 3½ hours, adding more water when necessary.

Preheat the oven to cool 300°F (Gas Mark 2, 150°C).

Lift the basins out of the saucepan. Remove the foil covers and place the basins in the oven. Bake the bread for 15 minutes. This will remove any excess moisture from the bread. Remove the basins from the oven and turn the bread out on to a wire rack. Serve warm or cold.

New England Wedding Cake

An old American recipe for a very rich and moist wedding cake, New England Wedding Cake, as with most fruit cakes, improves with keeping. When storing the cake, before wrapping it in aluminium foil, pierce the top and bottom with a skewer and dribble 4 tablespoons of brandy over both surfaces.

ONE 12-INCH CAKE

2 lb. [5⅓ cups] currants
1 lb. [2⅔ cups] sultanas or raisins
1 lb. [2⅔ cups] glacé cherries
10 fl. oz. [1¼ cups] brandy
10 fl. oz. [1¼ cups] medium dry
  sherry
1 lb. [2 cups] plus 1 teaspoon
  butter
1 lb. [4 cups] flour
1 teaspoon ground cloves

Serve this fabulous New England Soda Bread warm with lots of butter and cheese.

1 teaspoon ground cinnamon
1 teaspoon grated nutmeg
1 lb. [2 cups] sugar
12 eggs, separated
4 oz. [⅔ cup] candied citron peel,
  very thinly sliced

In a large mixing bowl, combine the currants, sultanas or raisins and cherries with the brandy and sherry. Cover the bowl and set it aside to soak for 30 minutes, stirring occasionally.

With the teaspoon of the butter, lightly grease a 12-inch cake tin. Line the inside of the tin with a double layer of grease-proof or waxed paper. Cut out a strip of heavy brown paper 1-inch wider than the depth of the tin and long enough to fit round the tin twice. Tie the brown paper around the tin. Place a double thickness of brown paper or newspaper on a baking sheet wide enough to hold the cake tin. Set aside.

Preheat the oven to cool 300°F (Gas Mark 2, 150°C).

Sift the flour, cloves, cinnamon and nutmeg into a large mixing bowl. Set aside.

In another large mixing bowl, cream the remaining butter and the sugar together with a wooden spoon until the mixture becomes light and fluffy.

Add the egg yolks, one at a time, beating well between each addition. Add 1 tablespoon of the flour mixture with

each egg yolk. Using a metal spoon, fold in the remaining flour mixture. Stir in the reserved fruit with the brandy and sherry.

In another large mixing bowl, beat the egg whites with a wire whisk or rotary beater until they form stiff peaks.

With the metal spoon, gently fold the egg whites into the cake mixture. Cover the bottom of the cake tin with one-quarter of the cake mixture. Place one-third of the citron over the top in a layer. Continue making layers in the same way until all the cake mixture and citron have been used up, ending with a layer of the cake mixture.

Place the cake in the oven and bake for 1 hour. Reduce the oven temperature to very cool 275°F (Gas Mark 1, 140°C) and bake for another hour.

Check the cake and, if it is browning too much, place a piece of aluminium foil over the top. Cracks may have appeared in the top of the cake, but these will close up when the cake is cooled. Continue to bake for another 2 hours, or until a skewer inserted into the centre of the cake comes out clean.

Remove the cake from the oven and leave it to cool in the tin until it is completely cold. Remove the greaseproof or waxed paper from the bottom and sides of the cake.

Leave the cake on the rack for at least 6 hours before wrapping in aluminium foil and storing.

Serve New Haven Baked Aubergines [Eggplant] with salad for lunch.

New Haven Baked Aubergines [Eggplant]

A delicious first course particularly popular in the northeastern states of the United States, New Haven Baked Aubergines [Eggplant] is a tasty mixture of minced [ground] pork, mushrooms and sour cream. The recipe given below will serve four people as a first course or, served with a mixed salad and crusty bread, two people as a light lunch.

2-4 SERVINGS

2 medium-sized aubergines
  [eggplant]
2½ teaspoons salt
2 fl. oz. [¼ cup] olive oil
1 teaspoon vegetable oil
1½ oz. [3 tablespoons] butter
1 large onion, finely chopped
1 lb. mushrooms, wiped clean and
  sliced
6 oz. cooked pork, minced [ground]
3 fl. oz. [⅜ cup] sour cream
½ teaspoon black pepper
½ teaspoon ground allspice
1 oz. [½ cup] fresh breadcrumbs
1 oz. [¼ cup] Parmesan cheese,
  grated
½ teaspoon paprika

Cut the aubergines [eggplant] in half, lengthways. With a sharp knife, make cuts in the pulp to within ¼-inch of the skin. Sprinkle the aubergines [eggplant] with 2 teaspoons of the salt and set aside for 30 minutes to dégorge.

Squeeze the aubergines [eggplant] to remove as much liquid as possible and pat them dry with kitchen paper towels. Set aside.

In a large frying-pan, heat the olive oil over moderate heat. When the oil is hot, place the aubergine [eggplant] halves, cut sides down, in the pan and cook them for 7 to 8 minutes or until they are light brown. Turn the halves over and cook them for 8 to 10 minutes on the other sides. With a slotted spoon, remove the aubergine [eggplant] halves from the pan and set aside on kitchen paper towels to cool slightly.

Preheat the oven to fairly hot 375°F (Gas Mark 5, 190°C). With the teaspoon of vegetable oil, lightly grease a baking dish large enough to hold all of the aubergine [eggplant] halves in one layer. Set aside.

Wipe out the frying-pan with kitchen paper towels. Add 1 ounce [2 tablespoons] of the butter to the pan and melt it over moderate heat. When the foam subsides,

add the onion and cook, stirring occasionally, for 5 to 7 minutes or until it is soft and translucent but not brown. Add the mushrooms and cook, stirring occasionally, for 3 minutes.

Stir in the pork, sour cream, the remaining salt, the pepper and allspice and mix well. Cook the mixture, stirring occasionally, for a further 3 minutes. Remove the pan from the heat and set aside.

Using a spoon, scoop out the aubergine [eggplant] flesh, leaving the skins intact. Chop the flesh very finely and add it to the mixture in the frying-pan. Stir well to blend.

In a small bowl, combine the breadcrumbs and grated cheese, stirring well to mix. Set aside.

Spoon the pork and mushroom mixture into the aubergine [eggplant] skins and arrange the stuffed halves in the prepared baking dish. Sprinkle over the breadcrumb and cheese mixture. Cut the remaining butter into small pieces and dot them over the breadcrumb mixture. Place the dish in the oven and bake the aubergines [eggplant] for 10 to 15 minutes or until the top is golden brown.

Remove the dish from the oven. Sprinkle over the paprika and serve.

New Orleans Barbequed Pork Chops

New Orleans Barbequed Pork Chops is a good main dish to serve for an informal supper party. Accompany it with rice and sweetcorn.

6 SERVINGS

1 teaspoon butter
1 large onion, thinly sliced and pushed out into rings
6 loin pork chops, cut 1-inch thick
1½ teaspoons salt
1 teaspoon black pepper
BARBECUE SAUCE
2 fl. oz. [¼ cup] red wine vinegar
4 fl. oz. [½ cup] tomato ketchup
2 teaspoons sugar
½ teaspoon ground cloves
1 teaspoon celery seeds
½ teaspoon dry mustard
1 bay leaf

Preheat the oven to moderate 350°F (Gas Mark 4, 180°C). With the teaspoon of butter, lightly grease a shallow baking dish large enough to hold the pork chops in one layer. Arrange the onion rings in the dish.

Rub the pork chops all over with the salt and pepper and place them in the dish on top of the onion rings.

In a medium-sized mixing bowl, combine all of the sauce ingredients, mixing well to blend. Pour the sauce over the pork chops and place the dish in the oven. Bake the pork chops for 1 hour, or until they are tender when pierced with the point of a sharp knife.

Remove the dish from the oven and transfer the chops to a warmed serving dish. Remove and discard the bay leaf. Spoon over the sauce and serve at once.

New Orleans Lamb Cutlets

One of the nicest ways to serve lamb cutlets, New Orleans Lamb Cutlets are grilled [broiled] and served with risotto and grilled [broiled] bananas. A crisp green salad is the only accompaniment required.

4 SERVINGS

2 oz. [¼ cup] butter
1 onion, sliced
8 oz. [1⅓ cups] long-grain rice, washed, soaked in cold water for 30 minutes and drained

A succulent and spicy recipe from the American Deep South, New Orleans Barbequed Pork Chops is a delicious supper dish.

19 fl. oz. [2⅜ cups] boiling chicken
  stock
½ teaspoon salt
8 lamb cutlets
4 bananas, sliced lengthways

In a medium-sized saucepan, melt half
the butter over moderate heat. When the
foam subsides, add the onion and fry,
stirring occasionally, for 5 to 7 minutes
or until the onion is soft and translucent
but not brown. Add the rice, reduce the
heat to low and cook, stirring frequently,
for 5 minutes. Pour in the boiling stock
and add the salt. Cover the pan, reduce
the heat to low and simmer the rice for
20 minutes or until it is tender and all the
liquid has been absorbed.

Meanwhile, preheat the grill [broiler]
to high.

Grill [broil] the cutlets for 2 minutes
on each side. Add the bananas to the grill
[broiler] pan and grill [broil] the bananas
and cutlets for 2 to 3 minutes longer on
each side or until the bananas are brown
and the cutlets are tender. Remove the
grill [broiler] pan from the heat.

Remove the rice mixture from the heat
and stir in the remaining butter. Turn the
risotto out on to a warmed serving dish.
Place the lamb cutlets on top and garnish
with the bananas.

Serve immediately.

New Potatoes Cooked in Butter

*This is one of the most delicious ways to
cook tiny new potatoes. The potatoes should
be of uniform size and should not be peeled
but scrubbed well with a stiff brush to
ensure that they are perfectly clean.*

4 SERVINGS
2 oz. [¼ cup] butter
1 lb. small new potatoes, scrubbed
  and dried on kitchen paper towels
1 teaspoon salt
1 tablespoon finely chopped fresh
  parsley

In a medium-sized saucepan melt the
butter over moderate heat. When the foam

subsides add the potatoes. Cover the pan,
reduce the heat to low and shake the pan
well so that all the potatoes are covered
with the butter. Cook, shaking the pan
occasionally, for 25 to 30 minutes or until
the potatoes are tender.

Sprinkle with the salt and parsley.
Transfer the potatoes to a warmed serving
dish and serve immediately.

New Potatoes with Sour Cream and Caviar

*For this dish you will need rather large new
potatoes. They can either be served as an
accompaniment to a special dish or alone as
a separate course.*

4 SERVINGS
4 large new potatoes, scrubbed
1 teaspoon salt
½ teaspoon black pepper
5 fl. oz. [⅝ cup] sour cream
4 teaspoons black caviar
1 tablespoon finely chopped fresh
  parsley

Place the potatoes in a large saucepan. Cover with cold water and add the salt. Place the pan over moderately high heat and bring the water to the boil. Reduce the heat to low and cook the potatoes for 15 to 20 minutes, or until they are tender.

Using a slotted spoon, remove the potatoes from the pan and drain them on kitchen paper towels. Using a teaspoon, scoop out about one-quarter of each potato. Sprinkle the cavity with the pepper. Place one-quarter of the sour cream in each cavity and top with 1 teaspoon of the caviar.

Sprinkle with the parsley and serve at once.

New Zealand Kiwi Fruit

This is another name for CHINESE GOOSEBERRY.

Newcastle Potted Salmon

An old English recipe, Newcastle Potted Salmon is an excellent way to serve salmon. Other fish, such as trout and carp, may be potted in the same way and stored for several days in a cool dry place. Serve the potted salmon with toast and lemon wedges as a first course.

THREE 4-OUNCE POTS

1 lb. fresh salmon
1½ teaspoons salt
1½ teaspoons black pepper
½ teaspoon ground mace
¼ teaspoon ground cloves
5 oz. [⅝ cup] butter
4 peppercorns
2 bay leaves

Preheat the oven to moderate 350°F (Gas Mark 4, 180°C). Season the salmon well with half the salt and pepper and the mace and cloves. Place the fish in a small casserole and dot it with 1 ounce [2 tablespoons] of the butter, cut into small pieces. Sprinkle the peppercorns over the fish and lay the two bay leaves on top.

Place the casserole in the centre of the oven and bake for 30 to 40 minutes, or until the fish flakes easily when tested with a fork.

Remove the casserole from the oven. Remove the fish from the casserole and remove and discard the skin and bones. Strain the cooking liquid and reserve. Place the fish in a mortar with 2 ounces [¼ cup] of the remaining butter and pound it with a pestle. Add a little of the strained

Newcastle Potted Salmon makes an excellent first course.

cooking liquid to make the pounding easier. Alternatively, put the fish, butter and cooking liquid in an electric blender and blend until smooth. Mix in the remaining salt and pepper.

When the fish has been thoroughly pounded, pack it into three 4-ounce pots, leaving a ¼-inch space at the top. Set aside to cool.

In a small saucepan melt the remaining butter over low heat. Remove the pan from the heat and set aside to cool for 5 minutes.

Pour one-third of the melted butter into each pot. Cover the pots with aluminium foil and put them in the refrigerator to chill for at least 2 hours.

Remove the pots from the refrigerator and serve immediately.

Newington Snow

A light, refreshing dessert, Newington Snow is made from a mixture of sugar, water, lemon juice and egg whites. Serve with cream or fresh fruit.

4 SERVINGS

2 tablespoons cornflour [cornstarch] dissolved in the juice of 2 lemons
3 oz. [⅜ cup] sugar
grated rind of 1 lemon
8 fl. oz. [1 cup] water
3 egg whites

Low Cal

Rinse a 1-pint mould with cold water and set aside.

Place the cornflour [cornstarch] mixture, sugar and lemon rind in a large saucepan and pour over the water. Place the pan over moderate heat and bring the mixture to the boil, stirring constantly. Boil for 1 minute, without stirring. Remove the pan from the heat and set aside to allow the mixture to cool completely.

In a medium-sized mixing bowl, beat the egg whites with a wire whisk or rotary beater until they form stiff peaks.

Using a metal spoon, fold the egg whites into the lemon mixture. Spoon the mixture into the prepared mould and place the mould in the refrigerator. Chill the mixture for 4 hours or until it is set.

Remove the mould from the refrigerator and run a knife around the edge. Turn the dessert out on to a serving dish and serve at once.

Niçoise, à la

A la Niçoise (nee-swahz) is a garnish prepared from ingredients from the region around Nice. The garnish consists of tomatoes, garlic, capers, lemon juice

and olive oil. Anchovies are sometimes included, either whole or in the form of ANCHOVY BUTTER.

Nigerian Jollof Rice

Nigerian Jollof Rice is a festive dish often served at weddings in Nigeria. Serve it with a green salad or steamed broccoli with lots of chilled lager.

4 SERVINGS

2 tablespoons vegetable oil
1 large onion, finely chopped
1 green chilli, finely chopped
1 lb. lean stewing beef, cut into 1-inch cubes
1 bay leaf
14 oz. canned peeled tomatoes
2 teaspoons salt
½ teaspoon black pepper
1¼ pints [3⅛ cups] water
1 x 4 lb. chicken, boned, skinned and cut into 1-inch pieces
8 oz. [1⅓ cups] long-grain rice, washed, soaked in cold water for 30 minutes and drained
2 tablespoons chopped fresh parsley

In a large saucepan, heat the vegetable oil over moderate heat. When the oil is hot, add the onion and chilli and fry, stirring occasionally, for 5 to 7 minutes or until the onion is soft and translucent but not brown.

Add the beef cubes and cook, stirring occasionally, for 6 to 8 minutes or until they are browned all over.

Add the bay leaf, tomatoes with the can juice, 1 teaspoon of the salt, the pepper and 5 fluid ounces [⅝ cup] of the water. Cover the pan, reduce the heat to low and simmer for 45 minutes.

Add the chicken pieces and stir well to incorporate them with the other ingredients. Recover the pan and simmer, stirring occasionally, for a further 1 hour or until the chicken and beef are tender when pierced with the point of a sharp knife.

Meanwhile, put the rice in a large saucepan. Pour over the remaining water and add the remaining salt. Bring the water to the boil over high heat. Cover the pan, reduce the heat to very low and simmer for 15 minutes, or until the rice is tender and all the liquid has been absorbed.

Remove the pan from the heat. Stir the cooked rice into the beef and chicken mixture and remove the pan from the heat. Remove and discard the bay leaf.

Transfer the mixture to a warmed serving dish. Sprinkle with the parsley and serve immediately.

Nitzanei-kruv be'dvash

HONEYED BRUSSELS SPROUTS

A reputedly life-sustaining combination, Nitzanei-kruv be'dvash (nitz-an-ay kroov bed-vash) is Brussels sprouts cooked in honey, orange juice and spices. It is a delicious and unusual vegetable dish to serve with roast beef.

4 SERVINGS

1½ lb. Brussels sprouts, trimmed
2 fl. oz. [¼ cup] fresh orange juice
1 teaspoon salt
1 oz. [2 tablespoons] butter
¼ teaspoon mixed spice or ground allspice
¼ teaspoon ground ginger
2 fl. oz. [¼ cup] clear honey

With a sharp knife, cut a cross in the base of each sprout.

Put the orange juice, salt, butter, mixed spice or allspice, ginger and honey into a large saucepan and stir well.

Bring the mixture to the boil over moderate heat. Add the sprouts and stir well with a wooden spoon. Reduce the heat to low, cover the pan and simmer for 15 to 20 minutes or until the sprouts are tender.

Remove the pan from the heat. Transfer the sprouts and cooking liquid to a warmed serving dish and serve at once.

Nivernaise, à la

A la Nivernaise (ah lah nee-vair-nayz) is a French garnish. It consists of small glazed carrots, turnips and onions, plain boiled potatoes and braised lettuce.

Njursaute

SWEDISH SAUTEED KIDNEYS

Easy to make and absolutely delicious, Njursaute (new-ver-eh-saw-tay) is a simple but sophisticated first course.

4 SERVINGS

1 oz. [2 tablespoons] butter
1 small onion, finely chopped
8 oz. mushrooms, wiped clean and sliced
1 lb. calf's kidneys, thinly sliced
3 fl. oz. [⅜ cup] Madeira
4 slices buttered toast

In a large frying-pan, melt the butter over moderate heat. When the foam subsides, add the onion and mushrooms and fry, stirring occasionally, for 5 to 7 minutes or until the onion is soft and translucent but not brown. With a slotted spoon transfer the onion and mushrooms to a warm dish and keep hot.

Add the kidney slices to the fat in the pan and fry for 2 to 3 minutes on each side or until they are tender but still slightly pink inside.

Using a slotted spoon, transfer the kidney slices to the plate with the mushrooms and onion. Keep hot.

Add the Madeira to the pan, increase the heat to high and, stirring occasionally, boil rapidly for 2 minutes.

Return the kidneys, onion and mushrooms to the pan. Stir to mix. Cook for 2 to 3 minutes or until the mixture is heated through.

Place the slices of toast on warmed separate serving plates. Spoon the kidney mixture on to the toast slices and serve immediately.

Nkontomire Fro

STEWED SPINACH WITH FISH

A very popular West African dish, Nkontomire Fro (n'kon-tom-ear-ay froh) is ideal for a light supper or lunch. Serve it with crusty bread and butter.

4-6 SERVINGS

4 fl. oz. [½ cup] water
1½ teaspoons salt
2 lb. spinach, chopped
2 tablespoons vegetable oil
1 onion, finely chopped
1 garlic clove, crushed
4 large tomatoes, blanched, peeled and coarsely chopped
¼ teaspoon black pepper
¼ teaspoon cayenne pepper
2 cod fillets, cooked and flaked
4 oz. [⅔ cup] dried shrimps
6 oz. canned mackerel, drained and flaked
1 tablespoon paprika

(Low Cal)

In a large saucepan, bring the water and 1 teaspoon of the salt to the boil over high heat. Add the spinach, cover the pan and reduce the heat to low. Cook for 8 to 10 minutes or until the spinach is pulpy. Remove the pan from the heat and drain the spinach. Reserve 8 fluid ounces [1 cup] of the cooking liquid. Set aside.

In a large frying-pan, heat the oil over moderate heat. When the oil is hot, add the onion and garlic and fry, stirring occasionally, for 5 to 7 minutes or until the onion is soft and translucent but not brown. Add the tomatoes, the remaining salt, the pepper and cayenne and, stirring occasionally, cook for 5 minutes.

Stir in the cod, shrimps, mackerel and paprika. Pour over the reserved cooking liquid, reduce the heat to low and simmer for 15 minutes.

Add the spinach, cover the pan and simmer for a further 10 minutes, stirring occasionally.

Remove the pan from the heat and transfer the mixture to a warmed serving dish. Serve at once.

Noce de Vitello Farcito

VEAL STUFFED WITH MEAT

This is a wonderfully rich meat dish and is ideal for a dinner party. Serve Noce de Vitello Farcito (noh-chay dee vee-tell-oh fahr-see-toh) with steamed broccoli, petits pois and new potatoes. If you like, the cooking juices may be used as the base for a sauce. Pour off the fat from the tin, leaving behind the sediment. Add 1 or 2 tablespoons of flour and stir to make a smooth paste. Stir in a mixture of 6 fluid ounces [¾ cup] of water and 6 fluid ounces [¾ cup] of Marsala. Place the tin over moderate heat and, stirring constantly with a wooden spoon, bring the sauce to the boil. Add more liquid, if necessary, to make a coating sauce. Strain the sauce into a warmed sauceboat and serve.

6-8 SERVINGS

2 lb. large veal escalopes
juice of ½ lemon
3 fl. oz. [⅜ cup] olive oil
STUFFING
8 oz. chicken, boned, skinned and cut into strips
2 oz. calf's liver, cut into strips
2 oz. cooked tongue, cut into strips
3 oz. cooked ham, cut into strips
1 medium-sized cooking apple, peeled, cored and grated
4 fl. oz. [½ cup] Marsala
2 egg yolks
1 teaspoon salt
1 teaspoon black pepper
4 oz. French beans, trimmed, blanched and drained

First make the stuffing. In a medium-sized mixing bowl, combine the chicken, liver, tongue, ham and apple. Pour over the Marsala and set aside to soak for 15 minutes at room temperature.

Drain the meats and apple in a colander and return them to the bowl. Add the egg yolks and half the salt and pepper and beat the mixture with a wooden spoon until it is well combined. Set aside.

Preheat the oven to moderate 350°F (Gas Mark 4, 180°C).

Lay the escalopes out on a board, overlapping the edges of the escalopes slightly, to make a 12-inch square. Using a meat mallet or your clenched fist, beat the overlapping edges together to form a slight seal. Sprinkle over the remaining salt and

pepper and the lemon juice and rub the seasonings in with your fingertips.

Place one-third of the stuffing in the middle of the meat. Cover with half the French beans and cover these with another third of the stuffing. Place the remaining French beans on the stuffing and cover with the remaining stuffing.

Fold the top and bottom sides of the escalope square over the stuffing so that they just meet. Turn in the sides to make a neat parcel. Tie the meat with string in four or five places along its length and twice around its width.

Place the meat in a roasting tin. Pour over the oil and place the tin in the oven.

Roast the meat for 1 hour or until a skewer inserted into the centre passes easily through the stuffing.

Remove the tin from the oven. Remove the meat from the tin and place it on a heated serving dish. Remove and discard the string.

Serve immediately.

Noekkelost

Noekkelost (noh-kehl-uhst) is a Norwegian semi-hard, round cheese, made with whole or skimmed milk. It comes in four different grades: Herfet, Halvfet, Kvartfet and Mager. Helfet is the richest in cream and Mager has none. Noekkelost is very similar to the Dutch cheese,

Noce de Vitello Farcito makes a marvellous meal, accompanied by steamed broccoli.

Gouda, and is quite easily obtainable.

The name Noekkelost is derived from the Norwegian word for keys, *nokkel,* as the cheese used to be branded with crossed keys, the coat of arms of the city of Leyden in Norway.

Noggin

Once commonly used in England as a liquid measure, a noggin equals approximately 5 fluid ounces [$\frac{5}{8}$ cup].

The photograph on the preceding pages shows three classic French noisette recipes — from left to right, Noisettes d'Agneau à la Clamart, Noisettes d'Agneau Ismail Bayeldi and Noisettes d'Agneau Milanaise. Serve with red wine and lots of French bread for a delightful and elegant meal.

Noisettes

Noisettes (nwah-zet) are boned chops from the best end of neck of lamb or, less commonly, from loin of pork.

Most butchers will prepare noisettes for you, but you may prepare them yourself. Buy best end of neck of lamb containing as many cutlets as you need. Ask the butcher to chine the meat. Remove the chine bone and cut between each rib bone until the ribs can be easily removed.

The meat is now completely boneless. Roll it up, starting from the thick end and rolling towards the flap. Tie it securely with string at 1½-inch intervals. Cut the meat between each piece of string to make the noisettes.

Noisettes can be pan fried in butter or grilled [broiled]. Timing depends on the thickness of the noisettes and on how well-cooked you like your lamb.

As a general guide, if the noisettes are not too thick cook them for 4 to 6 minutes on each side. They should then be brown on the outside and still slightly pink inside.

Noisettes d'Agneau Arlésienne

BONED LAMB CHOPS WITH AUBERGINE [EGGPLANT] AND TOMATO SAUCE

A mouth-watering dish of lamb noisettes served with an aubergine [eggplant] and tomato sauce, Noisettes d'Agneau Arlésienne (nwah-zet dah-nyoh ahr-lay-zee-yen) may be accompanied by buttered new potatoes and French beans.

4 SERVINGS

3 tablespoons vegetable oil
1 large or 2 small aubergines [eggplants], sliced and dégorged
3 onions, sliced and pushed out into rings
1 garlic clove, crushed
1 lb. tomatoes, blanched, peeled and chopped or 14 oz. canned peeled tomatoes
1 teaspoon salt
½ teaspoon black pepper
1 bay leaf
1 oz. [2 tablespoons] butter
8 lamb noisettes
1 tablespoon chopped fresh parsley

In a medium-sized saucepan, heat 2 tablespoons of the oil over moderate heat. When the oil is hot, add the aubergine [eggplant] slices, one of the onions and the garlic and fry, stirring occasionally, for 5 to 7 minutes, or until the onion is soft and translucent but not brown.

Add the tomatoes and, if they are canned, the can juice, the salt, pepper and bay leaf, and simmer, stirring occasionally, for 30 minutes or until the mixture is thick. Remove and discard the bay leaf. Set aside and keep warm.

In a medium-sized frying-pan, heat the remaining oil over moderate heat. When the oil is hot, add the remaining onions and fry, stirring occasionally, for 5 to 7 minutes or until they are soft and translucent but not brown. Remove the pan from the heat and, using a slotted spoon, transfer the onion rings to a plate lined with kitchen paper towels. Set aside and keep hot.

Return the pan to the heat and add the butter. When the foam subsides, add the noisettes and fry them for 4 to 6 minutes on each side or until they are tender but still slightly pink inside.

With a slotted spoon remove the noisettes from the pan and arrange them on a warmed serving dish in a circle. Remove and discard the string. Pour the aubergine [eggplant] and tomato mixture into the centre of the circle. Top the noisettes with the onion rings. Sprinkle with the parsley.

Serve immediately.

Noisettes d'Agneau à la Clamart

BONED LAMB CHOPS IN PASTRY CASES WITH PUREED PEAS

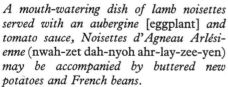

A classic French dish, Noisettes d'Agneau à la Clamart (nwah-zet dah-nyoh ah lah klah-mahr) is usually served with Noisette Potatoes. No other accompaniment is necessary.

4 SERVINGS

1½ oz. [3 tablespoons] plus 1 teaspoon butter
1 teaspoon salt
1 lb. fresh peas, weighed after shelling
8 lamb noisettes
PASTRY
4 oz. [1 cup] flour
⅛ teaspoon salt
1½ oz. [3 tablespoons] butter
1 tablespoon vegetable fat
1 to 2 tablespoons iced water

Preheat the oven to fairly hot 400°F (Gas Mark 6, 200°C).

Using the teaspoon of butter, lightly grease 8 patty tins and set aside.

To make the pastry, sift the flour and salt into a medium-sized mixing bowl. Add the butter and the vegetable fat and cut them into small pieces with a table knife. With your fingertips, rub the fats into the flour until the mixture resembles fine breadcrumbs.

Add 1 tablespoon of the iced water and, using the knife, mix it into the flour mixture. With your hands, mix and knead the dough until it is smooth. Add more water if the dough is too dry. Pat the dough into a ball, cover it with greaseproof or waxed paper and chill it in the refrigerator for 30 minutes.

On a lightly floured surface, roll out the dough to a circle about ¼-inch thick. Using a 3-inch pastry cutter, cut the dough into circles and line the prepared patty tins with them. Place a circle of aluminium foil or greaseproof or waxed paper inside each dough case. Half fill each one with dried beans or rice and place the patty tins in the oven. Bake blind for 10 minutes. Remove the foil or paper and beans or rice and continue baking for 5 minutes or until the pastry is golden brown.

Remove the patty tins from the oven and allow the tartlets to cool slightly in their tins. Turn off the oven. Cover the tartlets lightly with aluminium foil to prevent them from drying out and return them to the oven to keep warm.

Meanwhile, half fill a medium-sized saucepan with cold water. Add the salt, cover the pan and bring the water to the boil over high heat. Add the peas and when the water comes to the boil again reduce the heat to low. Cook the peas, uncovered, for 15 to 20 minutes or until they are tender.

Remove the pan from the heat and drain the peas in a colander. Using the back of a wooden spoon push the peas through a strainer back into the saucepan, or purée them in a food mill or electric blender. Add 1 tablespoon of the remaining butter and place the pan over low heat. Cook, stirring constantly, for 5 minutes or until the butter has been absorbed and the pea purée is hot and smooth. Remove the pan from the heat.

Remove the pastry cases from the oven and spoon equal portions of the pea purée into each one. Return the pastry cases to the oven to keep warm while you fry the noisettes.

In a large frying-pan, melt the remaining butter over moderate heat. When the foam subsides, add the noisettes and fry them for 4 to 6 minutes on each side or until they are tender but still slightly pink inside.

Remove the pan from the heat. Using a slotted spoon, remove the noisettes from the pan and place them on top of the pea-filled pastry tartlets. Remove the string. Serve immediately.

Noisettes d'Agneau Ismail Bayeldi

BONED LAMB CHOPS WITH VEGETABLES AND RICE

A beautiful dish perfect for a dinner party, Noisettes d'Agneau Ismail Bayeldi (nwah-zet dah-nyoh ish-myle bah'ell-dee) *was adapted by the French from Middle East cuisine. The dish needs no accompaniment other than a good rosé or red wine.*

4 SERVINGS

sufficient vegetable oil for deep-frying
2 large aubergines [eggplants], **sliced and dégorged**
juice of ½ lemon
8 lamb noisettes
2 garlic cloves, halved
½ teaspoon black pepper
2 oz. [¼ cup] butter
4 medium-sized tomatoes, quartered

RICE
2 oz. [¼ cup] butter
2 medium-sized onions, finely chopped
1 green pepper, white pith removed, seeded and chopped
1 red pepper, white pith removed, seeded and chopped
8 oz. [1⅓ cups] long-grain rice, washed, soaked in cold water for 30 minutes and drained
1 teaspoon salt
½ teaspoon black pepper
¼ teaspoon cayenne pepper
¼ teaspoon crushed saffron threads, soaked in 2 tablespoons hot water
1 tablespoon lemon juice
18 fl. oz. [2¼ cups] hot chicken stock

Preheat the oven to moderate 350°F (Gas Mark 4, 180°C).

First, prepare the rice. In a medium-sized flameproof casserole, melt the butter over moderate heat. When the foam subsides, add the onions and peppers and cook, stirring occasionally, for 8 to 10 minutes, or until the onions are golden brown.

Stir in the rice and cook, stirring constantly, for 5 minutes. Add the salt, pepper, cayenne, the saffron mixture, lemon juice and chicken stock. Stir well and bring the liquid to the boil, stirring constantly.

Cover the casserole, remove it from the heat and place it in the centre of the oven. Bake the rice for 25 to 30 minutes, or until it is tender and has absorbed all the liquid.

Meanwhile, fill a deep-frying pan one-third full with oil and place it over moderate heat. Heat the oil until it registers 375°F on a deep-frying thermometer, or until a small cube of stale bread dropped into the oil turns golden in 40 seconds.

Add a few of the aubergine [eggplant] slices and fry them for 2 to 3 minutes or until they are crisp and lightly browned. With a slotted spoon, remove the slices from the pan and drain them on kitchen paper towels. Transfer the slices to a warmed plate, sprinkle with a little of the lemon juice and keep hot while you fry the remaining aubergine [eggplant] slices in the same way.

Set aside and keep hot.

Rub the lamb all over with the garlic. Discard the garlic and rub the salt and pepper over the meat.

In a large frying-pan, melt the butter over moderate heat. When the foam subsides, add the lamb noisettes and fry them for 4 to 6 minutes on each side, or until they are tender but still slightly pink inside.

With a slotted spoon, remove the noisettes from the pan. Remove and discard the string from each noisette and keep them hot.

Add the tomato quarters to the pan and fry them, turning frequently with a slotted spoon, for 3 minutes or until they are heated through but still firm.

Remove the pan from the heat and set aside. Keep warm.

Remove the casserole from the oven and spoon the rice mixture into a large, shallow warmed serving dish. Arrange the lamb noisettes in a row on top of the rice mixture. Surround with the fried aubergine [eggplant] slices, garnish with the tomato quarters and serve immediately.

Noisettes d'Agneau Milanaise

BONED LAMB CHOPS WITH SPAGHETTI AND TOMATO SAUCE

One of the best and most interesting ways of preparing lamb noisettes, Noisettes d'Agneau Milanaise (nwah-zet dah-nyoh meel-ah-nays) *should be served with grated Parmesan cheese and accompanied by a crisp green salad.*

4 SERVINGS

2 tablespoons olive oil
1 onion, finely chopped
1 garlic clove, crushed
14 oz. canned peeled tomatoes
2 tablespoons tomato purée
1 bay leaf
2 teaspoons salt
½ teaspoon black pepper
½ teaspoon dried oregano
1 tablespoon chopped fresh basil or ½ teaspoon dried basil
4 oz. [½ cup] butter
2 oz. mushrooms, wiped clean and sliced
2 oz. lean cooked ham, cut into julienne strips
3 pints [7½ cups] water
8 oz. spaghetti
8 lamb noisettes
2 tablespoons chopped fresh parsley

In a medium-sized saucepan, heat the oil over moderate heat. When the oil is hot, add the onion and garlic and fry, stirring occasionally, for 5 to 7 minutes or until the onion is soft and translucent but not brown.

Stir in the tomatoes and the can juice, the tomato purée, bay leaf, 1 teaspoon of the salt, the pepper, oregano and basil and simmer, stirring occasionally, for 20 minutes, adding a little cold water if the sauce becomes too thick.

Meanwhile, in a large frying-pan melt 1 ounce [2 tablespoons] of the butter over moderate heat. When the foam subsides, add the mushrooms and fry, stirring occasionally, for 3 minutes. Add the ham and cook for a further 3 minutes. Remove the pan from the heat and, using a slotted spoon, transfer the mushrooms and ham to the tomato sauce. Set the frying-pan aside without rinsing. It will be used to cook the noisettes.

In a large saucepan, bring the water to the boil over high heat. Add the remaining salt and the spaghetti. Reduce the heat to moderate and cook for 10 to 12 minutes or until the spaghetti is 'al dente' or just tender.

Remove the pan from the heat and drain the spaghetti in a colander. Return the spaghetti to the pan and stir in 1 ounce [2 tablespoons] of the butter. Set aside and keep warm.

Add the remaining butter to the frying-pan and return the pan to moderate heat. When the foam subsides, add the noisettes and fry them for 4 to 6 minutes on each side or until they are tender but still slightly pink inside. Remove the pan from the heat and, using a slotted spoon, transfer the noisettes to a warmed serving dish, arranging them in a large circle. Remove and discard the string.

Place the spaghetti in the centre of the circle and spoon over the tomato sauce. Sprinkle with the parsley and serve immediately.

Noisettes d'Agneau Monegasque

BONED LAMB CHOPS WITH MUSHROOMS AND TOMATO SAUCE

A simple but tasty dish, Noisettes d'Agneau Monegasque (nwah-zet dah-nyoh mon-ay-gahsk) may be served with Duchess Potatoes and a crisp green salad.

4 SERVINGS

2 tablespoons olive oil
1 onion, finely chopped
1 garlic clove, crushed
1 lb. tomatoes, blanched, peeled and chopped or 14 oz. canned peeled tomatoes
2 teaspoons chopped fresh basil or ½ teaspoon dried basil
1 bay leaf
½ teaspoon salt
½ teaspoon black pepper
2 tablespoons tomato purée
8 circles of warm toasted bread, 3-inches in diameter
2 oz. [¼ cup] butter
8 large mushroom caps, wiped clean
8 lamb noisettes
4 fl. oz. [½ cup] dry white wine

In a large saucepan, heat the oil over moderate heat. When it is hot, add the onion and garlic. Fry, stirring occasionally, for 5 to 7 minutes or until the onion is soft and translucent but not brown.

Add the tomatoes and, if they are canned, the can juice, the basil, bay leaf, salt, pepper and tomato purée. Reduce the heat to low and simmer, stirring occasionally, for 30 minutes, adding a little water if the tomato sauce becomes too thick.

Meanwhile, arrange the slices of toast on a serving dish and keep warm.

In a large frying-pan, melt the butter over moderate heat. When the foam subsides, add the mushrooms and fry them, stirring occasionally, for 3 to 4 minutes or until they are tender. Using a slotted spoon, transfer the mushrooms to a plate lined with kitchen paper towels. Set aside and keep warm.

Add the noisettes to the pan and fry them for 4 to 6 minutes on each side, or until they are tender but still slightly pink inside. Using tongs, remove the noisettes from the pan and place them on top of the toast slices. Remove and discard the string. Top each noisette with a mushroom. Keep warm.

Add the wine to the pan and stir well, scraping the brown bits from the bottom of the pan with a wooden spoon. Increase the heat to high and boil the wine until it has reduced by half. Stir in the tomato sauce, reduce the heat to moderate and cook for a further 5 minutes, stirring occasionally. Remove and discard the bay leaf.

Remove the pan from the heat and pour the sauce into a warmed sauceboat.

Serve the noisettes immediately, with the sauce.

Noisettes d'Agneau au Sauce Champignon

BONED LAMB CHOPS WITH MUSHROOM SAUCE

These are tender succulent noisettes of lamb, still slightly pink on the inside, served with a sauce of mushrooms and marjoram. Serve Noisettes d'Agneau au Sauce Champignon (nwah-zet dah-nyoh oh sohs sham-peen-yon) with sautéed potatoes and steamed, buttered broccoli.

4 SERVINGS

1½ oz. [3 tablespoons] butter
8 oz. mushrooms, wiped clean and sliced
8 lamb noisettes
2 shallots, finely chopped
3 fl. oz. [⅜ cup] dry white wine
½ teaspoon dried marjoram
10 fl. oz. [1¼ cups] brown sauce
½ teaspoon salt
½ teaspoon black pepper

A simple classic, Noisettes d'Agneau Monegasque is excellent with salad and Duchess Potatoes.

A blend of prunes, potatoes and pork, Noisettes de Porc aux Pruneaux is a warming supper dish.

In a large frying-pan, melt 1 ounce [2 tablespoons] of the butter over moderate heat. When the foam subsides, add the mushrooms and cook them, stirring occasionally, for 3 to 4 minutes or until they are soft. Using a slotted spoon, transfer the mushrooms to a dish and keep warm.

Add the noisettes to the pan and fry them for 4 to 6 minutes on each side, or until the lamb is tender but still slightly pink inside.

With a slotted spoon, transfer the noisettes to a warmed serving dish. Remove the string and keep hot.

Add the shallots to the butter in the pan and fry, stirring occasionally, for 3 to 5 minutes, or until they are soft and translucent but not brown. Increase the heat to moderately high. Add the wine and marjoram and bring the mixture to the boil. Boil until the wine has almost evaporated. Reduce the heat to moderate and add the brown sauce, salt, pepper and mushrooms. Cook, stirring occasionally, for 5 to 8 minutes or until the sauce is hot. Taste the sauce and add more salt and pepper if necessary.

Remove the pan from the heat and stir in the remaining butter, a little at a time. Transfer the sauce to a warmed sauceboat and serve immediately, with the noisettes.

Noisettes de Porc aux Pruneaux

BONED PORK CHOPS WITH PRUNES AND CREAM

Noisettes of pork are thick pieces of loin of pork, boned and tied with string. They are one of the most tender and tasty cuts of pork. Serve Noisettes de Porc aux Pruneaux (nwah-zet d'pohr oh proo-noh) with buttered beans.

4 SERVINGS

6 oz. dried prunes, soaked overnight in 10 fl. oz. [1¼ cups] dry white wine
4 pork noisettes
2 tablespoons seasoned flour, made with 2 tablespoons flour, ½ teaspoon salt and ½ teaspoon black pepper
1 oz. [2 tablespoons] butter
1 lb. Duchess Potatoes, kept warm
1 teaspoon redcurrant jelly
5 fl. oz. single cream [⅝ cup light cream]
½ teaspoon salt
½ teaspoon black pepper

In a medium-sized saucepan bring the prunes and wine to the boil over moderate heat. Cover the pan, reduce the heat to low and simmer for 30 minutes or until the prunes are tender.

Remove the pan from the heat. Using a slotted spoon, transfer the prunes to a dish. Slit open the prunes and remove the stones. Set the prunes aside and keep warm. Reserve the wine.

Preheat the oven to very cool 275°F (Gas Mark 1, 140°C).

Coat the noisettes with the seasoned flour, shaking off any excess.

In a large frying-pan, melt the butter over moderate heat. When the foam subsides, add the noisettes and cook them for 10 minutes on each side or until they are tender and thoroughly cooked.

Meanwhile, fill a large forcing bag, fitted with a ½-inch star nozzle, with the Duchess Potatoes. Pipe four circles of the potatoes, about the size of the noisettes, on to a warmed serving dish. Fill in the centres with more potato.

With a slotted spoon, remove the noisettes from the pan and place them on top of the potato 'nests'. Remove and discard the string from the noisettes. Arrange the prunes around the noisettes. Cover the dish with aluminium foil and place it in the oven.

Pour off all the fat from the frying-pan. Add the reserved wine and bring it to the boil over high heat, scraping up the brown bits from the bottom of the pan with a wooden spoon. Boil for 3 to 4 minutes or until the wine has reduced by half.

Reduce the heat to low. Add the jelly, cream, salt and pepper and cook, stirring occasionally, for 3 minutes or until the sauce has thickened slightly. Remove the pan from the heat.

Remove the serving dish from the oven. Pour a little of the sauce over the noisettes. Pour the remaining sauce into a warmed sauceboat and serve immediately.

Noisette Potatoes

Noisette (nwah-zet) Potatoes are peeled potatoes which are cut with a small ball scoop to the size of hazelnuts (hence the name). The potatoes are quickly cooked in butter until they are tender and lightly browned. They may be served as a garnish or vegetable accompaniment to meat or fish dishes.

Noix de Veau aux Fruits

TOPSIDE OF VEAL WITH FRUIT

A delicate dish of veal and fruit, Noix de Veau aux Fruits (nwah d' voh oh froo-wee) is attractive and simply delicious. Serve this dish with creamed potatoes and broccoli.

6 SERVINGS

3 lb. noix de veau (trimmed topside [top round] of veal)
1 teaspoon salt
½ teaspoon black pepper
1 tablespoon chopped fresh chives
½ tablespoon chopped fresh sage
1 oz. [2 tablespoons] butter
4 oz. streaky bacon, diced
4 tablespoons Cognac
6 fl. oz. [¾ cup] chicken stock
2 medium-sized apples, cored and thinly sliced
2 medium-sized oranges, thinly sliced
8 oz. grapes, peeled and seeded
4 fl. oz. [½ cup] dry white wine
1 tablespoon beurre manié

Preheat the oven to moderate 350°F (Gas Mark 4, 180°C).

Rub the veal all over with the salt, pepper, chives and sage. Set aside.

In a large flameproof casserole, melt the butter over moderate heat. When the foam subsides, add the bacon and fry, stirring frequently, for 5 minutes, or until the bacon is crisp and has rendered most of its fat.

With a slotted spoon transfer the bacon to a plate and keep warm.

Place the veal in the casserole and cook, turning frequently, for 6 to 8 minutes, or until the meat is brown all over.

Pour in the Cognac and the chicken stock and bring to the boil. Add the diced bacon, cover the casserole and transfer it to the centre of the oven. Braise for 1 hour.

Remove the casserole from the oven and add the apples, oranges and grapes. Return the casserole to the oven and

braise for a further 30 minutes, or until the veal is cooked and the apples are tender. Remove the casserole from the oven.

Using two large forks, transfer the veal to a warmed serving dish. With a slotted spoon, transfer the bacon and fruit to the dish. Set aside and keep hot while you prepare the sauce.

Place the casserole over high heat and add the wine. Bring the contents of the casserole to the boil and boil for 3 to 5 minutes or until the liquid has reduced by about one-third. Stir in the beurre manié a little at a time. Cook the sauce, stirring constantly, for a further 3 minutes, or until it is smooth and thick.

Remove the pan from the heat and strain the sauce into a warmed sauceboat. Serve immediately.

Nonpareille

Nonpareille (nohn-pahr-aye) is a French word which literally means unequalled or peerless.

It is the name of a large pear which grows in France, as well as the name of small capers pickled in vinegar and the tiny, multi-coloured grains of sugar known as 'hundreds and thousands' in Britain.

Noodles

Noodles are a type of pasta which were introduced into Italy by the explorer Marco Polo after he had visited China in the thirteenth century. They are now widely eaten all over Europe and America, and can be made at home or bought.

Noodles are made with flour, water and eggs, and come in a variety of shapes and sizes, fresh or dried. Fresh noodles should be cooked as soon as possible after they have been made. Dried noodles, usually bought ready packed, may be stored in a cool, dry place for several months.

To cook 1 pound of fresh or dried noodles, bring 6 pints [7½ pints] of salted water to the boil in a large saucepan over high heat. Add the noodles and, stirring once or twice with a fork, cook them for 6 to 8 minutes, or until they are 'al dente', or just tender. Remove the pan from the heat and drain the noodles in a colander.

Chinese noodles differ in that they are made with a mixture of wheat flour and rice flour, and shaped into long strips, some as thick as spaghetti and some extremely thin. Chinese noodles may be partially cooked and deep-fried until crisp, or cooked, drained and lightly fried with vegetables or meat.

Cooked noodles may be served plain or buttered and seasoned as an accompaniment to meat or fish dishes, or cooked with cheese, sauces, vegetables or meat and served as a complete meal.

Noodles with Brown Butter

This is a simple dish which may be served with grated Parmesan cheese and a green salad, or as an accompaniment to a veal casserole.

6 SERVINGS

3 oz. [⅜ cup] butter
1 teaspoon white wine vinegar
1 lb. noodles, cooked and drained
2 tablespoons dry brown breadcrumbs

In a small saucepan, melt the butter over moderate heat. Allow the butter to bubble and become golden brown in colour. Stir in the vinegar and cook the butter for a further 20 seconds. Remove the pan from the heat.

Preheat the grill [broiler] to high.

Put the noodles in a large, shallow, flameproof serving dish. Pour the butter over the noodles and, using two forks, toss the noodles until they are all coated with the butter. Sprinkle the breadcrumbs over the top. Place the dish under the grill [broiler] for 3 to 4 minutes or until the noodles are very hot and the breadcrumbs are crisp.

Remove the dish from under the grill [broiler] and serve immediately.

Noodles with Ham

A quick supper dish, Noodles with Ham may be sprinkled with grated Parmesan cheese just before serving. Serve the noodles with a dish of creamed or chopped spinach.

4-6 SERVINGS

1 lb. noodles, cooked, drained and kept warm
2 oz. [¼ cup] butter, cut into small pieces
½ teaspoon salt
½ teaspoon black pepper
1 teaspoon dried basil
2 oz. proscuitto, cut into thin strips
6 oz. cooked lean ham, cut into thin strips
1 small garlic sausage, cut into thin strips
2 large tomatoes, blanched, peeled, seeded and cut into strips

Easy and quick to make, Noodles with Ham is a colourful and tasty supper dish.

In a large saucepan, heat the noodles and butter over very low heat. When the butter has melted, using two forks, toss the noodles until they are coated with the butter. Add the salt, pepper, basil, proscuitto, ham, sausage and tomatoes. Increase the heat to moderate and cook the noodle mixture, stirring frequently with a wooden spoon, for 6 to 8 minutes or until it is very hot.

Remove the pan from the heat. Transfer the noodle mixture to a heated serving dish and serve immediately.

Noodles with Mushrooms

This dish is easy to prepare and is very good served with a veal casserole.

6 SERVINGS

1 lb. noodles, cooked and drained
2 oz. [¼ cup] butter, melted
4 oz. mushrooms, wiped clean and chopped
¼ teaspoon dried basil
¼ teaspoon dried marjoram
½ teaspoon freshly ground black pepper

Preheat the oven to warm 325°F (Gas Mark 3, 170°C).

Place the noodles in a deep ovenproof serving dish and pour over the butter. Sprinkle the mushrooms, basil, marjoram and pepper over the noodles and, using two forks, toss the noodles until they are coated with the butter and the mushrooms are evenly distributed. Cover the dish with aluminium foil and place it in the oven. Bake the noodles for 20 minutes.

Remove the dish from the oven and serve immediately.

Noodle Pudding with Apples

A delightful, but filling, pudding, Noodle Pudding with Apples may be served with Crème à la Vanille.

4-6 SERVINGS

2 eggs, lightly beaten with 2 tablespoons milk
2 tablespoons sugar
¼ teaspoon salt
¼ teaspoon ground cinnamon
¼ teaspoon ground mixed spice or allspice

A marvellously filling pudding for winter, Noodle Pudding with Apples is a delightful mixture of fruits, spices and noodles.

2 large cooking apples, peeled, cored and grated
2 oz. [⅓ cup] raisins
12 oz. fine noodles, cooked and drained
1 oz. [2 tablespoons] butter, melted

Preheat the oven to moderate 350°F (Gas Mark 4, 180°C).

In a large mixing bowl, combine the egg mixture, sugar, salt, cinnamon, mixed spice or allspice, apples, raisins and noodles. With a wooden spoon, stir the noodle mixture until the ingredients are well mixed.

Spoon the noodle mixture into a deep ovenproof dish and pour over the melted butter.

Place the dish in the oven and bake for 45 minutes or until the pudding is firm to the touch and lightly browned on top.

Remove the dish from the oven and serve the pudding immediately.

Norfolk Dumplings

These dumplings are a filling accompaniment to a beef stew, especially if seasoned and flavoured with a teaspoon of herbs. Norfolk Dumplings may also be left plain, and served with jam, honey sauce or brown sugar and melted butter.

If they are to be served with a stew they should be cooked in stock in a saucepan with a tight-fitting lid. Sweet dumplings may be boiled in water or they may be steamed, but either way the lid of the pan must be tight-fitting and should not be removed before the cooking time is completed.

6-8 SERVINGS

½ oz. fresh yeast
½ teaspoon sugar
7 fl. oz. [⅞ cup] lukewarm water
12 oz. [3 cups] flour
1 teaspoon salt

Crumble the yeast into a small mixing bowl and mash in the sugar with a kitchen fork. Add 1 tablespoon of the water and cream the water and yeast together to form a smooth paste. Set the bowl aside in a warm, draught-free place for 15 to 20 minutes, or until the yeast mixture has risen and is puffed up and frothy.

Sift the flour and the salt into a warmed, large mixing bowl. Make a well in the centre and pour in the yeast mixture and the remaining water. Using your fingers or a spatula gradually draw the flour into the water and yeast mixture. Continue mixing until all the flour is incorporated and the dough comes away from the sides of the bowl.

Turn the dough out on to a floured board or marble slab and knead it for about 8 minutes, reflouring the surface if the dough becomes sticky. The dough should be elastic and smooth.

Rinse, thoroughly dry and lightly grease the large mixing bowl. Shape the dough into a ball and return it to the bowl. Dust the top of the dough with a little flour and cover the bowl with a clean, damp cloth. Set the bowl in a warm, draught-free place and leave it for 1 to 1½ hours, or until the dough has risen and almost doubled in bulk.

Turn the risen dough out of the bowl on to a floured surface and knead for 4 minutes. Break off small pieces of dough and roll them into 1-inch balls between the palms of your hands. Set the dough balls aside and keep warm.

Half fill a large saucepan with hot water and place it over high heat. Place the dough balls in a steamer, making sure they do not touch each other. If the dough balls will not fit in one layer, cut out a circle of greaseproof or waxed paper slightly smaller than the circumference of the steamer, grease it on both sides with a little vegetable oil and use it to divide the dough balls. Cover the steamer. If the lid does not fit tightly, place a strip of aluminium foil around the edge of the steamer so that it does.

Place the steamer over the saucepan of hot water. When the water boils reduce the heat to moderate so that the water simmers.

Steam the dumplings for 15 to 20 minutes. Remove the lid from the steamer, take out one dumpling and break it. The dumpling should be light and open-textured. If the dumpling is slightly under-cooked in the centre, cover the steamer again and steam for a further 4 minutes.

Remove the steamer from the heat. Transfer the dumplings to a warmed serving dish and serve immediately.

Norfolk Fruit Chutney

Made with fresh apricots, peaches and apples, Norfolk Fruit Chutney is delicious served with cold meat or cheese. You may, if you like, crack open the apricot stones, remove and peel the kernels and add them to the chutney with the sugar. Store the chutney for at least 6 weeks before serving.

Norfolk Fruit Chutney, made with fresh fruit, is delicious with cheese or cold meat.

ABOUT 8 POUNDS

2 lb. apricots, halved, stoned and chopped
2 lb. tart cooking apples, peeled, cored and chopped
4 medium-sized peaches, peeled, halved, stoned and chopped
2 medium-sized onions, finely chopped
8 oz. [1⅓ cups] raisins
2-inch piece fresh root ginger, peeled and finely diced
¾ teaspoon grated nutmeg
¾ teaspoon ground allspice
¾ teaspoon dry mustard
finely grated rind of 1 large lemon
juice and finely grated rind of 2 oranges
1¼ pints [3⅛ cups] white wine vinegar
1 lb. [2 cups] sugar
1 lb. [2⅔ cups] soft brown sugar

In a very large saucepan, or preserving pan, combine the apricots, apples, peaches, onions, raisins, ginger, nutmeg, allspice, mustard, lemon rind, orange juice and rind and 1 pint [2½ cups] of the vinegar.

Place the pan over moderately high

heat and bring the mixture to the boil, stirring constantly. Reduce the heat to low and simmer, stirring occasionally, for 1 to 1½ hours or until the fruit mixture is very soft and pulpy.

Stir in the sugars and the remaining vinegar and simmer, stirring occasionally, for 40 to 50 minutes, or until the chutney is very thick.

Remove the pan from the heat. Ladle the chutney into clean, warm dry jars. Wipe the jars clean with a damp cloth and seal them with their vacuum-sealed lids.

Label the jars and store them in a cool, dry, dark place for 6 weeks before serving.

Norma's Breakfast Breads

Small, easy to make little breads, Norma's Breakfast Breads are delicious served with butter and jam for breakfast, or with salad meals.

6 BREADS

½ oz. fresh yeast
¼ teaspoon sugar
2 tablespoons lukewarm water
12 oz. [3 cups] strong white flour
¼ teaspoon bicarbonate of soda [baking soda]
1 teaspoon salt
1 oz. [2 tablespoons] ghee or clarified butter
6 fl. oz. [¾ cup] lukewarm milk
1 large egg, well beaten
2 teaspoons vegetable oil
1 egg yolk, well beaten with 2 tablespoons milk
2 tablespoons sesame seeds (optional)

Crumble the yeast into a small mixing bowl and mash in the sugar with a kitchen fork. Add the water and cream the yeast and water together to make a smooth paste. Set the bowl aside in a warm, draught-free place for 15 to 20 minutes, or until the yeast mixture is puffed up and frothy.

Sift the flour, soda and salt into a large mixing bowl. Add the ghee or clarified butter and rub it into the flour with your fingertips until the mixture resembles fine breadcrumbs.

Make a well in the centre of the flour mixture and pour in the lukewarm milk, the egg and the yeast mixture. Using a spatula or your fingers, mix the liquids together, gradually drawing in the flour mixture. When all the flour mixture has been incorporated and the dough comes away from the sides of the bowl, turn the dough out on to a lightly floured board or marble slab.

With your hands, knead the dough for 10 minutes, or until it is smooth and elastic, adding a little more flour if the dough is too sticky.

Rinse, thoroughly dry and lightly grease the mixing bowl. Shape the dough into a ball and place it in the bowl. Cover the bowl with a clean, damp cloth and set it aside in a warm, draught-free place for 1½ to 2 hours, or until the dough has risen and almost doubled in bulk.

Preheat the oven to very hot 450°F (Gas Mark 8, 230°C).

Using the teaspoons of vegetable oil grease two large baking sheets and set them aside.

Turn the risen dough out of the bowl on to a lightly floured board and knead it for 5 minutes. Divide the dough into 6 equal pieces and shape the pieces into balls. Arrange the balls on the floured board and cover with a clean, damp cloth. Set aside in a warm, draught-free place for 20 to 25 minutes, or until the dough has risen and almost doubled in bulk.

With the heel of your hand, flatten and spread each ball into an oval shape approximately ¼-inch thick. Transfer the ovals to the prepared baking sheets.

With a pastry brush, coat the top of the dough ovals with the egg yolk and milk mixture. Sprinkle over the sesame seeds if you are using them.

Place the baking sheets in the centre of the oven and bake the breads for 10 to 15 minutes, or until they have risen slightly and are cooked and golden brown.

Remove the baking sheets from the oven. Let the breads cool on the baking sheets for 10 minutes. Remove them from the baking sheets and serve hot, or transfer them to a wire rack to cool completely before serving.

Normande, à la

A la Normande (ah lah nawr-mahnd) is a French culinary name for a garnish and for a sauce for fish. The fish is poached in white wine and garnished with oysters, mussels, mushrooms, crayfish, truffles and croûtons. The sauce is a VELOUTE made with a concentrated fish stock (FUMET), mushroom essence, oyster liquor, egg yolks and cream.

A la Normande may also describe dishes of meat and poultry which have been cooked in cider or with apples and served with a sauce flavoured with CALVADOS.

Normandy Cheese Spread

A rich, creamy mixture, Normandy Cheese Spread is excellent served on thin slices of

black bread. If Calvados is unavailable, Cognac can be substituted. If kept covered in the refrigerator, the spread will keep for 2 to 3 days.

8 OUNCES [1 CUP]

3 oz. roquefort cheese, crumbled
3 oz. full fat cream cheese
1 oz. [2 tablespoons] butter, softened
⅛ teaspoon black pepper
¼ teaspoon grated nutmeg
2 tablespoons Calvados
2 tablespoons chopped pickled walnuts

In a small mixing bowl, mash the roquefort, cream cheese and butter together with a wooden spoon until the mixture is smooth. Beat in the pepper, nutmeg and Calvados. Stir in the pickled walnuts.

Serve at once, or cover the bowl with aluminium foil and place it in the refrigerator until required.

Normandy Pear Tart

Pears encased in a rich walnut pastry and topped with whipped cream and nuts, Normandy Pear Tart is served cold and is absolutely delicious.

4-6 SERVINGS

PASTRY
10 oz. [2½ cups] flour
½ teaspoon salt
3 oz. [⅜ cup] butter, cut into walnut-sized pieces
2 oz. [¼ cup] vegetable fat
4 oz. [½ cup] plus 2 tablespoons castor sugar
1½ oz. [¼ cup] walnuts, finely chopped
2 egg yolks, lightly beaten
3 tablespoons iced water
1 egg white, lightly beaten
FILLING
2 oz. [¼ cup] sugar
5 fl. oz. [⅝ cup] water
4 large pears, peeled, halved and cored
5 fl. oz. double cream [⅝ cup heavy cream], stiffly whipped
2 tablespoons chopped walnuts

First make the pastry. Sift the flour and salt into a large mixing bowl. Add the butter and the vegetable fat and cut them into small pieces with a table knife. Rub the fats into the flour with your fingertips until the mixture resembles coarse breadcrumbs. Mix in 4 ounces [½ cup] of the sugar and the finely chopped walnuts.

Add the egg yolks with a spoonful of the water and mix it in with the knife. With your hands, mix and knead the dough until it is smooth. Add more water if the dough is too dry. Wrap the dough

in greaseproof or waxed paper and place it in the refrigerator to chill for 30 minutes.

Meanwhile make the filling. In a medium-sized saucepan, dissolve the sugar in the water over low heat, stirring constantly. When the sugar has dissolved, increase the heat to high and boil the syrup for 4 minutes.

Add the pear halves, reduce the heat to low and simmer the pears for 10 to 15 minutes or until they are tender but still firm. Remove the pan from the heat. Set aside to cool.

Preheat the oven to fairly hot 375°F (Gas Mark 5, 190°C).

On a lightly floured board, roll out two-thirds of the dough into a circle large enough to line a 9-inch flan ring. Lift the dough on the rolling pin and lay it over the flan ring. Gently ease the dough into the ring. Trim off any excess dough.

With a slotted spoon, remove the pears from the pan. Arrange the pear halves, narrow ends towards the middle and cut sides down, in the dough case. Dampen the edges of the dough.

On a lightly floured board, roll out the remaining dough into a circle large enough to fit over the top of the tart. Using a 3-inch pastry cutter, cut a hole in the centre of the dough circle. Discard the small circle of dough. Lift the dough on the rolling pin and lay it over the tart. Using your fingers, gently press the dough edges together. Trim off any excess dough.

With a pastry brush, brush the top of

Melting walnut pastry and tender pears combine to make Normandy Pear Tart a delightful dessert. Serve it with extra cream if you like.

the dough with the egg white and dust with the remaining 2 tablespoons of castor sugar.

Place the tart in the top of the oven and bake for 30 to 35 minutes or until the pastry is firm to the touch.

Remove the tart from the oven and set it aside to cool completely. When it is cold, carefully remove the tart from the flan ring.

Spoon the whipped cream into the centre of the tart and sprinkle with the chopped walnuts. Serve at once.

Normandy Pork

Lean pork fillet stuffed with a fragrant filling and braised in cider, Normandy Pork is a delicious dish.

4 SERVINGS

2 lb. pork fillet, cut into 8 pieces
2 oz. [¼ cup] butter
1 large onion, finely chopped
1 small apple, peeled, cored and very finely chopped
4 oz. pork sausage meat
2 oz. [1 cup] fresh breadcrumbs
1 tablespoon chopped fresh parsley
1 teaspoon chopped fresh sage or ½ teaspoon dried sage
1 teaspoon salt
½ teaspoon black pepper
1 egg, lightly beaten
10 fl. oz. [1¼ cups] cider
½ to 1 oz. [1 to 2 tablespoons] beurre manié

Ask the butcher to partly slit the pieces of fillets and bash them to make escalopes.

Preheat the oven to moderate 350°F (Gas Mark 4, 180°C).

Lay each piece of meat out flat and set aside.

In a large frying-pan, melt half the butter over moderate heat. When the foam subsides, add the onion and fry, stirring occasionally, for 5 to 7 minutes or until it is soft and translucent but not brown.

Remove the pan from the heat and, using a slotted spoon, transfer the onion to a large mixing bowl. Add the apple, sausage meat, breadcrumbs, parsley, sage, half the salt, half the pepper and the egg. Using your hands, knead and mix the ingredients well.

Spoon equal amounts of the stuffing over each pork piece, smoothing it out evenly. Roll up the pieces and tie them with string.

In the same frying-pan, melt the remaining butter over moderate heat. When the foam subsides add the pork rolls and fry them, turning frequently, for 4 to 5 minutes, or until they are evenly browned. Using tongs, transfer the pork rolls to a large flameproof casserole. Pour over the cider. Cover the casserole and place it in the oven. Bake for 1 hour or until the meat is very tender when pierced with the point of a sharp knife.

Remove the casserole from the oven and, using a slotted spoon, transfer the pork rolls to a warmed serving dish. Remove and discard the string. Keep hot while you make the sauce.

Place the casserole over moderately high heat and boil the cooking liquid for 5 minutes or until it is well reduced. Stir in the remaining salt and pepper. Using a wooden spoon, stir in the beurre manié, a little at a time, and continue cooking, stirring constantly, until the sauce is fairly thick and smooth. Remove the casserole

Stuffed with apple, herbs and pork sausage meat, Normandy Pork is cooked in a cider sauce.

from the heat and pour the sauce over the pork rolls. Serve at once.

Norrländsk Laxsoppa

This Swedish salmon soup is not as expensive as it sounds, since only the head and bones of the salmon are used. Serve Norrländsk Laxsoppa (nawr-lensk lax-soppah) as an unusual first course.

4 SERVINGS

head and bones from a large salmon, cleaned and eyes removed
2½ pints [6¼ cups] water
1 teaspoon salt
6 peppercorns, crushed
bouquet garni, consisting of 4 parsley sprigs, 1 thyme spray and 1 bay leaf tied together
1 strip of lemon rind
3 tablespoons pearl barley, soaked in water for 8 hours or overnight and drained
3 medium-sized carrots, scraped and cut into thin slices
½ small turnip, peeled and chopped
1 small onion, finely chopped

Unfortunately! North Country Cake must be kept for one week before eating.

2 small leeks, white part only, cut into ½-inch slices
1 tablespoon chopped fresh parsley
1 teaspoon chopped fresh dill or ½ teaspoon dried dill

In a large saucepan, bring the salmon head and bones, water, salt, peppercorns, bouquet garni and lemon rind to the boil over moderate heat. Reduce the heat to low and simmer for 30 minutes.

Remove the pan from the heat. Pour the contents of the pan through a strainer into a large mixing bowl. Reserve the salmon head and discard the bones and flavourings.

Rinse and dry the saucepan. Return the strained stock to the pan. Add the pearl barley, carrots, turnip, onion and leeks and place the pan over moderate heat. When the liquid boils, cover the pan, reduce the heat to low and simmer for 30 minutes or until the vegetables are tender.

Meanwhile, remove the flesh from the salmon head. Reserve the flesh and discard the bones.

Add the parsley, dill and reserved flesh to the saucepan and cook for a further 3 minutes. Remove the pan from the heat.

Pour the soup into a heated soup tureen. Serve immediately.

North Country Cake

A no-nonsense cake made with very basic ingredients, this heavy, moist cake is saturated with stout or ale and left to mature for a week before serving.

ONE 9-INCH CAKE

1 tablespoon butter
1 lb. [4 cups] plus 1 tablespoon flour
¼ teaspoon salt
8 oz. [1 cup] lard or vegetable fat, cut into walnut-sized pieces
12 oz. [2 cups] soft brown sugar
10 oz. [1⅔ cups] sultanas or seedless raisins
8 oz. [1⅓ cups] currants
4 oz. [⅔ cup] chopped mixed candied peel
1 teaspoon mixed spice or ground allspice
10 fl. oz. [1¼ cups] stout or brown ale
5 eggs, lightly beaten
1 teaspoon bicarbonate of soda [baking soda]

Preheat the oven to moderate 350°F (Gas Mark 4, 180°C).

Grease a 9-inch cake tin with half the butter. Line the base and sides of the tin with greaseproof or waxed paper and grease the paper with the remaining butter. Sprinkle with the tablespoon of flour, tipping and rotating the tin to coat the base and sides evenly. Knock out any excess flour and set aside.

Sift the remaining flour and the salt into a large mixing bowl. Using your fingertips, rub the lard or vegetable fat into the flour until the mixture resembles fine breadcrumbs.

Stir in the sugar, sultanas or seedless raisins, currants, candied peel and mixed spice or ground allspice.

In a medium-sized mixing bowl, beat 2 fluid ounces [¼ cup] of the stout or ale, the eggs and soda together with a wire whisk or rotary beater until the mixture is very frothy.

Make a well in the centre of the flour and fruit mixture and pour in the egg mixture. Using a metal spoon, fold them into each other, mixing until they are thoroughly combined.

Pour the batter into the prepared tin, smoothing out the top with a flat-bladed knife. Place the tin in the oven and bake for 1 hour.

Reduce the oven temperature to cool 300°F (Gas Mark 2, 150°C) and continue baking for a further 1 hour, or until a skewer inserted into the centre of the cake comes out clean.

Remove the tin from the oven.

Turn the cake out on to a board and return it, upside-down, to the tin. Using a skewer, pierce the bottom of the cake all over. Pour the remaining stout or ale slowly over the cake. Set the cake aside to cool.

When the cake is completely cold, remove it from the tin and wrap it securely in aluminium foil.

Leave the cake for 1 week before serving.

Northern Lights

A simple but filling dessert, Northern Lights are sweet crêpes filled with jam and cream. Serve them hot after a light meal or for tea.

4-6 SERVINGS

5 oz. [1¼ cups] sweet Crêpe batter
8 tablespoons blackberry, redcurrant or strawberry jam
5 fl. oz. double cream [⅝ cup heavy cream], stiffly whipped
2 tablespoons icing [confectioners'] sugar, sifted

Fry the crêpes according to the instructions in the basic recipe and keep them warm.

Put a spoonful of jam and a spoonful of whipped cream in the centre of each crêpe. Roll them up and place them on warmed serving dishes. Sprinkle with the icing [confectioners'] sugar. Serve immediately.

Northumberland Puddings

Easy to make and economical, if you omit the brandy, Northumberland Puddings are filling moulded milk puddings. Serve them hot with a wine sauce or cold with a lemon sauce.

4-6 SERVINGS

2 oz. [¼ cup] plus 1 tablespoon butter, melted
2 tablespoons castor sugar
1 pint [2½ cups] milk
1 vanilla pod
4 oz. [1 cup] flour
4 oz. [⅔ cup] currants
4 oz. [⅔ cup] chopped mixed candied peel
2 fl. oz. double cream [¼ cup heavy cream], lightly whipped
1 tablespoon brandy

Using the tablespoon of butter, grease 8 small dariole moulds. Set aside.

In a medium-sized saucepan, dissolve the sugar in the milk over low heat, stirring constantly. Scald the milk (bring to just under boiling point). Remove the pan from the heat, add the vanilla pod and set the milk aside to infuse for 20 minutes. Remove the vanilla pod, wash and dry it and set aside for future use.

In a small mixing bowl, mix the flour with 6 fluid ounces [¾ cup] of the hot

milk. Pour the flour and milk mixture into the pan with the rest of the milk. Return the pan to moderately low heat and cook the mixture, stirring constantly, until it comes to the boil and is thick and smooth. Remove the pan from the heat. Set aside to cool.

Preheat the oven to moderate 350°F (Gas Mark 4, 180°C).

When the milk and flour mixture is completely cold and has become a stiff paste, turn the mixture into a medium-sized mixing bowl. Break up the paste using a kitchen fork. Using a wooden spoon, beat in the remaining melted butter, the currants and candied peel. Fold in the cream and brandy. Spoon the mixture into the buttered moulds.

Place the moulds in a baking tin. Put the tin in the oven and bake the puddings for 15 minutes.

Remove the moulds from the oven. Run a knife around the edge of the puddings and turn them out on to a serving dish. Serve immediately or set aside to cool.

Norvégienne, à la

A la Norvégienne (nohr-vay-jee-ehn) is a name given to various dishes, but most commonly it is used to describe a dessert like BAKED ALASKA which is ice-cream on a sponge base, covered with meringue or an omelet soufflé mixture and set in a hot oven.

The name is also used to describe certain cold fish and seafood dishes.

Norwegian Cream

Simple but delicious, Norwegian Cream is a baked custard decorated with whipped cream and chocolate caraque and served well chilled.

6 SERVINGS

3 tablespoons apricot jam
2 whole eggs plus 2 yolks
1 tablespoon sugar
1 pint [2½ cups] milk
1 vanilla pod

5 fl. oz. double cream [⅝ cup heavy cream], stiffly whipped
1 oz. Chocolate Caraque

Preheat the oven to warm 325°F (Gas Mark 3, 170°C). Spread the apricot jam over the bottom of an 8-inch soufflé dish. Set aside.

In a medium-sized mixing bowl, beat the eggs, egg yolks and sugar together with a wooden spoon. Set aside.

In a medium-sized saucepan, scald the milk with the vanilla pod (bring to just under boiling point) over moderate heat. Remove the pan from the heat and set aside to infuse for 20 minutes. Remove and discard the vanilla pod.

Pour the milk over the eggs and sugar mixture, stirring until the mixture is well blended. Strain the mixture over the jam in the soufflé dish. Cover the dish with aluminium foil. Place the soufflé dish in a baking tin half filled with hot water. Place the tin in the centre of the oven and bake for 50 to 60 minutes, or until the custard is just set.

Remove the tin from the oven and take out the soufflé dish. Set it aside to cool. When the custard is cool, place it in the refrigerator to chill for 2 hours, or until it is completely cold.

Remove the soufflé dish from the refrigerator.

Decorate the top with the whipped cream and chocolate caraque. Serve immediately.

Norwegian Cucumber and Potato Soup

This refreshing hot cucumber, dill and potato soup from Norway tastes delicious served as a first course or as the main dish for a light lunch with hot crusty rolls and butter. For a more decorative effect, float thin cucumber slices or curls of cucumber skin on the soup.

6 SERVINGS

1 oz. [2 tablespoons] butter
2 shallots, finely chopped
4 small potatoes, peeled and diced
1 tablespoon flour
1¾ pints [4⅜ cups] chicken stock
1 tablespoon lemon juice
1 teaspoon salt
½ teaspoon black pepper
1 bay leaf
1 tablespoon finely chopped fresh dill, or 1 teaspoon dried dill
2 medium-sized cucumbers, peeled and thickly sliced
8 fl. oz. [1 cup] sour cream

In a large, heavy saucepan, melt the butter over moderate heat. When the foam subsides, add the shallots and fry, stirring occasionally, for 3 to 4 minutes, or until they are soft and translucent but not brown. Add the potatoes and fry, stirring constantly, for 4 minutes.

Sprinkle over the flour and stir well. Gradually add the chicken stock, stirring constantly. Stir in the lemon juice, salt, pepper, bay leaf, dill and cucumbers. Bring the soup to the boil, stirring constantly.

Cover the pan, reduce the heat to low and simmer for 30 minutes, stirring occasionally.

Remove the pan from the heat. Pour the soup into a large, fine wire strainer held over a large mixing bowl. Using the back of a wooden spoon, rub the vege- tables through the strainer until only a dry pulp is left. Discard the pulp in the strainer.

Alternatively, remove and discard the bay leaf and blend the soup in an electric blender.

Pour the soup back into the saucepan. Stir in the sour cream and return the pan to low heat. Cook the soup, stirring con- stantly, for 3 to 4 minutes, or until it is hot.

Remove the pan from the heat. Pour the soup into a warmed soup tureen or individual soup bowls and serve im- mediately.

Norwegian Fish Pudding

A delicious hot fish pudding, Norwegian Fish Pudding may be served with a shrimp and tomato salad and crisp Melba Toast and butter for a lunch or dinner party. Served in small quantities, the pudding makes an excellent first course.

4 SERVINGS

4 oz. [½ cup] plus 2 teaspoons butter, softened
1 oz. [⅓ cup] fine dry white breadcrumbs
2 tablespoons flour
1 teaspoon cornflour [cornstarch]
10 fl. oz. single cream [1¼ cups light cream]
1 lb. halibut steaks, poached, skinned, boned and flaked
8 oz. cod fillets, poached, skinned, boned and flaked
1 teaspoon salt
½ teaspoon black pepper
¼ teaspoon cayenne pepper
¼ teaspoon dried dill
finely grated rind of 1 lemon
4 eggs, separated

Preheat the oven to moderate 350°F (Gas Mark 4, 180°C).

With the 2 teaspoons of butter, generously grease a 3-pint [2-quart] soufflé or baking dish. Sprinkle in the breadcrumbs and press them lightly on to the sides and bottom of the dish. Shake out any excess breadcrumbs and set the dish aside.

In a medium-sized saucepan, melt 2 ounces [¼ cup] of the remaining butter over moderate heat. Remove the pan from the heat and, with a wooden spoon, stir in the flour and cornflour [cornstarch] to make a smooth paste. Gradually stir in the cream, being careful to avoid lumps.

Return the pan to the heat and cook the sauce, stirring constantly, for 2 to 3 minutes or until it thickens. Do not allow the sauce to boil. Remove the pan from

Norwegian Cucumber and Potato Soup and Norwegian Fish Pudding both are light and refreshing and make an ideal first course.

the heat and set aside.

In a large mixing bowl, beat the fish and the remaining butter together with a wooden spoon until the mixture is well combined. Stir in the sauce. Beat in the salt, pepper, cayenne, dill, lemon rind and egg yolks.

In a medium-sized mixing bowl, beat the egg whites with a wire whisk or rotary beater until they form stiff peaks.

With a metal spoon, carefully fold the egg whites into the fish mixture.

Spoon the mixture into the prepared dish and place the dish in a roasting tin half filled with hot water.

Place the tin in the centre of the oven and bake the pudding for 45 to 50 minutes, or until it is golden brown on top and a skewer inserted into the centre comes out clean.

Remove the tin from the oven. Lift the dish out of the tin and serve the pudding immediately, from the dish.

Norwegian Soda Bread

Quick and easy to make, Norwegian Soda Bread should be eaten with plenty of butter and is excellent with soup.

TWO 6-INCH LOAVES

2 oz. [¼ cup] plus 1 teaspoon
  unsalted butter, melted

8 oz. [2 cups] rye flour
8 oz. [2 cups] wholewheat flour
1 teaspoon baking powder
1½ teaspoons bicarbonate of soda
  [baking soda]
1 teaspoon salt
1 tablespoon soft brown sugar
8 fl. oz. [1 cup] buttermilk
1 egg, lightly beaten

Preheat the oven to hot 425°F (Gas Mark 7, 220°C).

Grease a large baking sheet with the teaspoon of butter and set aside.

Sift the rye flour, wholewheat flour, baking powder, soda and salt into a large mixing bowl. Stir in the sugar.

In a medium-sized mixing bowl, mix together the remaining melted butter and the buttermilk. Make a well in the centre of the flour mixture and pour in the buttermilk mixture and the egg. Using your fingertips or a spatula, gradually draw the flour mixture into the liquids. Continue mixing until all the flour is incorporated and the dough comes away from the sides of the bowl.

Transfer the dough to a floured board and knead it lightly. Divide the dough in half and shape each piece into a flat round shape, approximately ½-inch thick.

Place the dough rounds on the baking sheet.

Place the baking sheet in the oven and

bake for 20 to 25 minutes, or until the loaves are browned.

Remove the baking sheet from the oven. Allow the loaves to cool slightly and serve warm, or transfer them to a wire rack to cool completely.

Norwegian Venison Steaks

A simple way to cook venison, Norwegian Venison Steaks are marinated, then cooked until tender and served with a creamy sauce. Serve with mashed potatoes and steamed broccoli. The quality of venison varies and the meat can be very tough, so test it after 20 minutes cooking and adjust the cooking time accordingly.

4 SERVINGS

4 venison steaks, 1-inch thick
1 teaspoon salt
½ teaspoon black pepper
1 onion, finely chopped
1 celery stalk, trimmed and finely
  chopped
1 tablespoon chopped parsley
1 bay leaf
  finely pared rind of 1 lemon
2 tablespoons olive oil
6 fl. oz. [¾ cup] red wine
1½ oz. [3 tablespoons] butter
6 juniper berries, crushed
  juice of ½ lemon

Norwegian Venison Steaks make a hearty, tasty dinner dish.

---

5 fl. oz. single cream [⅝ cup light cream]

Rub both sides of the steaks with the salt and pepper. Place them in a shallow dish. Sprinkle the onion, celery and parsley over the top. Add the bay leaf and lemon rind. Pour over the olive oil and wine. Cover the dish and set it aside in a cool place to marinate for 24 hours.

Preheat the oven to warm 325°F (Gas Mark 3, 170°C).

Remove the meat from the marinade and pat it dry on kitchen paper towels. Reserve the marinade.

In a large flameproof casserole, melt the butter over moderate heat. When the foam subsides, add the steaks. Reduce the heat to moderately low and fry the steaks for 10 minutes on each side or until they are well browned.

Remove the casserole from the heat, cover it and place it in the oven. Bake for 20 to 40 minutes, or until the meat is very tender when pierced with the point of a sharp knife.

Remove the casserole from the oven. Using tongs, transfer the meat to a warmed serving dish. Keep hot while you make the sauce.

Strain the marinade through a fine wire strainer and return it to the casserole. Discard the contents of the strainer. Set the casserole over high heat and bring the marinade to the boil, stirring constantly. Stir in the juniper berries, lemon juice and cream. Remove the casserole from the heat.

Taste the sauce and add more salt and pepper if necessary.

Pour the sauce over the meat and serve at once.

Nougat

Nougat (noo-gah) is a white or pink sweet [candy] made from nuts and honey or a sugar syrup, or a combination of both. Nougat used to be made from walnuts, but blanched and sometimes roasted almonds are mainly used today. The sweet [candy] can be hard, or soft and chewy. The most popular type is nougat Montelimar, (mon-tay-lee-mahr) which is white nougat containing chopped nuts and candied fruit such as cherries and angelica.

There is another type of nougat, called nougat parisien, nougat brun or caramel nougat. This is made by dissolving castor sugar over heat with chopped nuts, usually almonds, until a pale brown caramel is obtained. The caramel is turned out on to an oiled slab and quickly moulded, while it is still hot, into the required shapes — sweets [candies], basket shapes to contain desserts, thin slabs to cover cakes, decorative leaves or flowers, and so on.

Nougat Ice-Cream

   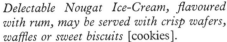

Delectable Nougat Ice-Cream, flavoured with rum, may be served with crisp wafers, waffles or sweet biscuits [cookies].

4-6 SERVINGS

1 pint single cream [2½ cups light cream]
1 vanilla pod
1 egg yolk
1 tablespoon custard powder
4 oz. [½ cup] plus 3 tablespoons sugar
1½ teaspoons gelatine, dissolved in 2 tablespoons hot water
1 egg white
4 oz. [1 cup] flaked blanched almonds, lightly toasted
2 tablespoons rum

Set the thermostat of the refrigerator to its coldest setting.

In a small saucepan, scald the cream with the vanilla pod (bring to just under boiling point) over moderate heat. Remove the pan from the heat, cover it and set the cream aside to infuse for 20 minutes.

In a medium-sized mixing bowl, beat the egg yolk, custard powder, 3 tablespoons of the sugar and 2 tablespoons of the scalded cream together with a wooden spoon until the mixture is smooth. Remove and discard the vanilla pod from the remaining cream and pour the cream, in a thin stream, on to the egg mixture, stirring constantly.

Return the cream mixture to the saucepan and place the pan over low heat. Cook the custard, stirring constantly, for 5 minutes, or until it is smooth and thick.

Remove the pan from the heat and stir in the dissolved gelatine. Set the custard aside to cool completely, pour it into a bowl, cover and chill in the refrigerator for 1 hour.

Remove the bowl from the refrigerator and pour the custard into a chilled freezing tray. Place the tray in the frozen food storage compartment of the refrigerator and freeze for 30 minutes.

Remove the tray from the refrigerator and spoon the custard into a medium-sized, chilled mixing bowl. Beat it for 1 minute with a wire whisk or rotary beater. Set aside.

In a small mixing bowl, beat the egg white with a wire whisk or rotary beater until it forms stiff peaks. With a metal spoon, fold the egg white into the custard and combine the mixture thoroughly.

Nougat in its many forms: some covered with chocolate, others with mixed fruit and nuts and one with almonds.

For Nougatine Cakes, cut the cake into four pieces and cut the pieces in half again to make eight cakes.

Add the flaked almonds to the golden brown caramel and stir well to coat the nuts thoroughly.

When the praline is cool, break it into pieces and pound it to a fine powder in a mortar with a pestle.

Spoon the custard mixture back into the freezing tray and return it to the frozen food storage compartment. Freeze for 1 hour, or until the ice-cream is firm to the touch.

While the ice-cream is freezing, prepare the nougat. In a small saucepan, melt the remaining sugar over low heat, stirring occasionally. Stir in the flaked almonds and increase the heat to moderately high. Boil the caramel, without stirring, until it is a rich golden brown colour. Do not allow the caramel to darken too much, or it will burn and taste bitter.

Remove the pan from the heat. Pour the caramel on to an oiled marble slab or hard surface and set it aside to cool and harden completely.

When the caramel is completely cooled, crush it to a fine powder with a rolling pin or mallet, or break it into pieces and pound it in a mortar with a pestle. Set aside.

Remove the ice-cream from the refrigerator and turn it into a medium-sized, chilled mixing bowl. Beat the ice-cream with a wire whisk or rotary beater for 2 minutes, or until it is completely smooth. Beat in the crushed caramel mixture and the rum and combine the mixture thoroughly.

Spoon the mixture back into the freezer tray and return it to the frozen food storage compartment of the refrigerator. Freeze the ice-cream for 1 hour, or until it is firm.

Remove the freezer tray from the refrigerator. Spoon the ice-cream into individual chilled serving glasses and serve immediately.

Nougatines

Nougatines (noo-gah-teen) are small orange-coloured sweets [candies] flavoured with honey, made in the Haute Seine region of France.

Nougatines are also small square GENOISE SPONGE cakes, layered with praline cream and iced with chocolate fondant.

Nougatine Cakes

Rich little Génoise sponge cakes layered with praline cream and iced with chocolate fondant, Nougatine (noo-gah-teen) Cakes are delicious served with afternoon tea or coffee.

8 CAKES

SPONGE CAKES
4 oz. [½ cup] plus 1 teaspoon unsalted butter, melted
4 oz. [1 cup] plus 2 tablespoons flour
5 oz. [⅝ cup] castor sugar
4 eggs, at room temperature
¼ teaspoon vanilla essence

PRALINE CREAM
4 oz. [½ cup] castor sugar
4 oz. [1 cup] flaked blanched almonds, lightly toasted
4 oz. [½ cup] unsalted butter, softened
4 oz. icing sugar [1 cup confectioners' sugar], sifted
2 fl. oz. double cream [¼ cup heavy cream], stiffly whipped

ICING
4 oz. dark [semi-sweet] chocolate, broken into small pieces
12 oz. Fondant, softened, diluted with 6 tablespoons of sugar syrup and kept hot
8 blanched almonds

Preheat the oven to fairly hot 375°F (Gas Mark 5, 190°C).

With the teaspoon of butter, grease an 8- x 10-inch cake tin. Sprinkle in 2 tablespoons of the flour. Tip and rotate the tin to distribute the flour evenly, shaking out any excess. Set the tin aside.

Place the sugar, eggs and vanilla essence in a medium-sized heatproof mixing bowl. Place the bowl in a pan half filled with hot water and set the pan over low heat. Beat the mixture with a wire whisk or rotary beater until it is pale and frothy and thick enough to make a ribbon trail on itself when the whisk is lifted.

Remove the pan from the heat. Lift the

bowl from the pan. Sift in the remaining flour and fold it in gently with a metal spoon. Gradually pour in the remaining melted butter, stirring constantly.

Spoon the batter into the prepared cake tin, smoothing it down with a flat-bladed knife. Place the tin in the centre of the oven and bake the cake for 20 to 30 minutes, or until the centre springs back when lightly pressed with a fingertip.

Remove the tin from the oven and let the cake cool in the tin for 30 minutes. With a sharp knife, cut the cake across into four pieces and cut the pieces in half to make eight cakes.

Transfer the cakes to a wire rack to cool completely. Meanwhile, make the praline filling. In a small saucepan, melt the sugar over low heat, stirring occasionally. When the sugar has melted, increase the heat to moderately high and boil the syrup, without stirring, for 1 to 2 minutes, or until it is a rich golden brown colour. Do not allow the syrup to darken too much, or it will taste bitter. Add the almonds and stir to coat them thoroughly with the syrup.

Remove the pan from the heat and pour the mixture on to an oiled marble slab or hard, cold surface. Set the mixture aside to cool and harden completely. When it is cool, crush it to a fine powder with a rolling pin, or break it into pieces and pound it to a fine powder in a mortar with a pestle. Set aside.

In a medium-sized mixing bowl, beat the butter, icing [confectioners'] sugar and cream together with a wooden spoon until the mixture is smooth. Beat in the crushed praline and blend it in thoroughly. Set aside.

To make the icing, in a small mixing bowl set over a pan half filled with boiling water, melt the chocolate, stirring occasionally. When the chocolate has melted, beat in the fondant, a little at a time, beating until the mixture is well blended. Keep the mixture hot over the pan of water, stirring frequently.

With a sharp knife, slice one of the sponge cakes across into three layers. With

When the chocolate has melted the fondant may be beaten in, with a wooden spoon, a little at a time.

Slice each cake into three layers and spread a little of the praline cream over the first two layers.

Spread the hot chocolate fondant icing over the top and sides of each cake to cover it completely.

a flat-bladed knife, spread a little of the praline cream over the first two layers and sandwich them together. Place the third layer on top. Repeat the process with the remaining cakes, using up all the praline cream.

Using a flat-bladed knife, quickly spread the hot chocolate fondant icing over the top and sides of the cakes to cover them completely. Place an almond half in the centre of each cake.

Place the cakes on a serving plate and leave them for 30 minutes before serving.

Nouilles au Gratin
NOODLES WITH BREADCRUMBS AND CHEESE

An easy-to-prepare supper dish for the family, Nouilles au Gratin (nwee oh gra-tan), could be served with French beans and a tomato salad.

6 SERVINGS

1 lb. noodles, cooked, drained and kept hot
2 oz. [¼ cup] butter, cut into small pieces
1 oz. [¼ cup] Parmesan cheese, grated
2 oz. [½ cup] Gruyère cheese, grated
3 tablespoons dry white breadcrumbs
¼ teaspoon black pepper

Preheat the grill [broiler] to high.

Place the noodles in a heatproof serving dish. Stir in half the butter. Sprinkle the grated cheeses, breadcrumbs and pepper over the noodles. Dot the top of the dish with the remaining butter.

Place the dish under the grill [broiler] and grill [broil] for 3 to 4 minutes or until the cheeses have melted and the top is a light golden brown.

Remove the dish from under the heat and serve immediately.

Nouilles à la Lyonnaise
NOODLES WITH ONIONS

Nouilles à la Lyonnaise (nwee ah lah lee-oh-nayz) complements the rich taste of a beef pot roast or goulasch very well.

4 SERVINGS

1 lb. noodles, cooked and drained
3 oz. [⅜ cup] butter
½ teaspoon black pepper
¼ teaspoon grated nutmeg
2 small onions, thinly sliced and pushed out into rings

Preheat the oven to warm 300°F (Gas Mark 2, 150°C).

Place the noodles in a large shallow ovenproof dish.

Cut 1 ounce [2 tablespoons] of the butter into small pieces and dot the noodles with them. Sprinkle the pepper and nutmeg over the noodles and place the dish in the oven. Bake for 10 minutes.

Meanwhile, in a small frying-pan, melt the remaining butter over moderate heat. When the foam subsides, add the onions and cook them, stirring occasionally, for 5 to 7 minutes or until they are soft and translucent but not brown. Remove the pan from the heat.

Remove the dish of noodles from the oven and stir well. Pour the onion mixture over the noodles. Increase the oven temperature to moderate 350°F (Gas Mark 4, 180°C). Return the dish to the oven and bake the noodles for a further 15 minutes or until the onions are slightly crisp.

Remove the dish from the oven and serve immediately.

Nova Scotia Potato Patties

Nova Scotia Potato Patties, made with potatoes, turnip, carrots and shallots, may be served with a hot tomato sauce for a light meal, or on their own as an accompaniment to roast or grilled [broiled] meat or fish.

4 SERVINGS

1 lb. potatoes, peeled, cooked and drained
4 small carrots, scraped, cooked and drained
1 small turnip, peeled, chopped and cooked
1 tablespoon finely chopped fresh parsley
2 small shallots, very finely chopped
1 small egg, well beaten
1 teaspoon salt
½ teaspoon black pepper
¼ teaspoon grated nutmeg
2 tablespoons flour
2 egg yolks, well beaten with 2 tablespoons milk
2 oz. [⅔ cup] dry white breadcrumbs
2 fl. oz. [¼ cup] vegetable oil

Place the potatoes, carrots, turnip, parsley and shallots in a large mixing bowl. Using a potato masher or a large fork, mash the ingredients to a purée.

With a wooden spoon, beat in the egg, salt, pepper, nutmeg and flour. Combine the mixture thoroughly.

With lightly floured hands, break off pieces of the mixture and shape them into patties.

Place the patties, in one layer, on a large plate and put them in the refrigerator to chill for 1 hour.

Place the egg yolk and milk mixture on one plate and the breadcrumbs on another.

Remove the patties from the refrigerator and dip them first in the egg yolk mixture and then in the breadcrumbs, coating them thoroughly and shaking off any excess crumbs.

In a large frying-pan, heat the oil over moderate heat. When the oil is hot, add the patties, a few at a time, and fry them for 3 to 4 minutes on each side, or until the outsides are crisp and golden brown.

Using a fish slice or spatula, remove the patties from the frying-pan and drain them well on kitchen paper towels. Transfer the patties to a warmed serving dish and keep them hot while you fry the remaining patties in the same way, adding more oil to the pan if necessary.

Serve hot.

Nova Scotia Salmon Cream

A tasty snack to serve for supper, Nova Scotia Salmon Cream is quick and easy to prepare.

4 SERVINGS

7 oz. canned salmon, drained and flaked
1 oz. [2 tablespoons] unsalted butter
2 tablespoons tarragon vinegar
1 teaspoon soft brown sugar
¼ teaspoon salt
⅛ teaspoon black pepper
⅛ teaspoon cayenne pepper
½ teaspoon paprika
3 fl. oz. double cream [⅜ cup heavy cream]
4 slices hot buttered toast

Put the salmon and butter into a medium-sized saucepan. Place the pan over low heat and cook the mixture for 5 minutes, stirring frequently. Pour the vinegar into the pan and stir in the sugar, salt, pepper, cayenne and paprika. Stir the cream into the salmon mixture and cook for a further 1 minute.

Remove the pan from the heat and spoon equal amounts of the mixture over the slices of toast. Serve at once.

Noyau

Noyau (nwah-yoh) is a liqueur of French origin which has a strong bitter-sweet taste, rather like bitter almonds. The liqueur, which is white, pink or pale orange in colour, is chiefly made from a mixture of the extracts of peach and apricot kernels, though some varieties are made purely from the extract of cherry kernels.

Noyau Cream

This rich, creamy dessert is flavoured with Noyau liqueur and sprinkled with flaked almonds. Serve it in small quantities

---

Flavoured with Noyau liqueur, Noyau Cream is delightful served either with raspberries or crisp biscuits.

accompanied by sweet biscuits [cookies] or fresh fruit such as black cherries, raspberries or peaches.

4 SERVINGS

15 fl. oz. double cream [1⅞ cups heavy cream]
1 tablespoon arrowroot dissolved in 2 fl. oz. [¼ cup] milk
2 oz. [¼ cup] plus 1 tablespoon castor sugar
2 fl. oz. [¼ cup] Noyau liqueur
1 oz. [¼ cup] flaked blanched almonds

In a medium-sized saucepan, combine the

cream, the dissolved arrowroot and 2 ounces [¼ cup] of the sugar.

Set the pan over moderate heat and cook the mixture, stirring constantly with a wooden spoon, for 4 to 5 minutes, or until the mixture is thick and smooth.

Remove the pan from the heat. Stir in the liqueur. Spoon the cream into a medium-sized glass serving dish and sprinkle over the remaining sugar and the flaked almonds.

Set the dessert aside to cool to room temperature, and then chill it in the refrigerator for at least 1 hour before serving.

Ntroba Forowee

GHANAIAN STEWED AUBERGINE [EGGPLANT] WITH SHRIMPS

An unusual West African method of cooking aubergine [eggplant] with ham and shrimps, Ntroba Forowee (nat-row-bah froy) can be served with plain boiled rice and a green salad or as an accompaniment to grilled [broiled] meat.

4 SERVINGS

1 aubergine [eggplant], peeled, cubed and dégorged
1½ teaspoons salt
3 tablespoons peanut oil
1 large onion, sliced
2 tomatoes, blanched, peeled, seeded and diced
1 tablespoon tomato purée
1 teaspoon black pepper
5 fl. oz. [⅝ cup] chicken stock
8 oz. cooked ham, cut into strips
4 oz. shrimps, shelled
1 tablespoon chopped fresh parsley

Place the aubergine [eggplant] and 1 teaspoon of the salt in a medium-sized saucepan. Pour over enough water to cover. Place the saucepan over moderate heat and bring the water to the boil. Cover the pan, reduce the heat to low and cook the aubergine [eggplant] for 10 to 15 minutes or until it is soft. Remove the pan from the heat and drain the aubergine [eggplant] cubes in a colander.

Transfer the aubergine [eggplant] cubes to a medium-sized mixing bowl. Using a kitchen fork, mash the cubes until they form a purée. Set aside.

In a large saucepan, heat the oil over moderate heat. When it is hot, add the onion and fry, stirring occasionally, for 5 to 7 minutes or until it is soft and translucent but not brown.

Add the tomatoes, tomato purée, the remaining salt, the pepper, the aubergine [eggplant] purée and stock and cook, stirring occasionally, for 10 to 15 minutes or until the mixture has thickened.

Stir in the ham and shrimps and cook for 3 to 4 minutes or until they are hot.

Transfer the mixture to a warmed serving dish. Sprinkle with the parsley and serve immediately.

Nudeln mit Käse

NOODLE AND CHEESE RING

A moulded noodle custard flavoured with cheese, Nudeln mit Käse (nood-dl' mit kay-zeh) should be served with stewed beef or buttered mixed vegetables.

4 SERVINGS

1 teaspoon butter
8 fl. oz. [1 cup] milk
3 egg yolks
½ teaspoon salt
¼ teaspoon white pepper
⅛ teaspoon cayenne pepper
1 tablespoon chopped fresh parsley
4 oz. [1 cup] Emmenthal or Gruyère cheese, grated
8 oz. noodles, cooked and drained

Preheat the oven to warm 325°F (Gas Mark 3, 170°C). Using the butter, lightly grease a 2-pint [1½-quart] ring mould. Set aside.

In a small saucepan, scald the milk over moderate heat (bring to just below boiling point). Remove the pan from the heat.

In a medium-sized mixing bowl, beat the egg yolks, salt, pepper, cayenne and parsley together with a wooden spoon. Slowly add the hot milk, stirring constantly. Stir in the grated cheese and the noodles.

Spoon the mixture into the prepared mould. Place the mould in a baking tin half filled with hot water. Place the tin in the oven and bake for 45 to 50 minutes or until the custard has set.

Remove the mould from the oven. Run

Succulent with vegetables, Ntroba Forowee also contains shrimps and ham. Serve this tasty dish with boiled rice and a green salad.

a sharp knife around the edge and un-mould the custard ring on to a warmed serving dish.

Serve immediately.

Nuits St. Georges

The village of Nuits St. Georges lies at the southern tip of the Côte de Nuits, one of the major wine areas of BURGUNDY. The village produces both red and white wines, but it is for its red wine, also called Nuits St. Georges, that it is best known.

Nun's Salad

A simple dish, Nun's Salad is so called because of the use of black and white ingredients. Serve it as a light supper dish or as a first course.

4 SERVINGS

1 lb. cooked chicken, diced
12 spring onions [scallions], white part only, chopped
1 lb. potatoes, peeled, cooked and diced
2 oz. [⅓ cup] seedless raisins
8 oz. large black grapes, halved and seeded

2 oz. [⅔ cup] large black olives, halved and stoned
½ teaspoon salt
¼ teaspoon black pepper
1 large apple, peeled, cored and diced
6 fl. oz. [¾ cup] mayonnaise

In a large salad bowl, combine the chicken, spring onions [scallions], potatoes, raisins, half the grapes, the olives, salt, pepper and apple. Pour over the mayonnaise and, using two large spoons, toss the salad, mixing the ingredients well.

Arrange the remaining grape halves decoratively over the top. Place the bowl in the refrigerator and chill the salad for 30 minutes before serving.

Nuremburg Chocolate Pudding

A favourite with children, Nuremburg Chocolate Pudding is a perfect dessert for a family supper. Serve with whipped cream.

6 SERVINGS

1 teaspoon vegetable oil
6 slices white bread, crusts removed and cubed

The black and white ingredients give Nun's Salad its unusual name.

8 fl. oz. double cream [1 cup heavy cream]
4 oz. [½ cup] butter
6 oz. [1 cup] ground almonds
6 oz. [¾ cup] sugar
6 oz. dark [semi-sweet] cooking chocolate, melted with 1 teaspoon vegetable oil
½ teaspoon instant coffee powder
6 eggs

Grease a 2-pint [1½-quart] metal mould with the teaspoon of oil. Set aside.

In a small mixing bowl, soak the bread in the cream for 5 minutes. Set aside.

In a medium-sized mixing bowl, cream the butter with a wooden spoon until it is soft and fluffy. Gradually beat in the almonds, sugar, chocolate and coffee powder and mix the ingredients together until they are thoroughly combined.

Add the soaked bread cubes with the cream to the butter mixture and beat until the mixture is smooth and creamy. Beat in the eggs, one at a time, making sure that each one is absorbed before adding the next.

Pour the mixture into the prepared mould. Cut out a circle of aluminium foil 4-inches wider in diameter than the rim of the mould. Make a 1-inch pleat across the centre of the circle and place the foil over the rim of the mould. With a piece of string, securely tie the foil circle around the rim of the mould.

Half fill a large saucepan with boiling water. Place the mould in the saucepan. Cover the pan and steam the pudding for 1½ to 2 hours over low heat, or until it is well risen and just firm to the touch. Add more water to the pan as it evaporates.

Remove the saucepan from the heat. Take out the mould and remove the aluminium foil. Run a knife around the edge of the mould. Place a serving dish, inverted, over the top of the mould. Reverse the two and give a slight shake. The pudding should slide out easily. Serve immediately.

Nuremburg Spice Squares

This is a variation of a traditional German cake (Lebkuchen) which is very similar to Gingerbread. Serve these delicious spicy squares with unsalted butter.

36 SQUARES

1 teaspoon butter
12 oz. [3 cups] flour
½ teaspoon salt
1 teaspoon baking powder
½ teaspoon ground ginger
½ teaspoon ground cinnamon
¼ teaspoon grated nutmeg
½ teaspoon ground cloves
2 tablespoons cocoa powder
3 large eggs
6 oz. [1 cup] soft brown sugar
6 fl. oz. [¾ cup] clear honey

Preheat the oven to moderate 350°F (Gas Mark 4, 180°C). Using the teaspoon of butter, grease a 9-inch square baking tin. Set aside.

Sift the flour, salt, baking powder, spices and cocoa powder into a large mixing bowl. Set aside.

In a medium-sized mixing bowl, beat the eggs, sugar and honey together with a wooden spoon until the ingredients are well combined. Make a well in the centre of the flour mixture and pour in the sugar and honey mixture. Mix the ingredients together until all the flour is incorporated and the batter is smooth.

Turn the batter into the prepared tin and smooth it down with a flat-bladed knife.

Place the tin in the oven and bake for 30 minutes or until a skewer inserted into the centre of the cake comes out clean.

Remove the tin from the oven and set the cake aside to cool completely before cutting into approximately 1½-inch squares and serving.

Nursery Cakes are sweet, Nusscreme Torte is sophisticated and both call for second helpings every time.

Nursery Cakes

Little squares of chewy biscuit [cookie] *crust, glacé cherries and milk, Nursery Cakes are ideal for a children's tea-party, and are very quick and easy to prepare.*

36 CAKES

3 oz. [⅜ cup] plus 1 teaspoon butter, melted
8 oz. crushed shortbread biscuits [2 cups crushed shortbread cookies]
2 oz. [⅓ cup] soft brown sugar
4 oz. [⅔ cup] walnuts, chopped
4 oz. [⅔ cup] sultanas or seedless raisins
6 oz. [1 cup] glacé cherries, halved
8 fl. oz. [1 cup] sweetened condensed milk

Using the teaspoon of butter, grease a 9-inch square baking tin and set aside.

Place the crushed biscuits [cookies] and sugar in a large mixing bowl. Pour on the remaining melted butter and, using a wooden spoon, mix the ingredients together thoroughly. Press the mixture into the bottom of the prepared tin. Place the tin in the refrigerator to chill for 30 minutes.

Remove the tin from the refrigerator. Sprinkle the walnuts and sultanas or seedless raisins evenly over the biscuit crust. Arrange the cherries on the top and pour over the milk. Set aside for 30 minutes.

Preheat the oven to warm 325°F (Gas Mark 3, 170°C).

Place the tin in the oven and bake for 10 to 15 minutes or until the visible milk has set.

Remove the tin from the oven and set aside to cool completely. When the cake is cold, cut it into 1½-inch squares and serve.

Nusscreme Torte

NUT AND CREAM CAKE

Chocolate-flavoured whipped cream sandwiched between light sponge cake layers, Nusscreme Torte (nooss-krem tohr-tuh) *comes from the land of delicious cakes, Austria. Serve the cake with strong black coffee to brighten up your mid-morning break.*

ONE 9-INCH CAKE

2 oz. [¼ cup] plus 1 teaspoon butter, melted and cooled
4 tablespoons flour, sifted
5 eggs, separated
3 oz. [⅜ cup] castor sugar
3 tablespoons finely chopped walnuts
3 tablespoons finely chopped Brazil nuts
finely grated rind of 1 lemon

FILLING

10 fl. oz. double cream [1¼ cups heavy cream]
2 oz. icing sugar [½ cup confectioners' sugar]
1 tablespoon Crème de Cacao
2 oz. [⅓ cup] hazelnuts, finely chopped

Preheat the oven to warm 325°F (Gas Mark 3, 170°C). Using the teaspoon of butter, grease a 9-inch round cake tin. Sprinkle the tin with one tablespoon of the flour, tipping and rotating the tin to coat the sides and base evenly. Knock out any excess flour and set the tin aside.

In a large mixing bowl, beat the egg yolks and half the sugar together with a wire whisk or rotary beater until the mixture is pale and thick. Set aside.

In another large mixing bowl, beat the egg whites with a wire whisk or rotary beater until they form soft peaks. Gradually add the remaining sugar, beating constantly, and continue beating until the mixture forms stiff peaks.

Using a metal spoon, gently fold the egg white mixture into the egg yolk and sugar mixture. Set aside.

In a small mixing bowl, combine the remaining flour, the walnuts, Brazil nuts and lemon rind. Using the metal spoon, very carefully fold the flour mixture and the remaining butter into the egg and sugar mixture.

Spoon the batter into the prepared cake tin and place it in the centre of the oven. Bake for 25 to 30 minutes, or until the cake springs back when lightly pressed with a fingertip.

Remove the cake from the oven and leave it to cool in the tin for 10 minutes. Then turn it out on to a wire rack to cool completely.

Meanwhile, make the filling. In a large mixing bowl, beat the cream with a wire whisk or rotary beater until it is thick but not stiff. Add the icing [confectioners'] sugar and Crème de Cacao. Continue beating until the cream mixture forms stiff peaks.

Using a sharp knife, slice the cake into two layers. With a flat-bladed knife, spread half of the filling on to the bottom half of the cake. Place the other half of the cake on top. Spread the remaining filling over the cake and sprinkle over the hazelnuts. Serve immediately.

Nusspastete

GERMAN NUT PASTRY ROLL

A delicious flaky pastry, stuffed full with nuts and honey, Nusspastete (nooss-pah-stay-tay) *is very rich and should be served in small slices. If you do not have a large enough baking sheet, divide the roll in half and bake it on two baking sheets.*

ONE 16-INCH ROLL

½ oz. fresh yeast
2 oz. [¼ cup] plus ½ teaspoon sugar
6 fl. oz. [¾ cup] lukewarm milk
1 lb. [4 cups] plus 1 tablespoon flour
1 teaspoon salt
1 teaspoon ground cardamom
10 oz. [1¼ cups] plus 1 tablespoon butter
2 eggs, lightly beaten

FILLING

12 oz. [2 cups] hazelnuts, chopped
4 oz. [⅘ cup] almonds, blanched and chopped
4 oz. [⅔ cup] soft brown sugar
2 tablespoons chopped glacé cherries
1 tablespoon chopped candied angelica
1 tablespoon sultanas or seedless raisins
grated rind of 1 lemon
½ teaspoon ground cinnamon
¼ teaspoon mixed spice or ground allspice
2 tablespoons double [heavy] **cream**
4 fl. oz. [½ cup] clear honey
3 tablespoons dark rum

GLAZE

1 egg, lightly beaten

Crumble the yeast into a small bowl and mash in ½ teaspoon of the sugar with a fork. Add 2 to 3 tablespoons of the milk and cream the milk and yeast together. Set the bowl aside in a warm, draught-free place for 15 to 20 minutes or until the yeast mixture is puffed up and frothy.

Sift 1 pound [4 cups] of the flour, the salt, cardamom and remaining sugar into a large mixing bowl. Add 2 ounces [¼ cup] of the butter and cut it into small pieces with a table knife. With your fingertips, rub the butter into the flour mixture until the mixture resembles fine breadcrumbs. Add the yeast mixture, the remaining milk and the eggs. Mix well to make a soft dough (add more milk if necessary). Cover the bowl with a cloth and place it in the refrigerator to chill for 50 minutes.

Allow the remaining 8 ounces [1 cup] of butter to soften slightly and form it into an oblong about ½-inch thick. Set aside.

Turn the dough out on to a floured

board and knead it for 10 minutes or until it becomes smooth and elastic. Using both hands, stretch and pull the dough out into an oblong about 12- x 8-inches.

Place the butter in the centre and fold the dough over to enclose the butter completely. Pull and roll out the dough to a strip about 5- x 15-inches. Fold the bottom third up and the top third down. Cover the dough and place it in the refrigerator to rest for 10 minutes. Repeat the rolling and folding twice more. Cover the dough and leave it in the refrigerator for 1 hour.

Using the remaining tablespoon of butter, grease a large baking sheet. Sprinkle with the remaining tablespoon of flour and tip and rotate the sheet to coat evenly. Knock out any excess flour and set aside.

In a large mixing bowl, combine the hazelnuts, almonds, sugar, glacé cherries, angelica, sultanas or seedless raisins, lemon rind, cinnamon and mixed spice or allspice. Mix the ingredients together well with a wooden spoon. Stir in the double [heavy] cream.

In a small saucepan, heat the honey over moderately low heat for 2 to 3 minutes or until it is thin. Remove the pan from the heat and pour the honey into the nut mixture. Stir until the fruit and nuts are thoroughly coated with the cream and honey. Stir in the rum. Set aside.

Remove the dough from the refrigerator and turn it out on to a lightly floured board. Pull and roll out the dough into a large rectangle, approximately $\frac{1}{4}$-inch thick. Trim the sides of the rectangle.

Spread the filling over the surface of the dough leaving a margin of 1-inch all round. Carefully roll it up Swiss [jelly] roll style.

Transfer the roll to the prepared baking sheet. Cover with a clean, damp cloth and set aside in a warm, draught-free place for 2 hours, or until the roll has risen and almost doubled in bulk.

Preheat the oven to very hot 425°F (Gas Mark 7, 220°C).

Using a pastry brush, lightly glaze the roll with the beaten eggs. Place the baking sheet in the oven and bake for 20 minutes. Reduce the oven temperature to moderate 350°F (Gas Mark 4, 180°C) and bake for a further 20 to 25 minutes, or until the roll is golden brown. Remove the sheet from the oven and transfer the roll to a wire rack to cool completely before serving.

Nuss Schlagsahne

NUT CREAM

Nuss Schlagsahne (nooss schlahg-eh-sahn-neh), a mixture of nuts and cream, makes a lovely dessert. Serve with fresh fruit, or biscuits [cookies].

4-6 SERVINGS

2 oz. [½ cup] walnuts
2 oz. [½ cup] pistachio nuts
2 oz. [⅓ cup] blanched almonds
2 teaspoons arrowroot dissolved in 1 tablespoon milk
10 fl. oz. single cream [1¼ cups light cream]
2 egg yolks
4 oz. [½ cup] castor sugar
1 tablespoon orange-flavoured liqueur
10 fl. oz. double cream [1¼ cups heavy cream]
1 teaspoon lemon juice
GARNISH
2 tablespoons finely ground pistachio nuts

Using a blender or pestle and mortar, blend or pound the walnuts, pistachio nuts and almonds together until they are coarsely ground. Set aside.

In a large mixing bowl, combine the dissolved arrowroot with the single [light] cream. Set aside.

Place the egg yolks and sugar in a medium-sized heatproof mixing bowl set over a pan of hot water. Set the pan over low heat and, using a wire whisk or rotary beater, beat the mixture until it is pale and thick enough to make a ribbon trail on itself when the whisk is lifted.

Remove the pan from the heat and the bowl from the pan.

Using a wooden spoon, stir the egg mixture into the cream mixture. Stir in the liqueur and the ground nuts. Set aside to cool slightly.

In a medium-sized mixing bowl, beat the double [heavy] cream and lemon juice together with the wire whisk or rotary beater until the mixture is thick but not stiff. With a metal spoon, fold the cream into the nut mixture.

Spoon the mixture into a 2-pint [1-quart] serving dish or into individual dishes. Sprinkle the top with the ground pistachio nuts. Place the dish or dishes in the refrigerator to chill for at least 1 hour before serving.

Nut

Nut is the name given to any seed or fruit consisting of a soft, usually edible, kernel surrounded by a hard, woody shell. The nut is a valuable source of protein and fat,

and because of this it has constituted an important part of man's diet almost since the beginning of time.

Western vegetarians often use nuts as a substitute for meat, and in some parts of the world, nuts (GROUNDNUTS and COCONUTS for example) form a staple part of the diet of the people.

Nuts such as ALMONDS, BRAZIL NUTS, CASHEWS, HAZELNUTS, PECANS, PISTACHIOS and WALNUTS are called dessert nuts and are used extensively in desserts and cakes and, increasingly, as flavourings in stews and meat stuffings.

Almonds, walnuts, peanuts and cashews may also be salted, spiced or devilled and served as appetizers.

Nut and Apple Cream

This is a light, nourishing dessert of apple purée and nuts in cream. If you like you can substitute plain yogurt for the cream to make the dessert even more nutritious.

4 SERVINGS

2 lb. green cooking apples, peeled, cored and sliced
1 teaspoon ground cinnamon
2 cloves
2 tablespoons sugar
grated rind and juice of ½ small lemon
2 oz. [⅓ cup] mixed nuts, chopped
5 fl. oz. double cream [⅝ cup heavy cream], stiffly whipped
1 teaspoon grated nutmeg

In a medium-sized saucepan, combine the apples, cinnamon, cloves and sugar. Set the pan over moderate heat and cook, stirring occasionally, for 10 to 15 minutes or until the apples are soft. Remove the pan from the heat. Remove and discard the cloves.

Using a wooden spoon rub the apples through a strainer into a medium-sized mixing bowl. Alternatively, place the apples in an electric blender and blend until smooth.

Stir in the lemon rind and juice and the nuts and fold in the whipped cream. Spoon the mixture into individual serving glasses. Sprinkle over the nutmeg and place the glasses in the refrigerator to chill for 1 hour before serving.

Nut Apple Jellies [Gelatins]

Nut Apple Jellies [Gelatins] are a light and pleasant-textured dessert, especially good in summer. Serve them plain or with whipped cream.

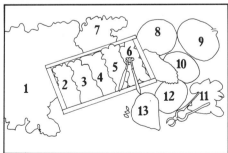

1 Sweet Chestnuts, 2 Pistachios, 3 Almonds, 4 Brazils, 5 Hazelnuts, 6 Pecans, 7 Peanuts, 8 Shelled Almonds, 9 Cashews, 10 Shelled Brazils, 11 Walnuts, 12 Shelled Hazelnuts, 13 Shelled Pistachios

6 SERVINGS

4 fl. oz. [½ cup] water
1 lb. [2 cups] sugar
  juice and finely grated rind of
  ½ lemon
3 lb. green cooking apples
6 oz. [1 cup] mixed nuts (walnuts,
  unsalted peanuts, almonds),
  chopped
2 fl. oz. [¼ cup] dark rum

In a large saucepan, combine the water, sugar, lemon juice and lemon rind. Place the pan over moderate heat and cook, stirring constantly, for 7 to 10 minutes or until the sugar has dissolved. Remove the pan from the heat and set aside.

Peel, core and quarter the apples and cut the quarters into thin slices. Drop the apple slices into the syrup as you cut them to prevent them from discolouring.

Return the pan to the heat, increase the heat to high and boil, stirring constantly, for 20 minutes or until the apples have become soft and translucent. Remove the pan from the heat and stir in the nuts and rum.

Pour the mixture into 6 small bowls and set aside to cool at room temperature.

When the jellies [gelatins] are cool, place them in the refrigerator to chill and become firm for at least 3 hours before serving.

Nut Brittle

Nut Brittle is a hard sweet [candy], made from nuts, sugar and butter. Peanuts are most commonly used to make the brittle, but any type of nut may be substituted. Nut Brittle made with mixed nuts is usually called NUT CLUSTERS.

Nut Butter

Nut Butter is a spread made by grinding roasted nuts in a blender or in a mortar with nut oil and salt.

The most famous nut butter is peanut butter but it can also be made from cashews, Brazil nuts and hazelnuts.

Nut and Cauliflower Flan

An inexpensive and easy-to-make dish, Nut and Cauliflower Flan may be eaten either hot or cold. Serve with a crisp green salad.

4-6 SERVINGS

1 x 9-inch Flan Case made with
  shortcrust pastry, baked blind
1 small cauliflower, trimmed and
  separated into flowerets
1½ teaspoons salt
2 eggs, lightly beaten
4 fl. oz. single cream [½ cup light
  cream]

3 oz. [½ cup] walnuts, chopped
¼ teaspoon black pepper
4 oz. [1 cup] Cheddar cheese, grated
1 oz. [2 tablespoons] butter
1 medium-sized onion, finely
  chopped
2 medium-sized tomatoes,
  blanched, peeled and sliced

Preheat the oven to moderate 350°F (Gas Mark 4, 180°C). Place the flan case on a baking sheet and set aside.

Place the cauliflower in a medium-sized saucepan and pour over enough water to cover. Add 1 teaspoon of the salt and place the pan over moderately high heat. Bring the water to the boil and cook the cauliflower for 9 to 12 minutes, or until it is just tender.

Remove the pan from the heat and drain the cauliflower in a colander. When the cauliflower is cool enough to handle, chop it finely. Set aside.

In a medium-sized mixing bowl, combine the eggs, cream, walnuts, the remaining salt, the pepper and grated cheese, beating until the ingredients are well blended. Set aside.

Nut and Cauliflower Pie is easy to make and to eat! Serve it cold with a crisp green salad.

Serve Nut and Chocolate Cookies as a snack with a glass of milk.

together with a wooden spoon until the mixture is light and fluffy. With a metal spoon, gradually fold in the flour. Mix in the syrup, almonds and chocolate chips.

Using your hands, form the mixture into walnut-sized balls. Place the balls on the greased baking sheets, spaced well apart. With a fork, slightly flatten the balls.

Place the baking sheets in the oven and bake for 15 to 20 minutes, or until the biscuits [cookies] are golden brown.

Remove the baking sheets from the oven and transfer the biscuits [cookies] to a wire rack. Allow the biscuits [cookies] to cool completely before serving.

Nut and Chocolate Sauce

Nut and Chocolate Sauce is a rich accompaniment to sponge puddings or ice-cream.
                                    8 FLUID OUNCES
6 oz. dark [semi-sweet] chocolate
2 tablespoons strong black coffee
2 tablespoons rum
2 oz. [½ cup] slivered almonds

In a small saucepan, melt the chocolate with the coffee and rum over low heat, stirring occasionally. When the chocolate has melted and the mixture is smooth remove the pan from the heat. Stir in the almonds and serve immediately.

Nut Clusters

This is the basic recipe for Nut Clusters. Add other nuts or use just one type if you prefer. Seeds such as sunflower seeds or sesame seeds can also be added to the mixture.
                                         2 POUNDS
1 teaspoon vegetable oil
8 oz. [2 cups] roasted, shelled peanuts
4 oz. [⅔ cup] hazelnuts, shelled
4 oz. [⅔ cup] unblanched almonds, chopped
1 lb. [2 cups] sugar

Using the teaspoon of oil, grease a large baking sheet. Set aside.

In a medium-sized mixing bowl, combine the nuts and stir well to mix. Set aside.

In a medium-sized saucepan, melt the sugar over low heat, stirring occasionally. Cook gently for 10 minutes or until the sugar syrup is golden brown.

In a small frying-pan, melt the butter over moderate heat. When the foam subsides, add the onion and cook, stirring occasionally, for 5 to 7 minutes, or until it is soft and translucent but not brown. Remove the pan from the heat and add the onion to the egg mixture. Set aside.

Arrange the cauliflower in the bottom of the flan case and cover with the sliced tomatoes. Pour the egg and cream mixture over the tomatoes and place the baking sheet in the centre of the oven.

Bake the flan for 30 to 35 minutes, or until the filling is golden brown and firm to the touch. Remove the flan from the oven and serve immediately.

Nut and Cheese Dressing

This is an unusual dressing for a fresh fruit salad. The cheese and nuts are a perfect accompaniment to fruit. This dressing may also be used for a green salad or a mixed salad of fruit and vegetables.
                                    8 FLUID OUNCES
4 fl. oz. [½ cup] olive oil
2 fl. oz. [¼ cup] fresh orange juice
2 tablespoons fresh lemon juice
1 teaspoon sugar

½ teaspoon salt
2 oz. Roquefort cheese, finely crumbled
2 oz. [⅓ cup] walnuts, chopped

In a small mixing bowl, combine all the ingredients. Beat them together well with a kitchen fork or spoon. Serve immediately or keep, covered, in the refrigerator until needed.

Nut and Chocolate Cookies

A favourite with children, Nut and Chocolate Cookies are easy to make.
                        24 BISCUITS [COOKIES]
4 oz. [½ cup] plus 2 teaspoons butter
2 oz. [¼ cup] soft brown sugar
8 oz. [2 cups] flour, sifted
2 tablespoons golden [light corn] syrup
3 oz. [½ cup] almonds, chopped
4 tablespoons chocolate chips

Preheat the oven to moderate 350°F (Gas Mark 4, 180°C). With the 2 teaspoons of butter, grease two baking sheets. Set aside.

In a medium-sized mixing bowl, cream the remaining butter and the sugar

Nut

Mix in the nuts. Remove the pan from the heat. Using an oiled teaspoon, drop spoonfuls of the mixture on to the greased baking sheet. Set aside to cool.

When the caramel has cooled and hardened, the nut clusters are ready to eat.

Nut and Cream Cheese Balls

These small cheese balls make tasty little cocktail snacks. Or you may serve them with a green salad.

4 SERVINGS

4 oz. cream cheese
$\frac{1}{8}$ teaspoon cayenne pepper
1 tablespoon finely chopped fresh chives
1 tablespoon finely chopped fresh parsley
$\frac{1}{2}$ teaspoon salt
$\frac{1}{4}$ teaspoon black pepper
2 oz. [$\frac{1}{3}$ cup] walnuts, chopped

In a small mixing bowl beat the cream cheese, cayenne, chives, parsley, salt and pepper together with a wooden spoon until the mixture is smooth. Stir in the chopped walnuts.

Place the bowl in the refrigerator to chill for 30 minutes.

Form the mixture into about 16 balls about 1-inch in diameter. Place the cheese balls on a serving dish and return them to the refrigerator to chill until you are ready to serve them.

Nut and Cream Cheese Puffs

Easy to make and delicious to eat, Nut and Cream Cheese Puffs may be served as a light supper snack accompanied by a green salad, or as an appetizer with drinks.

4-8 SERVINGS

8 oz. cream cheese
2 tablespoons mayonnaise
$2\frac{1}{2}$ oz. [$\frac{1}{2}$ cup] walnuts, chopped
1 medium-sized red pepper, white pith removed, seeded and finely chopped
8 oz. canned pineapple slices, drained and finely chopped
$\frac{1}{4}$ teaspoon salt
8 large Choux Puffs, cooled to room temperature

In a medium-sized mixing bowl, combine the cream cheese and mayonnaise, beating with a fork until they are blended. Stir in the walnuts, red pepper and pineapple and season with the salt. Set aside.

Gently cut off the tops of the choux puffs with a sharp knife. Spoon in the filling. Replace the tops, gently pressing the two parts of the puffs together.

Serve as soon as possible after filling.

Nut Croquettes

These tasty, bite-sized croquettes may be served as a nourishing supper dish or as part of a vegetarian meal. Serve the croquettes with tomato or mushroom sauce.

4 SERVINGS

1 oz. [2 tablespoons] butter
1 small onion, finely chopped
1 oz. [$\frac{1}{4}$ cup] plus 2 tablespoons flour
5 fl. oz. [$\frac{5}{8}$ cup] milk
4 oz. [1 cup] peanuts, finely chopped
1 small carrot, scraped and finely grated
$\frac{1}{4}$ teaspoon dried thyme
1 teaspoon celery salt
$\frac{1}{4}$ teaspoon black pepper
4 tablespoons vegetable oil

In a small saucepan, melt the butter over moderate heat. When the foam subsides, add the onion and fry, stirring occasionally, for 5 to 7 minutes or until it is soft and translucent but not brown. With a wooden spoon stir in 1 ounce [$\frac{1}{4}$ cup] of the flour to make a smooth paste.

Remove the pan from the heat and gradually add the milk, stirring constantly. Return the pan to the heat and, stirring constantly, bring the sauce to the boil. Boil the sauce for 1 minute or until it is very thick. Remove the pan from the heat.

Add the peanuts, carrot, thyme, celery salt and pepper and stir until the ingredients are thoroughly mixed.

Spoon the mixture into a medium-sized dish and set it aside to cool completely.

Nut and Cream Cheese Puffs and Nut and Cream Cheese Balls are so tasty.

Using a wet knife, cut the cold nut mixture into pieces 2-inches by 1-inch.

Place the remaining flour on a plate. Roll the nut pieces in the flour, rounding the edges against your hands. Shake off any excess flour.

In a large frying-pan, heat the oil over moderate heat. When the oil is hot, add half the croquettes and fry them, turning frequently with a fish slice or spatula, for 4 minutes or until they are deep golden brown on all sides. Using a slotted spoon, remove the croquettes from the pan and drain them on kitchen paper towels. Keep them warm while you cook the remaining croquettes in the same way.

Serve hot.

Nut and Date Biscuits [Cookies]

Crisp, delicately flavoured little biscuits [cookies], Nut and Date Biscuits [Cookies] are easy and quick to make. Serve them slightly warm from the oven or cold. Stored in an airtight tin, they will keep for several weeks.

ABOUT 30 BISCUITS [COOKIES]

8 oz. [2 cups] flour
$\frac{1}{8}$ teaspoon salt
1 teaspoon baking powder
$\frac{1}{8}$ teaspoon ground allspice
$\frac{1}{8}$ teaspoon ground cardamom
3 oz. [$\frac{3}{8}$ cup] butter, softened
4 oz. [$\frac{2}{3}$ cup] soft brown sugar
1 egg, well beaten with 1 tablespoon milk
4 oz. [$\frac{2}{3}$ cup] dates, stoned and finely chopped
2 tablespoons finely chopped hazelnuts
2 oz. [$\frac{1}{3}$ cup] Brazil nuts, finely chopped

Preheat the oven to moderate 350°F (Gas Mark 4, 180°C).

Line two medium-sized baking sheets with non-stick silicone paper and set them aside.

Sift the flour, salt, baking powder, allspice and cardamom into a small bowl and stir well to mix. Set aside.

In a medium-sized mixing bowl, cream the butter and sugar together with a wooden spoon until the mixture is smooth and fluffy.

Stir in half of the flour mixture and the egg and milk mixture. Combine thoroughly and stir in the remaining flour mixture, the dates and nuts. Lightly knead the dough until it is smooth. Cover the dough and chill it in the refrigerator for 30 minutes.

Remove the dough from the refriger-

Serve these Nut and Date Biscuits [Cookies] slightly warm with coffee for a mid-morning snack.

ator. Shape the dough into a ball and turn it out on to a lightly floured board or marble slab. Using a lightly floured rolling pin, roll out the dough into a circle about $\frac{1}{4}$-inch thick. With a 2-inch pastry cutter, cut the dough into circles. Gather the leftover dough and knead it lightly until it is smooth. Roll out and cut into circles as before.

Transfer the dough circles to the prepared baking sheets, spacing them slightly apart.

Place the baking sheets in the centre of the oven and bake for 15 minutes or until the biscuits [cookies] are golden brown.

Remove the baking sheets from the oven. Transfer the biscuits [cookies] to a wire rack to cool. Serve warm, or allow to cool completely before serving.

Nut Fritters

These crunchy little fritters may be made in a moment and served with honey or lemon sauce as a dessert.

4 SERVINGS

4 oz. [$\frac{2}{3}$ cup] ground almonds
4 oz. [$\frac{2}{3}$ cup] Brazil nuts, ground
3 eggs, lightly beaten
3 oz. [$\frac{3}{8}$ cup] sugar
$\frac{1}{4}$ teaspoon ground cinnamon
$\frac{1}{8}$ teaspoon ground mace
    sufficient vegetable oil for frying

In a medium-sized mixing bowl combine the almonds, Brazil nuts, eggs, sugar cinnamon and mace. Beat the mixture until the ingredients are thoroughly mixed.

Pour enough oil into a large frying-pan to make a 1-inch deep layer. Put the pan over moderately high heat. When the oil is hot, drop in tablespoonfuls of the nut mixture and fry them for 1 minute on each side or until they are golden brown.

Using a slotted spoon, remove the fritters from the oil and drain them on kitchen paper towels. Keep them warm while you fry the remaining fritters in the same way.

Transfer the fritters to a warmed serving dish and serve immediately.

Nut Meringues

These little Nut Meringues are filled with dates and cream. They are good to serve at tea and a wonderful way to use up extra egg whites.

16 MERINGUES

4 oz. [⅘ cup] chopped nuts
6 oz. Meringue Cuite, warm
4 oz. [⅔ cup] dates, stoned and
   chopped
8 fl. oz. double cream [1 cup heavy
   cream], stiffly whipped

Preheat the oven to very cool 250°F (Gas Mark ½, 130°C).

Line two large baking sheets with non-stick silicone paper. Set aside.

With a metal spoon, carefully fold the chopped nuts into the warm meringue cuite.

Drop tablespoonfuls of the meringue mixture on to the prepared baking sheets.

Place the baking sheets in the oven and bake the meringues for 1½ hours or until they are crisp on the outside and slightly sticky on the inside. If the meringues begin to brown too much and too early, open the door of the oven and continue baking. Halfway through the baking time, reverse the baking sheets so that the one that was on the bottom is on top.

Remove the baking sheets from the oven. Detach the meringues from the non-stick silicone paper and turn them upside-down. Gently press the undersides with your index finger to make a hollow. Place them on the baking sheets and return to the oven and continue baking for another 30 minutes.

Remove the baking sheets from the oven and allow the meringues to cool for 5 minutes. Using a palette or a table knife, carefully transfer the meringues to a wire rack to cool completely.

Fold the dates into the whipped cream. When the meringues are cool, sandwich them together with the cream and date mixture and serve immediately.

Nut Princesses

These rich little sweets [candies] should be served after dinner with freshly percolated coffee. They may be stored in an airtight tin for several weeks.

30 SWEETS [CANDIES]

6 oz. [¾ cup] sugar
6 oz. [1½ cups] slivered almonds
10 oz. Marzipan I or II
6 oz. dark [semi-sweet] cooking
   chocolate
1 tablespoon brandy
1 tablespoon butter, cut into pieces

Partially decorated, Nut Roll is almost ready to be served as a superb dinner party dessert. The dessert may be prepared in advance and chilled.

In a medium-sized saucepan, melt the sugar over low heat, shaking the pan constantly. When the sugar has melted and is beginning to turn a rich golden brown, quickly stir in the slivered almonds. Cook for 1 minute, being very careful not to let the sugar burn. Remove the pan from the heat and pour the mixture on to an oiled marble slab or hard surface. Leave to cool.

When the sugar and nut mixture has cooled and hardened, crush it with a mallet or wooden rolling pin. Set aside.

On a flat surface, roll out the marzipan with a floured rolling pin into a rectangle about ½-inch thick. Using a kitchen knife, cut the marzipan into 30 squares. Roll each square between the palms of your hands into a small ball. Set aside.

In a small saucepan, melt the chocolate with the brandy over low heat, stirring occasionally. Remove the pan from the heat and stir in the butter, one piece at a time.

Using a cocktail stick, spear the marzipan balls and dip them into the chocolate, coating them entirely. Then, using two table knives, roll the balls in the crushed sugar and nut mixture. Put the balls on a large baking sheet and set aside until the chocolate has cooled and hardened.

When the chocolate has set, serve the sweets [candies] or store them in an airtight tin.

Nut and Raisin Stuffing

A delicate-tasting stuffing that beautifully complements roast pork, veal and poultry, Nut and Raisin Stuffing is very easy and quick to prepare.

ABOUT 12 OUNCES

4 oz. [2 cups] fresh breadcrumbs
2 oz. [⅓ cup] raisins, chopped
2 oz. [⅓ cup] walnuts, chopped
2 oz. [¼ cup] butter, softened
1 egg, lightly beaten
½ teaspoon salt
¼ teaspoon black pepper
1 teaspoon paprika
   grated rind and juice of ½ lemon

In a medium-sized mixing bowl, combine all the ingredients, stirring with a wooden spoon until they are well blended. Use as required.

Nut Roll

An absolutely delicious confection, Nut Roll is made with a rich sponge cake and filled with cream and nuts. It is ideal for a party

dessert, and looks most impressive. Vary the taste with the use of different nuts.

ONE 12-INCH ROLL

1 teaspoon vegetable oil
3 eggs
3 oz. [½ cup] soft brown sugar
2 oz. [⅓ cup] hazelnuts, ground
2 oz. [1 cup] fresh white
   breadcrumbs
½ teaspoon rum essence
1 tablespoon cornflour [cornstarch]
FILLING
5 fl. oz. double cream [⅝ cup heavy
   cream]
2 tablespoons icing [confectioners']
   sugar
½ tablespoon rum
1½ oz. [¼ cup] hazelnuts, chopped
4 whole hazelnuts
4 walnut halves
4 whole blanched almonds

Preheat the oven to hot 425°F (Gas Mark 7, 220°C). Lightly grease an 8- x 12-inch Swiss [jelly] roll tin with half the oil. Line the tin with non-stick silicone paper or aluminium foil and brush with the remaining oil. Set aside.

Place the eggs and sugar in a large heatproof mixing bowl. Place the bowl over a pan half filled with hot water. Set the pan over low heat.

Using a wire whisk or rotary beater, beat the eggs and sugar together until the mixture is very thick and will make a ribbon trail on itself when the whisk is lifted. Remove the bowl from the saucepan. Using a metal spoon, fold in the ground hazelnuts, breadcrumbs and rum essence.

Pour the mixture into the prepared tin and smooth it down with a flat-bladed knife.

Place the tin in the centre of the oven and bake for 7 to 8 minutes or until the cake springs back when lightly pressed with a fingertip. Remove the tin from the oven.

Lay a piece of greaseproof or waxed paper, the same size as the cake, on a flat surface. Sprinkle it with the cornflour [cornstarch]. Turn the cake out on to the paper. Carefully remove the silicone paper or foil from the bottom of the cake.

With a sharp knife, make a shallow cut across the cake, about 2½-inches from the end, to make the rolling easier. With the help of the greaseproof or waxed paper, carefully roll up the cake, Swiss [jelly] roll style, with the paper inside. Set the roll aside to cool completely.

Meanwhile, make the filling. In a medium-sized mixing bowl, beat the cream with a wire whisk or rotary beater until it is thick. Add the sugar and rum. Continue whisking until the cream forms stiff peaks. Fold in the chopped hazelnuts.

Carefully unroll the cake. Discard the greaseproof or waxed paper and, using a flat-bladed knife, spread half the cream filling over the surface of the roll. Carefully roll it up again.

Place the roll on a serving plate. Spread the remaining cream filling over the top of the roll. Arrange the whole hazelnuts, walnuts and almonds decoratively on top.

Serve immediately.

Nut Sauce

This versatile Nut Sauce is especially good with crudités, or with freshly cooked hot vegetables, such as broccoli, cauliflower, and potatoes. The sauce may be kept in a screw-top jar in the refrigerator for up to three days.

12 FLUID OUNCES

2 oz. [⅓ cup] hazelnuts, toasted
2 oz. [½ cup] almonds, toasted
8 fl. oz. [1 cup] mayonnaise
4 fl. oz. [½ cup] sour cream
1 teaspoon lemon juice
¼ teaspoon salt
¼ teaspoon white pepper

Place the nuts in an electric blender or food mill and grind them very finely. Set aside.

In a medium-sized mixing bowl, combine the mayonnaise and sour cream, beating until they are well blended. Pour in the lemon juice, then stir in the ground nuts, salt and pepper. Mix the ingredients until they are thoroughly combined.

The sauce is now ready to use.

Nut and Sweet Potato Flan

Try this unusual flan, filled with sweet potatoes, fruit juices and nuts, for a light nourishing family dessert. Serve with a lemon or orange sauce, although it is just as good on its own.

4 SERVINGS

1 x 9-inch Flan Case, made with rich shortcrust pastry, baked blind and cooled
3 eggs
3 egg yolks
3 oz. [½ cup] soft brown sugar
1 lb. sweet potatoes, peeled, cooked and mashed
¼ teaspoon salt
4 fl. oz. double cream [½ cup heavy cream]
2 fl. oz. [¼ cup] fresh orange juice
1 tablespoon lemon juice
1 teaspoon vanilla essence

2 oz. [⅓ cup] brazil nuts, chopped
2½ oz. [½ cup] almonds, chopped
2 oz. [⅓ cup] sultanas or seedless raisins
1 teaspoon grated nutmeg

Preheat the oven to hot 425°F (Gas Mark 7, 220°C).

Place the flan case on a baking sheet and set aside.

In a large mixing bowl, beat the eggs, yolks and sugar together with a wooden spoon until the mixture is smooth. Add the potatoes, salt, cream, orange juice, lemon juice and vanilla essence. Beat well until the mixture is thoroughly combined. Stir in the nuts and sultanas or seedless raisins. Spoon the mixture into the flan case and sprinkle over the nutmeg.

Place the baking sheet in the oven and bake the flan for 10 minutes. Reduce the oven temperature to moderate 350°F (Gas Mark 4, 180°C) and bake the flan for a further 25 to 30 minutes or until the filling has set and the top is deep golden brown.

Remove the flan from the oven and serve at once.

Nut Waffles

Nut Waffles, deliciously light and crunchy, are traditionally served hot in the United States for breakfast with maple syrup, melted butter or jam. A waffle iron, electric or non-electric, is essential to make Nut Waffles. The number of waffles made and the amount of batter used for each depend on the size of your waffle iron.

6 LARGE WAFFLES

3 eggs, separated
2 oz. [⅓ cup] soft brown sugar
6 oz. [1½ cups] flour
2 teaspoons baking powder
½ teaspoon salt
3 oz. [½ cup] walnuts, ground
10 fl. oz. [1¼ cups] milk
4 oz. [½ cup] butter, melted

In a medium-sized heatproof mixing bowl placed over a pan of hot water, beat the egg yolks and sugar together with a wire whisk or rotary beater over low heat, until the mixture will form a ribbon trail on itself when the whisk is lifted. Remove the pan from the heat and set the bowl aside.

Sift the flour, baking powder and salt into a medium-sized mixing bowl. Stir in the walnuts. Make a well in the centre of the flour mixture and pour in the egg and sugar mixture, the milk and 3 ounces [⅜ cup] of the melted butter. Using a metal spoon, fold the ingredients together until the mixture forms a smooth batter.

Ideal for breakfast when served with maple syrup or jam and melted butter, Nut Waffles are very popular in the United States.

In a medium-sized mixing bowl, beat the egg whites with a wire whisk or rotary beater until they form stiff peaks. With the metal spoon, fold the egg whites into the batter. Cover the bowl and set aside for 10 minutes.

Heat a waffle iron over moderate heat. Brush some of the remaining melted butter over the iron. Pour about one-sixth of the waffle batter into the centre of the waffle iron. Close the top and cook over moderate heat for 2 to 3 minutes on each side, or until the waffle stops steaming. Tip the waffle out on to a serving platter. Keep it warm while you cook the remaining waffles in the same way, using the remaining melted butter.

Serve hot or cold.

Nutalie Flan

A delicious dessert, Nutalie Flan combines fruit and nuts with honey. Serve it either hot or cold with whipped cream.

6 SERVINGS

1 x 9-inch Flan Case made with shortcrust pastry, baked blind and cooled
3 large cooking apples, peeled, cored and thinly sliced
4 tablespoons clear honey
½ teaspoon ground cinnamon
1 tablespoon lemon juice
1 oz. [2 tablespoons] butter
3 oz. [½ cup] sultanas or seedless raisins
4 oz. [1 cup] toasted slivered almonds

Preheat the oven to moderate 350°F (Gas Mark 4, 180°C).

Place the flan case on a baking sheet and set aside.

Put the apples, honey, cinnamon, lemon juice and butter in a medium-sized saucepan. Place the pan over moderate heat and cook the apples, stirring occasionally, for 10 to 15 minutes, or until they are very soft.

Remove the pan from the heat and stir in the sultanas or seedless raisins and almonds. Spoon the mixture into the flan case.

Place the baking sheet in the oven and bake the flan for 15 minutes.

Remove the flan from the oven and serve at once or leave it to cool before serving.

Nutcracker

The nutcracker is a utensil for cracking nuts. It is usually made of metal or very hard wood.

Nutmeg

Nutmeg is the seed of the fruit of the nutmeg tree, an evergreen indigenous to the Molucca Islands in Indonesia.

The nutmeg is brownish in colour, about 1 inch in diameter and oval in shape. The honeycombed outer covering of the nutmeg is removed and marketed separately as MACE.

Nutmeg may be bought whole, grated or ground. The best and most pungent flavour is obtained from freshly grated whole nutmeg.

Nutmeg is used extensively in cooking as a flavouring for sweet and savoury dishes and many warm drinks.

Nutmeg Cream

Nutmeg Cream is a simple creamy sauce which tastes especially delicious served with poached pears, apples and apricots or fruit flans. It may be diluted with milk to make a nourishing drink.

ABOUT 10 FLUID OUNCES

6 fl. oz. [¾ cup] evaporated milk, chilled

3 fl. oz. [⅜ cup] orange juice

1 teaspoon grated nutmeg

In a medium-sized mixing bowl, beat the evaporated milk with a wire whisk or rotary beater until it is frothy. Gradually whisk in the orange juice. Stir the nutmeg into the mixture and pour the sauce into a sauceboat.

Chill the sauce in the refrigerator until you are ready to serve it.

Nutrition

Nutrition is the science of the nutrients in food. Nutrients provide energy, are necessary for the growth and repair of tissues and regulate body processes. So to live, we must not only eat but eat the right things.

CALORIES

The first requirement of the body is calories. Food is measured in units of heat called calories. One calorie equals the amount of heat needed to raise one gram of water one degree Centigrade. In food values this means that one gram of carbohydrate — sugar and starch — produces 3.7 calories; one gram of protein such as found in meat, fish, eggs and milk produces 4.1 calories; and one gram of fat such as found in butter, oil and lard produces 9.3 calories.

FATS

Fats are a necessary part of a normal diet.

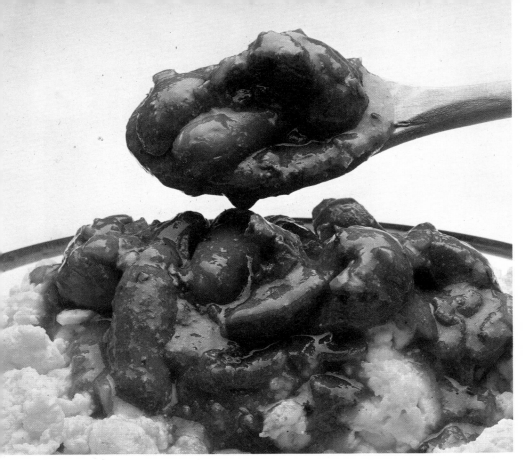

Nyrer med Karbonadepølser og Røraeg is rich and sophisticated.

They act as lubricants, fuel and as insulation against the cold. They play a vital role as carriers of the fat-soluble vitamins.

Both animal and vegetable fats should be included in the diet, the amount necessary varying according to the age, weight and occupation of the individual. Fats should probably not comprise more than 35% of the total daily intake of calories.

PROTEINS

Proteins are an essential part of a diet because they include many elements which the body requires for growing and rebuilding.

Proteins are complex combinations of amino acids. Some of the amino acids which the body does not require can be converted into those that it does. But there are some which cannot be made by the body and which must be included in the diet. The protein foods which contain these essential amino acids in the largest proportions are meat, fish, eggs, milk and cheese.

Amino-acids are also found in a wide variety of non-animal foods such as bread, cereals, nuts, pulses, beans, potatoes and other vegetables. Combinations of these foods provide excellent protein, for instance beans on toast or a bowl of cereal with milk.

For vegetarians to get enough of the essential amino acids they must eat not only a wide variety, but also a large quantity, of protein foods (including nuts and legumes).

Approximately 15 per cent of the daily intake of calories should be proteins.

CARBOHYDRATES

Carbohydrates include sugars and starches. They contribute heat and energy and when absorbed in a greater quantity then the body requires, they are converted into body fat.

In the Western world, the consumption of sweets and sweet drinks forms such a large part of the diet, particularly of children, that there is some danger that these children may be overfed and yet undernourished.

Most carbonhydrats should be taken as starchy foods rather than as sugars.

MINERALS, ENZYMES AND VITAMINS

The most important minerals are calcium, phosphorous and iron. See MINERALS.

Enzymes are organic catalysts — substances which induce change without being affected themselves and which do not form part of the resultant product. Vitamins are important as enzymes in the body, enabling it to function efficiently.

Vitamins are organic substances found in minute quantities in foods. Fat-soluble vitamins are A, D, E and K, and Vitamin C and the vitamins of the B group are water-soluble.

Vitamins are obtained from a wide variety of foods and providing the diet is varied and food is well prepared, the average person should not require vitamin supplements.

Nyrer med Karbonadepølser og Røraeg

KIDNEYS WITH SAUSAGES AND SCRAMBLED EGGS

A tasty combination of kidneys, sausages and eggs flavoured with Marsala, Nyrer med Karbonadepølser og Røraeg (nye-rer med kar-bon-add-pole og roar-agg) makes a perfect meal. Serve with crusty bread.

4 SERVINGS

4 oz. [½ cup] butter
1 large onion, finely chopped
8 lambs' kidneys, cleaned, and sliced
1 tablespoon flour
2 tablespoons tomato purée
4 fl. oz. [½ cup] chicken stock
2 fl. oz. [¼ cup] Marsala
14 oz. canned cocktail sausages, drained
2 oz. mushrooms, wiped clean and finely chopped
1 teaspoon dried thyme
2 teaspoons salt
1 teaspoon black pepper
6 eggs
2 fl. oz. [¼ cup] milk

In a flameproof casserole, melt 3 ounces [⅜ cup] of the butter over moderate heat. When the foam subsides, add the onion and cook, stirring occasionally, for 5 to 7 minutes, or until it is soft and translucent but not brown. Add the kidneys and cook, turning occasionally, for 5 to 8 minutes or until they are lightly and evenly browned.

With a wooden spoon, stir in the flour and cook, stirring constantly, for 2 minutes. Add the tomato purée, chicken stock and Marsala and stir well. Increase the heat to moderately high and bring the liquid to the boil, stirring constantly.

Add the sausages, mushrooms, thyme and half of the salt and pepper. Reduce the heat to low, cover the casserole, and simmer the mixture for 15 to 20 minutes, or until the kidneys are tender when pierced with the point of a sharp knife.

Meanwhile, prepare the scrambled eggs. In a medium-sized mixing bowl, combine the eggs and milk, beating with a fork until they are well blended. Beat in the remaining salt and pepper.

In a medium-sized saucepan, melt the remaining butter over moderate heat. When the foam subsides, add the egg mixture and cook, stirring constantly, for 5 minutes, or until the eggs are just set.

Remove the pan from the heat and spoon the scrambled eggs on to a warmed serving dish. When the kidneys are cooked, remove the pan from the heat and pour over the eggs. Serve immediately.